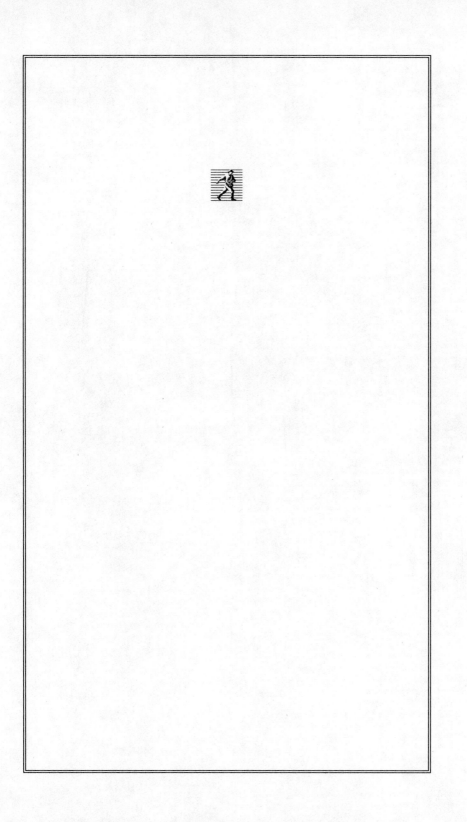

*Also by Marianne Williamson*

A RETURN TO LOVE

A WOMAN'S WORTH

ILLUMINATA

EMMA AND MOMMY TALK TO GOD

# MARIANNE WILLIAMSON

## THE
# HEALING
## OF
# AMERICA

SIMON & SCHUSTER

SIMON & SCHUSTER
ROCKEFELLER CENTER
1230 AVENUE OF THE AMERICAS
NEW YORK, NY 10020

COPYRIGHT © 1997 BY MARIANNE WILLIAMSON
ALL RIGHTS RESERVED,
INCLUDING THE RIGHT OF REPRODUCTION
IN WHOLE OR IN PART IN ANY FORM.

SIMON & SCHUSTER AND COLOPHON ARE REGISTERED TRADEMARKS
OF SIMON & SCHUSTER INC.

DESIGNED BY KAROLINA HARRIS

MANUFACTURED IN THE UNITED STATES OF AMERICA

1  3  5  7  9  10  8  6  4  2

LIBRARY OF CONGRESS CATALOGING-IN-PUBLICATION DATA
WILLIAMSON, MARIANNE, DATE.
THE HEALING OF AMERICA / MARIANNE WILLIAMSON.
P.   CM.
INCLUDES BIBLIOGRAPHICAL REFERENCES AND INDEX.
1. UNITED STATES—RELIGION.   2. SPIRITUALITY—UNITED STATES.
3. RELIGION AND CULTURE—UNITED STATES.   4. POLITICS AND RELIGION—
UNITED STATES.   I. TITLE.
BL2525.W495   1997
973—DC21                97-26308   CIP
ISBN 0-684-84270-X

*For Al*

# CONTENTS

WE have been preserved, these many years, in peace and prosperity. We have grown in numbers, wealth and power, as no other nation has ever grown. But we have forgotten God. We have forgotten the gracious hand which preserved us in peace, and multiplied and enriched and strengthened us; and we have vainly imagined, in the deceitfulness of our hearts, that all these blessings were produced by some superior wisdom and virtue of our own. Intoxicated with unbroken success, we have become too self-sufficient to feel the necessity of redeeming and preserving grace, too proud to pray to the God that made us!

It behooves us, then, to humble ourselves before the offended Power, to confess our national sins, and to pray for clemency and forgiveness.

—PRESIDENT ABRAHAM LINCOLN,
PROCLAIMING A DAY OF NATIONAL FASTING,
MARCH 30, 1863

# PREFACE

————

A s I wrote this book, my opinions about many things changed. Researching certain problems in America, I found that they were more intense than I had previously thought. I found myself yelling at things on C-Span, howling and raving around the room when I read certain newspaper articles, doubting even the most innocuous utterances of government officials, taking positions that previously I would have felt were cynical or negative.

I began to question what was going on inside myself. Maybe, I thought, I'm projecting unconscious rage at my father onto the U.S. government; perhaps I'm a huge hypocrite to criticize capitalism when it's given me, after all, such fabulous opportunities. Why am I complaining so much? Emotionally, the process was difficult. I began to feel like I was carrying around America's dirty laundry.

Then one day, having basically written what I wanted to write and having brought the book near conclusion, I found I was bouncing around my house like a child and playing in the backyard with my daughter's hula hoop—and she wasn't even home! Wow, I thought, thank God I finally got a good night's sleep, and thank goodness this book is finally just about written. But then I realized something more significant lay beneath my newly jauntier mood: I had gone through the process I was writing about

—I had faced the darkness, to the best of my ability, that all Americans are to some extent carrying around. And instead of finding further darkness on the other side, I had found that the darkness lifted.

I am an optimistic person, and I believe optimism is a moral imperative. But I don't believe in false positivism. You can't just pour a lot of feel-goodisms over your problems and think that that will make them go away. Healing is an emotional detox, in which disease can't be indefinitely stuffed down, its symptoms merely managed. We must bring our problems to light in order to be rid of them; lack of conscious awareness is the cause of our problems, and conscious awareness is the source of our healing.

Therein lies the power of truth: what is honestly looked at, no longer has the same power over us. Whether what is to be healed is a person or a nation, the healing process takes personal courage, and a willingness to face things not always easy to face.

The true healer is not always the Teller of Good News, which is why we have a problem when the healer has to run for reelection. Jimmy Carter was turned out of office when he tried to describe to America what he saw as our societal malaise. We ran right into the arms of someone who said that all things were shiny and great.

In many ways, Ronald Reagan's optimism reflected well on a positive aspect of the American character. We do have a magnificent capacity to transcend our problems, and we always have. But transcendence is very different from denial. What has happened in the last thirty years in America is that we have taken a load of accumulated problems and pushed them under the rug. We haven't cleaned up our house so much as added a room to put all of the dirty things in. The problem with this is that we're not a house but a living organism. Unhealthy factors have an inertia of their own, and ultimately produce all manner of disease that does not stay relegated to its primary site of origin.

You don't go to a doctor with a broken arm and say, "But my heart works great and my lungs are fine." So it is that in this book some might feel that perhaps I give short shrift to all the things that are working so well in America. The truth is, I'm as big a champion of what is right about this country as anyone. But I set out to write about the healing of America, and this I could not do without looking as clearly and honestly as I could at the disease.

The emotional, psychological, and spiritual aspects of healing have become well known. People who have been diagnosed with life-challenging illness statistically live twice as long after diagnosis, if they regularly attend support groups. What I hope to do with this book is to contribute in some way to a more open discussion of what is wrong in America, not negatively, but constructively. As a nation, we need a public context for discussing how we feel about things and what we think about those feelings in order that we might heal. To say that this has nothing to do with politics is no longer reasonable. Our capacity to think deeply, feel deeply, and pray is now scientifically proven to help heal the body; next on our agenda should be to use those same capacities to help heal our country.

It's easy to build an argument for how good things are in America. It's even easy to build an argument for how bad things are in America. That is because both are true.

But the things that are bad are just symptoms of a deeper malaise that has no place, as yet, in public conversation. Reasonable dissent and difficult but necessary soul-searching have been so invalidated within the public domain that they emerge only in shadow versions as almost psychotic paranoia.

Only when you *say* the truth can the truth set you free. This is not a negative process, but at times it is a difficult process. I once heard someone say, "The truth shall set you free, but first it will piss you off."

I have tried with this book, to the best of my ability, to tell the truth as I see it. Having done so, I now feel great, as though a psychic burden has been removed from my shoulders and I can now move on. It is my deepest wish that that experience, in some small way, might come about for all who read this book.

—MARIANNE WILLIAMSON

*I WAS fifteen years old when Martin Luther King, Jr., was shot. I was watching television in my family's den while waiting for my father to come home from work, when a news bulletin reported that King had been killed.*

*Shortly afterward, my father walked in the back door. I ran up to him crying, "Daddy, Daddy, Martin Luther King, Jr., was shot and killed!"*

*I saw a look on my father's face that I had never seen before. His eyes seemed to focus on something impossibly far away, and with an intensely pained expression on his face, he spat out the words, "Those bastards."*

*Confused, I thought, "What is he saying? How does he know? What does he mean, 'those' bastards?"*

*In that instant, I lost my innocence. That day changed history and it certainly changed me. I have never forgotten my father's eyes. I took another road than my father took, but I am looking for the same perfect world.*

# INTRODUCTION

# TOUGH MINDS, TENDER HEARTS

*"Our goal is to create a beloved community and this will require a qualitative change in our souls as well as a quantitative change in our lives."*
— MARTIN LUTHER KING, JR.

> *Out of Tao comes unity; out of unity comes two;*
> *from two comes three; from three all things come.*
> *The shade of Yin is on the back of everything; the*
> *light of Yang is on the face of everything. From*
> *their blending together balance exists in the world.*
> *The concept of Yin is ever present. It is the Mystic*
> *Female from whom the heavens and the earth*
> *originate.*
> *Constantly, continuously, enduring always.*
> *Use her!*
>
> —LAO TZU, *TAO TE CHING*

ACCORDING to ancient Chinese philosophy, the forces of yin and yang are like night to day, darkness to light, feminine to masculine, inner to outer, heart to head. They balance, border, and complete each other, forming together a unified whole.

To understand this dynamic is to be more fully aware of the rhythms that underlie all things. Our ultimate ground of being —what the Chinese call the Tao—is the mystical oneness out of which all worldly manifestation flows. To see how the greater oneness is in constant process of giving birth to two—that yin and yang might then come together again and give birth to another one—is to hold the key to greater understanding of anything in the world.

Anywhere there is Great Duality, there is yin and yang: the eternal and the temporal, women and men, philosophy and science, vision and politics. To seek their balance in any situation is to seek the healing of the world. For according to Taoist philosophy, when yin and yang are out of balance, there is tension, disharmony, and discord in the universe. To right the wrong, we must seek to reunite the pieces of the whole that have been torn asunder.

This book is about the yin and yang of American history, the Great Duality of our miraculous beginnings, the ultimate tearing apart of our vision from our politics, and an effort that can now begin in earnest to repair the resulting wounding of our collective soul.

Our Founders embodied the ideals of an extraordinary moment in history. Their philosophical vision was expressed in the Declaration of Independence and their political genius in the Constitution. The balance of their intellectual brilliance with personal courage, philosophical vision with political acumen, and mature serenity with revolutionary fervor created a doorway in a seemingly impenetrable wall of history. A paradigm so entrenched as to leave the common masses of humanity little hope of rising above the station in life into which they had been born, was abolished forever by a group of young Americans who stood up to what was then the most powerful military force in the world and said, "No. We have a better idea."

Most major institutions, from the U.S. government to the Christian Church to the scientific establishment, began with a small group of radicals whose thoughts were considered outrageous by holders of the status quo of their time. To use the

German philosopher Hegel's expression, they were "world-historic individuals" who took the wheel of history and steered it in another direction. They looked at the world with the pulsating spirit of spontaneity and hope for something better than that which had been before.

America was like a child who was born, grew, and turned out to be a genius. By the latter part of the nineteenth century, the Industrial Revolution raged throughout Europe and the United States, bursting forth from our foreheads seemingly fully grown. Railroads, electricity, factory production—scientific experimentation and technological prowess came to embellish our dreams and define our ambitions. As this rush of industrial expansion unfolded, the yang of human assertion and physical manifestation was extraordinary. We lost something precious, however, when the yin of greater wisdom, understanding, and perspective was subtly pushed to the side. By the beginning of the twentieth century, attention to the soul had been marginalized by a materialistic focus sweeping across the plains of America's consciousness like a windstorm that wouldn't stop.

Thus was torn asunder the brilliant balance from which America had been born. Money replaced justice as our popular ambition, and the authoritarian business models of the industrial age came to replace democracy as the main organizing principle of American society. We began to backslide, our vision to diffuse. The elements of higher truth and commitment to justice that so imbued our founding were slowly forced into exile in the corners of the American mind. They remained in our documents but no longer in our hearts. The very tyrannies from which we had fought to be free now reappeared among us, but this time we were the oppressors as well as the oppressed.

A fiery personal and political drama—still raging among us —began in earnest. America would be home to both slave owner and abolitionist, both conscienceless industrialist and labor reformer, both corporate polluter and world-class environmentalist. The tension itself is not inherently bad, because through it we have the freedom to grow. But we have lost our experience of the great Tao underlying our differences, the coagulating sense of American unity that makes our freedom to disagree all the more important. We have lost our sense that political debate is not what was meant to divide us as a nation, but rather to sustain us. We have left behind the delicate balance between the celebration of our diversity and the dedication to our unity, which lies at the heart of the American ideal.

Although the original ideals handed down to us by our Founders were almost perfect expressions of a commitment to human justice, America has never fully manifested those ideals. That does not mean that we are bad or hypocritical, but merely a nation still in the throes of a greater becoming. We have, from our beginning, been home to both noble and spiritually based political impulses, as well as to the most materialistic and selfish ones. Freedom means that we will be as a nation whatever we, the people, choose to be. The push and pull between two major aspects of our being is the overarching drama of our national life.

In America today, we have critical problems that will not go away without collective dedication and effort. We must apply ourselves to serious problems with a concentration and a sense of purpose that we do not always summon in more normal times. Those who would have us gloss over those problems or deny them do not help us respond. Those who would lead us into cynicism or anger lead us away from healing. We need deep understanding of our collective problems, we need faith, and we need love.

There is so much injustice in America, and such a conspiracy not to discuss it; so much suffering, and so much deflection lest we notice. We are told that these problems are secondary, or that it would cost too much to fix them—as though money is what matters most. Greed is considered legitimate now, while brotherly love is not. Millions of us see this as an unacceptable violation of spiritual truth. We must create the restoration of our collective conscience, and turn it into political will.

We are organized in the United States today according to obsolete social principles, obsolete because they reflect separation from spirit. They posit us as purely material rather than spiritual beings, and economically oriented rather than relationship-oriented people. We have viewed competition as the primary motivator of human creativity, though it is not. We have viewed the creation of wealth as the primary goal of human work, though it should not be. We have treated each other as anything but brothers, though that is what we are. These principles hold us back, keeping us limited to the lower energies of dense, material plane consciousness at a time when the species is ready to expand to new levels of awareness and experience. We must withdraw our attachment to those principles, reject their claim upon our imaginations, and assert for ourselves the right and ability to transform.

We are divinely created spiritual beings placed on earth for the purpose of creating the good, the true, and the beautiful. This goal, when embraced by the human heart, is a compelling force that motivates us to higher heights than any contest or economic stimulus could ever come close to matching. There are within each of us God-given talents that do not respond to market pressure yet spring to life in the presence of honor and respect. Spiritual law would have us serve each other rather than compete with each other, bless each other rather than condemn each other, and place our primary attention on the extension of brotherly love.

Awareness of spiritual law not only will determine the primary philosophical outlook of the century ahead but also will determine our future politics and economics as well. Either that, or we will suffer the consequences of our continued resistance to the rule of love, too long past the point when as a species we knew better.

The Declaration of Independence, the Constitution, the Bill of Rights, the Emancipation Proclamation, the Gettysburg Address, Kennedy's Inaugural Address, King's Letter from a Birmingham Jail—these are like ancient tablets on which are inscribed our fundamental yearnings and highest hopes. At the same time, the Trail of Tears, the Vietnam War, systemic racism and economic injustice, official hypocrisy, violence, and exalted militarism form a dark and seemingly impenetrable forcefield acting like a barrier before our hearts, keeping our hands from being able to grasp those tablets to our chest. It is the task of our generation to break through the wall before us, to atone for our errors and reactivate our commitment to the promulgation of our strengths. It is not just that we need our sacred tablets; our sacred tablets, to be living truths, need us.

We must begin in earnest an archeological dig into the American psyche, that we might retrieve the tablets on which are written the truths that set us free. This is not an easy assignment, for the layers of our denial are thick and encrusted. Billions of dollars are invested in our not seeing our own circumstances clearly; then, in our blindness, we continue to support the very system that blocks our vision.

Never has there been a time in our history when it was more imperative for the average citizen to think for him- or herself. Often, President Kennedy said, "we enjoy the comfort of opinion without the discomfort of thought." Everyone in America has opinions today, but too few of us are doing our very best thinking.

In the words of historian Henry Steele Commager, "The greatest danger confronting us is not any particular kind of thought, but absence of thought." We are allowing others not only to determine the answers to our problems, but even which questions we're asking. And in that lies real threat to our democracy.

I think America at this time is like someone who has gotten tired of being sad, so has decided to go back to pretending to be happy. Our political options range for the most part from complaining about what's wrong to denying what's wrong. Such limited options for national recovery result in a psychic pain that has sent most Americans into an unconscious throwing up of our hands. The purpose of this book is to help us get at the causes underlying our pain, and hopefully help encourage the reader to take part in the process of genuine healing.

There is a new prophetic voice in America, saying, as do all prophets, that we must repent—which literally means "re-think." This new prophetic voice is not a soloist but a choir. This time it will not be possible to silence one prophet, or even a few, and thereby stymie a broad-based impulse for decades. This time, a prophetic calling is seizing the hearts of a critical mass. It is a voice of group conscience and a redefinition of citizen activism in American democracy.

Our healing will not happen in a day, or a weekend, or a year. It will happen because of a massive turnaround in the way we view, and live, our lives. There is about to rise up among us, if we wish, a new American consciousness, and a renewed regard for the authority of the American citizen. That authority has not been taken from us so much as we have given it away. Therein lies America's disease. In reasserting the potential power of the American citizen, America will heal itself.

One way to promote healing is to look at the examples of great spirits who have gone before, in this country and elsewhere, who brought illumination to the darkness of their times. There have been those in history who personified perfectly, or very nearly, the balance of soul and political intelligence necessary to right the wrongs of history. From our Founders, to Mahatma Gandhi, to Martin Luther King, Jr., there are those to whom humanity can point and say, "There, they got it right." And we can look at the things they did and make their truths our own.

Our Founders had a job to do: to win freedom from the English, and forge the country's own political identity. Lincoln had a job to do: to preserve the Union, and make this a country worth fighting for. Gandhi had a job to do: to lead a nonviolent crusade for India's independence. Martin Luther King, Jr., had a job to do: to lead the struggle for American civil rights. None of those people whined. They just did it. They didn't give in, they created revolutions. They didn't curse the darkness, they became the light: passionately intelligent people in the service of a job at hand. They put aside their childish inclinations. They were not perfect; they were just like us when first they heard the call of history. They answered the plea for democracy and justice that has been made throughout the ages, and having answered it, were given all the strength they needed to bring forth the resurrection of good.

The Greek root of the word *politics* does not mean "of the government" but "of the *citizen.*" We need a new political gestalt in America: an expansion of the political arena to more accurately reflect not only what we do, but who we are and are becoming. Politics should include more than just changes in government; it should also include changes in *us.* We are what America *is.* There are internal as well as external aspects to a nation, and to the process of societal change. From hatred, racism, and cynicism to hope, creativity, and forgiveness, both the inner and the outer America are now political issues.

Martin Luther King, Jr., spoke often of our need to have "tough minds and tender hearts." He himself displayed that combination brilliantly. Many tough thinkers in America today lack heart, while too many tender hearts lack mental and intellectual acumen. Fuzzy thinking is just one step above not thinking. We must pool our intellectual and emotional strengths to create an elixir of healing for our national distress.

We have the yang; we must reclaim the yin. We have the intelligence; we must retrieve our souls. We will find a way to put the two together. And out of that union will flow such power of personal fortitude that a revolution of good will occur in America, a reassertion of hope and nonviolent authority. There is a wellspring of love and wisdom in each of us, which is itself, as both Gandhi and Dr. King proclaimed, a powerful political force. Our only true enemy is not people or institutions, but fear-laden thoughts that cling to our insides and sap us of our strength. We must make a stand for our better selves. We must recommit to essential truths, both spiritual and political.

In the words of Abraham Lincoln, in his 1862 Annual Message, "Fellow citizens, *we* cannot escape history. We will be remembered in spite of ourselves. No personal significance, or insignificance, can spare one or another of us. The fiery trial through which we pass, will light us down, in honor or dishonor, to the latest generation.... We shall nobly save, or meanly lose, the last best hope of earth."

To heal America now is a huge challenge for our generation, and as the psychological heirs of our Founders and Lincoln, we have what it takes to meet it. They looked to the power of a great idea—American democracy—and it inspired them to greatness. We can look to embrace that same idea—and if we do, it will inform our minds and ignite our hearts the same way it did theirs. Democracy is profoundly relevant to the evolution of humanity, and as such it carries the psychological momentum to create miracles in the strangest places.

"To some generations," President Franklin D. Roosevelt declared, "much is given. From some generations, much is expected. This generation has a rendezvous with destiny." Roosevelt's words, uttered in 1936, are relevant today. For our generation has a rendezvous with destiny as well; what we're now in the midst of deciding is whether we'll sleep through the date.

Our alternative is to choose to awaken.

# 1

# AMERICAN RENAISSANCE

*"These are times in which a genius would wish to live. It is not in the still calm of life, or in the repose of a pacific station, that great characters are formed. ... Great necessities call out great virtues."*

—ABIGAIL ADAMS,
LETTER TO JOHN QUINCY ADAMS,
JANUARY 19, 1780

WITHIN the next ten years, America will have a renaissance or a catastrophe. Something is going to happen to take us back to who we are. If America were an individual seeking counseling, a good therapist might say: "Number one, you're not really sober. Number two, you're obsessed with material things and your spiritual life is begging for attention. Number three, you rarely take responsibility for your own problems and project a lot of blame onto other people. Number four, you've neglected your kids. Number five, the size of the elaborate security system around your house shows paranoid tendencies. Number six, you have a lot of amends to make. Number seven, your attraction to generals is neurotic."

Whether the patient takes the cue or not remains to be seen. But for a person or for a nation, everything will erupt in time if we do not attend to the inner life.

## Radical Beginnings

The curtain is now set to rise on the drama of the twenty-first century; we hold in our minds the possible scripts for its beginning scenes. As Thomas Paine proclaimed in speaking about the

American Revolution, "We have it in our power to begin the world over again." So do we. Like our Founders before us, we live in one of those pregnant moments when a fundamental paradigm that has ruled one chapter of history is ready to pass and give way to another. Entire eras dovetail. At such times, the systems of life are more malleable than usual, and committed individuals have more power than they sometimes do to determine the course of history.

It is ours to decide where history goes now, and Western civilization has but two directions from which to choose: transformation or disintegration. Cultures that did not have the capacity to fundamentally rethink themselves when historical conditions demanded that they do so have collapsed and passed out of existence. It behooves us at times such as these to consider deeply the historical examples of those societies that faced the challenge and found a way to be reborn without first having to die.

The American Revolution was a stunning social rebirth. Our Founders repudiated systems of feudal authority that had been entrenched in Europe for centuries. The Americans declared all men to be endowed by rights given them not by a king, but by God. This was, and is, a radical declaration of individual authority. Power was deemed to be enthroned within each of us, to then be lent by us to government—not to suppress our individual freedom but rather to release it and harness it effectively.

Our Founders risked their lives to make that historic break from the past, boldly changing the course of human events. They reached beyond the accepted boundaries of what was to be expected from life and stretched the limits of human possibility. They left in their wake a compelling promise, not only to Americans but to people throughout the world, that a society could exist in which the individual talents and abilities of free, self-governed people could come together fruitfully, forming out of what is always potential chaos something creative and good.

Our Founders asserted the dramatic proposition that if ordinary people are deliberative and responsible, then they can run their own affairs. A problem in America today is not that we have lost our rights, but that we seem to have lost our passionate connection to their historical significance. The average American has too little sense of the radicalism of the American experiment or the meaning of fundamental democratic principles. We have forgotten—if we ever knew—how much those principles affect issues that matter in our daily lives.

A key to our ability to renew ourselves now is to seek to remember who we already are.

## *The New Enlightenment*

The American Founders were intellectual citizens of the Age of Enlightenment. At that time, the governing intellectual assumption was that all human knowledge and experience had come together in a great confluence, from which human beings could distill general principles of nature and society. The means of this distillation was the exercise of reason. The great intellectual model of the Enlightenment was Isaac Newton, who deduced and articulated the principles of what we have ever since called Newtonian physics. Many American statesmen with intellectual ambition—James Madison, Alexander Hamilton, John Adams, among them—aspired to become the Newton of politics and government.

Now, at the end of the twentieth century, the world has corrected and improved upon Newtonian science. Reality is not quite as solid or objective or deterministic as Newton thought.

Heisenberg, Bohr, and Einstein were thinkers as revolutionary in their time as Newton had been in his. While the thinkers of the Enlightenment exalted the faculty of reason, quantum mechanics proved some "unreasonable" things to be true: time flows at different rates for observers moving at different speeds, solid atoms are largely empty, subatomic phenomena are both particles and waves, particles seem to affect each other at a distance even in the absence of a known causal connection, and, according to Heisenberg's Uncertainty Principle, an object is affected by the act of being observed. As British physicist Sir James Jeans proclaimed, the world now turned out to be "not so much a great machine as a great thought."

Quantum physics gives human consciousness a much more central role in the larger scheme of the universe than did Newtonian physics. How we perceive and how we interpret things are more than mere symbolic powers, opening the modern mind to a more spiritual interpretation of reality than has been intellectually in vogue for centuries. "The more I study physics," said Einstein, "the more I am drawn to metaphysics." The rationalistic worldview of the Enlightenment is now repudiated by one more soulful, as the Renaissance itself was a repudiation in its time of an overly mystified Middle Ages. In every historical era there ensues a creative argument with the past, as every thesis is met by its antithesis, moving humanity backward or forward depending on who's in charge.

In the words of Thomas Jefferson,

I am not an advocate for frequent changes in laws and constitutions, but laws and institutions must go hand in hand with the progress of the human mind. As that becomes more developed, more enlightened, as new discoveries are made, new truths discovered and manners and opinions change, with the change of circumstances, institutions must advance also to keep pace with the times. We might as well require a man to wear still the coat which fitted him when a boy as civilized society to remain ever under the regimen of their barbarous ancestors.

As our Founders sought to apply the knowledge of Newton and the Age of Enlightenment to the politics of their time, we should try to apply the principles of modern physics and metaphysics to the politics of our time. The consciousness revolution of the twentieth century has already transformed both mainstream medicine and business: Harvard Medical School has hosted symposiums on the role of spirituality and healing in medicine, and highly paid corporate consultants call on business executives to turn their workplaces into "sanctuaries for the soul." Government is the only major American institution that doesn't seem to have heard yet that the world has unalterably changed.

The world of medicine has already been radically transformed by new paradigm thinking. Business is mid-process. Politics is next.

## Creative Chaos

Every corner of God's universe is being swept upward, as the door to a new millennium offers escape from the lower regions of thought still tugging so strongly and destructively at us.

We are exiting a Material Age, which has lasted for thousands of years, and are entering an Ideational Age. We are, as a species, shifting our focus from extrinsic to intrinsic value. We are living during dramatic times of historical transition, in which our psyches and our social orders are trying to adjust to the often violent shift from one primary mode of civilization to another.

Just as when we go from one country to another we use an adapter to convert our use of electrical energy, so we must now learn to convert our use of mental energy. We are moving into new territory where we are unable to plug into our own energy sources unless we learn how to convert our thinking. We need adapters—facilitators of the new consciousness—and most important, we need the willingness to adapt.

Where the Atlantic meets the Pacific, the waters are turbulent. When one major historical epoch meets another, the psychic and emotional waters are likewise turbulent. Navigating those waters is difficult, but mastering the waves brings an exhilaration that those living in less exciting times will never know.

I have wondered if, at the beginning of the Italian Renaissance, people looked at each other and said, "I think this is the Renaissance. Do you think it's the Renaissance?" They must have felt that something was in the air. Franklin and Adams and Jefferson must have known that the paintings showing them at the signing of the Declaration of Independence stood a good chance of being around for a while: the room must have had an intense reverberation. The air must have crackled. Their hearts must have known. For such were times when the world was recreated, when ages of dust were swept aside and civilization renewed itself.

This moment is such a time.

These transitional periods are always chaotic; there is no amount of legal or political maneuvering that can limit the explosion of human energy bursting forth at such times. No matter how much some people might try to hold back the tide of change today, the remedies of a materialistic order will have less and less effect on affairs now unfolding. The chaos of our times is a reflection of a profound and inexorable reorientation of the human mind. This explosion is coming from the deepest levels of the psyche: it is not orderly, and no amount of tight, repressive force can contain it. We can no more stop its energy than a parent can stop the explosion of hormones in an adolescent child. This transformation of human consciousness *is*—it is not up for a vote. No action—only principle—can govern chaos. Our lives will not be brought to order through anything but love.

An entirely new *Weltanschauung,* or worldview, is on the horizon. The outer world will no longer be looked to as the source of our power or our salvation. The belief that it ever was our salvation was a delusion fostered by the seductive, gross materialism of our technological, industrialized age. Transcendent philosophical traditions reveal that true power is sourced within, is ever-renewable through the grace of God, and is activated through human dedication to whole-centered rather than self-centered goals.

From alternative health practitioners, to corporate trainers teaching creative visualization techniques and spiritual basics as keys to business revitalization, to the Internet communications revolution that has already lessened the ability of the communications autocracy to control the flow of information, we Americans are in the process of building for ourselves a society no longer limited by a strict and rationalistic materialism. This effort annoys and angers those who would prefer that we enter the twenty-first century with no fundamental changes in our approach to being human. But history is not static. The twentieth-century *zeitgeist* was very different from its nineteenth-century predecessor, and the twenty-first century's *zeitgeist* promises to be very different still. There are millions of people throughout the world who have spent the last several years trying to unlearn a worldview that dominated Western civilization during the century now passing. That worldview has given us tremendous progress, but it cannot be said to have given us peace.

Dense human consciousness is beginning to lighten up. This is not prophecy, but rather a description of what is happening now. All structures and systems that remain primarily wedded to external substance have already begun and will continue to collapse around us. They are dinosaurs. They will be replaced by structures just as real—perhaps more real—but focused within the mind.

Western materialism—largely a product of Newtonian physics—and our economic obsessiveness—largely a product of the Industrial Revolution—will both be largely undermined by the natural flow of future developments. Western materialism will be forced to surrender to a new age of scientific and spiritual consciousness, and our economic points of view will surrender to the demands of the Information Age. Structures which seem very solid to us now are not as solid as they appear. Only that which is built on sacred principle is built on rock. All else is built on sand.

New attitudes based on the awareness of spiritual principles have been embraced now by enough Americans to turn the tenets of higher consciousness into a major force for social change. Political as well as social issues will come to bear the mark of this transformation as we continue our countdown to a new millennium. Therein lies great potential for the release of massive healing energies, here and around the world.

## The Soul's Frontier

There is now a new frontier, not of land but of consciousness. There is no outer ground to conquer, but there is an important inner journey that stretches out before us. There is a realm of being within us to rediscover, a path to take as perilous and demanding of courage, in its way, as that taken by the wagon train heading toward the Pacific Ocean in the nineteenth century.

—

The Great Seal of the United States, which appears on our dollar bill and was designed by Jefferson, Franklin, and Adams, illustrates our Founders' sense of America's destiny. The seal shows the Great Pyramid at Giza, with its missing capstone returned and illuminated. The Eye of Horus, the ancient Egyptian symbol for the consciousness of higher mind, is displayed within the capstone. Beneath the picture are written the words "*Novus Ordo Seclorum*"—new order of the ages. This Masonic symbolism reveals democracy's function as a vehicle for the realization of humanity's highest potential. It is incumbent on every generation of Americans to seek the ways in which our country can contribute to the enlightenment of humankind. Whether fear-based forces come at us from within or without, we must continue to proceed in the direction of opening doors for humanity.

As Abraham Lincoln wrote in his 1862 Annual Message, "The occasion is piled high with difficulty, and we must rise with the occasion. As our case is new, so we must think anew, and act anew. We must disenthrall ourselves, and then we shall save our country."

There is within every person a veiled, oceanic awareness that we are all much bigger than the small-minded personas we normally display. The expansion into this larger self, for the individual and the species, is the meaning of human evolution and the dramatic challenge of this historic time.

Evolution proceeds not through adaptation but through creativity. We must create who we want to be, rather than merely imitate who we have recently been. We can, and will, evolve to something much more than our present personalities, shedding the skin of our former selves. We are not only all equal but potentially equally brilliant. Within us all there is divinity hiding, waiting for its moment to be born into the world, the opportunity to come out of the shadows of our entrenched illusions.

Renaissance begins with the activation of forces of internal rebirth, spreading like light through each of us and out into the world.

Race relations, the decivilization of our cities, the violence among our youth and in our neighborhoods, the problem with our economy, even foreign policy—the most serious problems we face as a nation are not actually soluble through traditional political means because they are the wounds of an internal disease. To simply imprison more criminals is not going to stop crime; to tax or raise interest rates more or less is not going to make the American economy both abundant and just; and no amount of military might can ultimately control the bonfire of ethnic hatred if it continues to erupt like grassfire all around the world.

For the first time in decades, there seems to be a limit to the technological solutions to humanity's problems. A critical mass of Americans has come to understand that mere treatment of symptoms is not an adequate response to the diseases that plague us. A new law here and a new law there are little more than different sets of Band-Aids on a ripped-apart aorta. We need a new conceptualization of our problems and a revised understanding of what it will take to eradicate them. We must fundamentally change the way we think. Such a paradigm shift applied to the public realm amounts to a revolution in American political consciousness, though it has little to do with politics as we know it. We need a nonviolent assumption of the power of the soul to heal the pain of a world that has forgotten it has one.


## Political Salvation

We are now learning as much about waging peace as we have known for ages about waging war, and as much about the power of love to heal us as we have known about the power of hate to destroy us. The extraordinary technological changes on our horizon are mere adjuncts to the even greater explosion of possibilities within the human mind. It is not only our interconnectedness technologically that promises to shift the world we live in but, even more so, the realization of our interconnectedness humanly and spiritually. It is not new material resources that promise to arise in our midst, but rather resources of soul and creativity that promise to provide us with rich and exciting new frontiers.

The contrast between this exciting future and the way we govern ourselves couldn't be starker—or sadder. Politics in America has become just another business. It bombards us with a specific, and specifically limited, way of looking at the political process. It is more authoritarian than democratic, having less to do with us and more to do with them. Politics as we know it now is a materially based process focused through dense, fear-laden consciousness. But politics, like everything else, promises to change radically in the coming days, as a broad-based awakening of human awareness causes radical expansion of hope and possibility. Politics will become less concerned with governmental change, and more concerned with human change; less concerned with how to allocate our outer resources, and more concerned with harnessing the inner gold within each of us.

Renaissance is a social uprising centered not on our streets but in our minds, an outpicturing of years of accumulated internal shifts within millions of people. Many who have focused their political and social efforts solely on external change have come to see how superficial and temporary such change can ultimately be; many who have sought personal growth as a path to global transformation have begun to extend their efforts into the outer world.

The former group are America's social and political activists, while the latter are America's modern version of the spiritual contemplative. It is the balance and intersection of these two impulses—the political and the spiritual—that will foster the rebirth of American democracy and form the crux of a new revolutionary power.

This renaissance will come from neither the Left nor the Right. It is neither a bridge to the past nor a bridge to the future, but a bridge to who we most deeply are. The bridge to a better future is a shift in mass consciousness, to a part of ourselves we have tended to keep out of the public realm. That part of us is not interested in traditional politics. It is who we are when we are hushed in church, near tears when they blow the shofar on Yom Kippur, honest and vulnerable with our therapist. It is the part of us least acknowledged, maintained, or seemingly even valued at all by the social order we have created around us. It is the part of us that still hopes for miracles—and at times can even see them.

That place in each of us is the key to our personal and political salvation. For it is from that inner, sacred place that we genuinely join with others. From elsewhere within the personality we can forge alliances but we cannot merge. It is in joining that we emerge changed, having fertilized the garden that just might become our Eden. It is in joining that we turn back our lower natures, allowing the angels room to breathe within us. It is in Americans joining with other Americans that America will be healed.

Community is the launching pad for a missile of energy that propels us into renaissance. Through it we can intercept the nosedive that threatens American civilization. In business, medicine, education, psychology, religion, and even politics, we see the reflection of a basic spiritual and psychological principle: where people genuinely join, breakthroughs occur. Where people are separate from each other—when they are angry, polarized, and defensive—breakdown and disorder are inevitable. The way to heal social disorder is to reintroduce community. We don't need deeper analyses of our sicknesses so much as we desperately need a more passionate embrace of the only thing that heals them all.

Our culture has lost its sense of sacred connection to any power or authority higher than ourselves. We have lost our spiritual rudder, and without it we have neither individual nor collective wisdom. Our national conscience is barely alive as we slither like snakes across a desert floor toward any hole where money lies. Nothing short of an internal awakening will heal this wounded nation. Our children are prey to violence more vicious than that of most civilized countries, thousands of our young are themselves violent criminals, and millions of Americans can barely contain their rage much longer in the face of continued social and economic injustice. We see both major political parties steering the discussion of what truly ails us away from that which actually does, for they have no context for a higher discussion. They are not modern. They are now more alike than different, and neither is any longer home to truly serious political alternatives. They have become a game unto themselves. Our political salvation will not come from our political system as it now exists. It will come from deep within us.

## From They Can Do It to We Can Do It

Central to new paradigm thinking, in any area, is the notion that the power of the individual human mind is greater than the power of any external structure; that indeed, without the support of the mind all outer structures fail. Without the creative thinking of the worker and not just management, business falters;

without the spiritual and mental power of the patient and not just the doctor, healing falters; without positive intention and not just money, materialization falters; and without love and not just human will, all systems of life falter. Without the creative thinking, passion, positive intention, spiritual vision, and love of the individual citizen—not just government—America will falter. Politicians in America are twenty years behind the times: they seem to think that if you change the management, that's enough to change the company. They change the hardware but they ignore the software. Real change occurs not from the top down but from the bottom up. America's power emanates not from business, science, money, technology, or government; it stems from us.

The political status quo looks to the average American citizen for two things only: our votes and our money. It would be laughable if it were not so sad.

What America most needs, neither big government nor small government can address at the deepest level. While purveyors of conventional political wisdom present governmental action, or lack thereof, as the primary source of solutions to what ails us, a growing number of Americans sense that the key to genuine solutions is found in the realm of human consciousness. The problem with the current political dialogue is that it seeks to undo the damages we have suffered by means of the same dialectic that created them. To heal the havoc wreaked by a left-brain, paternalistic, authoritarian bias, we must be willing to question the bias itself.

It is not our new problems so much as our old thinking that obstructs America's healing. Old thinking is any thought that sees power in arousing hatred or blame, mirrors an "us versus them" mentality, emphasizes external over internal power, or lacks dedication to a universal, inclusive good. Old thinking does not value repentance, tends to trivialize prayer and spiritual devotion, and values top-down, authoritarian implementation of power.

The surrender of human consciousness to its own divine element is our greatest tool for change. It is more powerful than bullets and more effective than any army. Sacred power is the greatest power in the universe. We were born to extend the power of our spiritual source, and having deviated from that mission, we have become disconnected from our true selves. The fragmentation of our psyches is reflected in the fractured state of the world around us.

Americans do not wake up in the morning *longing* for a balanced budget. What we do most long for cannot be put in material terms. That is because it is not material. We're about to realize that our biggest problems, and our most powerful solutions, are not outside us but within, and therefore cannot adequately be addressed by a political system that only considers external events as real.

## Perchance to Dream

As a nation, we have a collective psyche, a common river of thoughts and feelings that runs through the soul of every American. We are bound together by a common tension between hopes for the blossoming of our highest potential and fears that, for whatever reason, such blossoming will never occur. Americans are less complacent than others when told that our dreams will not come true. We are not patient in the face of rejected dreams because we have always been told we have a right to have them. We were literally born into the promise, that this is a land where dreams come true.

The American dream, when best understood, is not a material thing. Rather, it is the fact that we have the right to dream at all.

It is the right to expect that our talents and abilities and diligence—not the prejudices of others—will determine the nature of the lives we live. Our right to dream whatever life we wish for ourselves, and our responsibility to respect the dreams of others, is the philosophical fulcrum of the American ideal. The American dream is both individual and collective. Even in the most oppressive societies, *some* people have the right to dream. What makes a free society different is that we are *all* supposed to have that right, and a reasonable opportunity to have our dreams come true.

We cannot pursue our happiness, or make manifest our glory, without the right to dream dreams for ourselves and our children. And that right must extend to everyone. Such is the philosophical basis for our belief in an America in which rigging the game of life is an abhorrence. Opportunity is not inherently good unless that opportunity is universal. None of us ultimately wins in America unless all of us have a chance.

The American dream is a dream in process, a not yet fully manifested image of a nation of people with equal access to their own creative powers. Many people in America have lived lives of very limited, even cruelly squelched dreams, not through any fault of their own but through accidents of history and various forms of obstruction and injustice. That has been true in the past, and it is true now. To deny this is not to honor the dream but to mock it. We must vigilantly and rigorously uncover the instances and seek to understand the circumstances where the dream has not been allowed to flourish. Where the violation of these rights occurred in the past, we should atone and seek to make remedy. Where they occur in the present, we should radically and immediately commit ourselves to change. If any Americans are denied the right to weave their dreams, then America itself isn't weaving hers. It is the job of every generation of Americans to further expand and fulfill the dream of freedom and justice for all.

In ending slavery, we committed to the dream. In giving women the right to vote, we committed to the dream. In passing child labor laws, we committed to the dream. In passing civil rights legislation, we committed to the dream. Every generation of Americans plays out the struggle between the forces that would expand the dream and those that would constrict it. Reinterpreting the American dream to mean very little more than a job that pays well is to rob the dream of its deeper meaning.

A national ideal is not an intellectual exercise. It is a sacred, emotional commitment. The statement that our "Creator ... created all men equal" and endowed them with "certain inalienable rights, that among these are life, liberty and the pursuit of happiness" is not an early American public relations slogan. It is a bright light shot like a laser through thousands of years of history. It is a principle for which millions of people have fought and died. These words are radical, revolutionary *force*. They can and have moved the mountains of history. They represent an ideational construct rooted firmly in what is essentially a religious truth, reflecting a national faith in the equality of souls. These words carry such emotional and philosophical power that should enough Americans truly embrace the principles behind them and try their best to live according to them, not one penny would have to be spent—nor ultimately one bullet have to be fired—to protect our interests and extend our most precious truths around the world.

Dreams do not extend through armies or diplomacy; they fly on the wings of passion. All great ideas reflect passion, but most modern education dishonors passion. We are not taught to love our "self-evident" truths, but merely perhaps to memorize them. For far too many of us, the embrace of essential American principles has not been a reenactment of a courageous, experiential response to the darkness of ancestral history, but merely a mechanical recitation of words. Poignantly, however, many millions of Americans would still willingly risk their lives for these principles. There is something in us well aware of an inutterably precious nugget of truth in the dream of our forefathers, which in some mysterious way still applies to each of us.

## Mind Asleep, Mind Awake

Just as the European Renaissance was a break from the stultifying effects of the domination of the Roman Catholic Church, today's renaissance is also a rebellion against a stultifying influence. But this influence today is in a way more difficult to overcome, for it is not institutionalized but systemic. It permeates all our institutions, from education to media, even politics. It is the deadening of the American mind. What the Catholic Church did to Europe during the Middle Ages much public education, the media, and politics do now: they tell us what to think rather than how to think, and ultimately teach us *not* to think.

In early America, people discussed politics in the taverns; the early equivalent of today's longshoreman was as well informed about political issues as was the colonial equivalent of today's business mogul. Democracy means that all of us must become engaged in the big picture of society's affairs. The price you pay for not thinking about something important in your life is that there will always be someone else eager to do your thinking for you. What you don't decide, they'll be happy to decide for you. And obviously, they may not love you.

We must reclaim lost ground. We must stand up, many millions of us, in full intellectual and emotional glory, and so express our own uniqueness in the service of a greater good that the forces that would constrict us are transformed in a great awakening. In the presence of people whose minds are awake, the Great Sleep cannot come upon us. Only in this way can we reassume the power of American citizenship.

That power, to be noble, must be the power of conscience and compassion. That is the only power that comes from God.

Looking around the world today, we see tremendous violence, killing, and assertion of brute force. From street gangs in America to chaos in the Balkans, power without conscience is exploding all around us. The next major unfolding in the progress of human liberty will emerge from our expanded capacity to love. The problem in America today is not that there are more insane people than usual; the problem is that the most fear-based among us are now the most well-organized, enthusiastic, and efficient. We must become as vigilant, focused, and effective at the expression of love's power as others now are in the expression of their hate.

We must live for the day, and work for the day, when human society realigns itself with the radical love of God. In a truly democratic paradigm, there is no love of power for power's sake. Power exists for one good reason and one good reason only: to provide the opportunity to extend the higher processes of life. In the hands of the immature, the purposes of power are greedy or authoritarian, used to increase the dominance of one individual or group over another. True democracy demands a very mature use of power, a deep appreciation for its positive value, and an equally serious vigilance against its misuse.

Americans have been seduced by the perks of power, whether governmental or economic, but not adequately educated in the responsibilities that come with it. That is beginning to change, as many of us have now seen whole worlds crash as a consequence of the misuse of power. We have seen the mighty fall. The contest that matters is not the one to determine whether or not we get power; the contest that matters is the one that occurs within ourselves once we have it. Money and power can easily seduce us into selfish or narcissistic behavior; as we transcend those temptations, however, we are given by material power the opportunity to move the world closer in the direction of good. Worldly power—financial and political—should not be avoided but, rather, used to extend the love of our Creator to every corner of the universe now darkened by its absence. Power should not support the status quo; it should always be cutting through yesterday's complacency to create tomorrow's safety for ourselves and our children.

## Rededication

In the most advanced stages of ancient Egyptian culture, the pharaoh was not just given his job for life. At regular intervals, he had to prove to his people that he still had what it took to do the job, displaying physical, moral, and mental strengths for all his subjects to witness. Similarly, statues of ancient Egyptian gods were reconsecrated yearly through prayer and rituals, as though it could not be taken for granted that the genuine *force* behind material substance would remain fully active without a regular reassertion of human devotion.

So it is that while Americans still go through the paces of our most revered rites of democracy—political campaigns, elections, inaugurations—there is among us the sinking feeling that these rites are losing their spiritual *force*. Anything, no matter how pure, becomes corrupted in the absence of honesty and integrity, or in the presence of malice and exploitation. Democracy is still a vital concept—in fact, more so now than ever; it is the perfect human organizing principle for an ideational age. What we must do now is recommit ourselves to it, so that the house that was built to hold our treasure might be rebuilt around it.

Darkness of various sorts has always sought to suck the spiritual lifeblood out of human civilization, while the love of God continues to pour forth upon us. Never before have the stakes been so high, humanity so challenged to make a decisive choice of which path to tomorrow we wish to take. Renaissance lies in choosing, as a political option, the power of love to heal the world. The problem is not that Americans do not hear our hearts. The problem is that we do not always heed the heart. A materialistic age has peripheralized its call.

But we need to hear that call now. The fabric of American society must be rewoven one loving stitch at a time: one child read to, one sick person prayed for, one elder given respect and made to feel needed, one prisoner rehabilitated, one mourner given comfort. These actions, when performed sincerely, emanate from spiritual ground that is itself the healing of our problems, as our separation from that ground of being has itself been our primary wound. Like the mythical lost continent of Atlantis, there is a ground now submerged beneath the subconscious waters, visible in ancient times perhaps but not visible now, set to rise again, to reappear. The level of consciousness that is the salvation of the human race is not something new, so much as very old yet forgotten. The ultimate height of human thinking and being is, in fact, the source point from which we all began. Our initial tenderness, wonderment, and innocence have been suppressed and marginalized by the world we have built—the world of secular, mechanistic "progress." It is only when we fall in love, marry, give birth, grieve openly, or prepare to die that we dare to show our real face. Our failure to be more authentically human is threatening to destroy the world.

In a country where our political right to live creatively is so

—

awesomely assured, there is yet within most of us the feeling that a beautiful instrument is in some way going unplayed. There is a saying in the Jewish prayer book, "Sad is he who does not sing, and when he dies his music dies with him." Something goes unsung in most Americans today, though there is yet within each of us the urging of an internal conductor, exhorting and preparing us to sing.

While earthly resources are finite, spiritual ones are not. Our gifts from God can be ignored but they can never be destroyed. In all of us there is divine potential and the natural propensity to reach for it. It is not our political rights but our God-given gifts that are the promise of deliverance from the problems of the world.

In a nation of 266 million, our healing is actually extremely personal. We must each mature into a deeper understanding of our lives and why we're living them, for such understanding is the womb out of which will come new life for American culture. We are all of us bound together. Just as our external movements have the power to affect others, so do our internal ones. As *we* become, so the country becomes. As each of us awakens to the preciousness of our individual right to make a difference in America—and our responsibility to try—we become a powerful wave of resistance to the forces that would tear us down. It is not just our capacity to say no to what we don't want that is our power to renew America. It is our deeper power to say yes to our own creative abilities and yes to the light within others, which is both the promise of democracy and its furtherance. Each generation brings forth new life, physically and spiritually, or life will stop. So it is that each of us must now commit to bring forth, on some level, new life in America.

## One Mind, One Heart

There is a scientific theory that the universe is like a hologram. Imagine that you have a photograph of someone, and you tear the picture down the middle. You now have two pictures: one of the person's left side and one of his or her right side.

But if you have a hologram and you break it in two, then you are left with two complete images, each slightly less clear than the original but total nevertheless. So it is that each of us contains within us not just a piece of the whole but a level of the whole *in its entirety.* That is why when we change, so does everything on some level, for better or for worse. This makes a conscious person feel more responsible for the world, yet also more hopeful. For what we do and what we are carry more influence than we might previously have imagined.

America's renaissance is a quantum phenomenon, whereby we change the society not only through awakening others but through our own awakening. Our own transformation influences the world, for all minds are joined. We need not stop in fear when we read a newspaper report of something that shouldn't be happening. If enough people read the same article and think the following thought: *"This should not be happening in America; I am committed to this not happening in America"*—then that alone contributes to a new vortex of power. A moral vortex. A motivational momentum. And *that* becomes political power.

Our problem today is that, first, although people are inundated with bad news all the time, the worst news of all remains hidden. The worst news is not just what is happening but what it *means* that certain things are happening—the bigger picture. The mainstream news often reports facts, but rarely does it reveal meaning. We must find meaning for ourselves; the search for it is the social artistry at the heart of a new politics.

---

Every awakened thought, meditation, and prayer is a vote to turn the world around. A new political power is trying to emerge, like bound hands breaking free. We must throw off the chains of careless, passive thinking by which we have been so insidiously constricted, and assert our emotional, psychological, and spiritual independence from the dominant thought forms of our culture. We must rethink the world before we can change it; until then, all progressive action will merely take us in circles. It is internal power which can give us a new footing in the external world; the only way out of our outer darkness is through inner light.

Gandhi stressed that society cannot be divided into watertight compartments; we are living at a time of "whole-systems transition," in which the only way to address a piece is if you have a powerful grasp of the whole. Everything affects everything, because all things emerge from consciousness.

To bring peace to America, we must find peace within ourselves. Hysterical, greedy, frantic, insecure, cowering, unclear, inebriated, obsessed minds will not bring forth an American renaissance.

Because of the incredible power of the electronic media, our thoughts are magnified a trillionfold. American pop culture is a context in which someone has a thought, and millions join them in that thought within minutes. This is the good news and the bad news also. We have become, through the electronic media, one global brain. Now we must become one heart.

## The Heart of America

The heart of America already dwells beneath the surface of things, like an underground territory, a morphic field of thoughts and feelings that feeds our hopes and understanding. It is an

inchoate sense in all of us that America—and each one of us—
is capable of great things.

If we desire an American renaissance, we must reeducate and
reempower ourselves. We must seek depth as well as breadth of
activity. Where we have no access to our deeper humanness, we
have no access to our greater intelligence. While myriad problems cry out for breakthrough solutions, we are stymied by our
tacit agreement to keep the cultural and political conversation
as sophomoric as possible, lest the average citizen actually be
called upon to think an issue through.

We must reclaim our capacity to think and feel as powerfully
and deeply as possible, and expand our capacity to love.

What matters now, and always, is whether God's love infuses
the things we do. What is not love is an illusion. It does not
matter how sophisticated an illusion is or how technologically
stunning the application of its power. We must seek to leave
illusions behind us.

The purpose of our lives is to bring forth on earth as perfect
an expression as we are capable of achieving of the goodness of
the human spirit. For us to mine that spirit in our children, and
exalt it in their nurturance; to devote our undertakings to the
flowing forth of that spirit in all things and all people, making
all else secondary to the achievement of that goal—this is the
calling that will renew America, for this is the call to awaken
our soul.

Democracy means we are free to do whatever we feel in our
hearts that we should do. The noble practice of democracy is
our willingness to do it. A threat to democracy is anything that
would have us believe that something else is more important.

Herein lies our renaissance.

# 2

# FIRST PRINCIPLES

*"Educate and inform the mass of the people.... En-*
*lighten the people generally, and tyranny and op-*
*pressions of body and mind will vanish like evil*
*spirits at the dawn of day."*
— THOMAS JEFFERSON

HISTORY is a series of phases, much like gates that delineate the march of human progress. With each phase of American history we have entered more deeply into the well of human possibilities, consciously and unconsciously creating our destiny as a nation. As we stood before every gate in the past, and as we stand before them now, we make the choices that define the meaning of history: would we choose "the angels of our better nature," to use Lincoln's phrase, or the demons of our lower selves to make manifest in the world?

America's history is a grand drama, though a relatively short one as yet—an expression of humanity at both its best and its worst. We are a land of contradictions. We were born of a stunning assertion of the human spirit in the face of tyranny, yet we built a country on the blood of Native Americans and slaves from Africa. We expanded our physical territory and our commitment to freedom, abolishing slavery, giving suffrage to women, banning child labor, and in many other ways remaining true to the goal of expanding democracy. Had the Industrial Revolution, with its gargantuan focus on material power, not occurred, then the magnificence of our original ideals might have continued to pull us upward and out of the devolutionary lure of history. But the Industrial Revolution did occur, and

---

while it allowed the world phenomenal opportunity for the eradication of material suffering, it also clearly fostered our spiritual forgetfulness. Material progress became an American god. We now had two lovers: our principles and our money. We endured the horrors of the Civil War, fought two World Wars, brilliantly helped to defeat Hitler, then imperialistically devastated Vietnam. We are blessed with more money and more technological resources than any other nation of the world, yet we give only .6 of one percent of our budget away to nations less fortunate than we. We are a nation that loves to say how much we love our children, yet children are less well cared for in America than in any of our industrialized counterparts.

What is important is not merely that we record history, or that we understand it from a seemingly objective perspective. What matters is that we take it personally, that we own our history in the deepest part of ourselves, that we might solidify its power where it is something to be proud of and transform it where it is not.

## *Claiming Our Inheritance*

We are the heirs of a philosophical and political fortune. America has fostered such genius and enlightened thinking in our relatively short history that we need less to reinvent wheels than to drive on the ones we have. We are like children of a most astounding legacy, who have forgotten where we came from. We don't need a lot of frantic action so much as we need depth of thought and historical knowledge.

Beginnings matter, for they determine the trajectory by which events tend to unfold. If Washington personified the yang of our beginnings—the father of our country who led the Revolutionary Army—then Jefferson was the yin, his mind the womb out of which we sprang. To know him, however slightly, is to know an important part of ourselves. Like all great souls, he has the power to teach and guide us from the grave.

The reason our Founders matter is because meaningful lives jump out of time, grab us by the heart and oblige us to try to emulate them. We are compelled by an adequate knowledge of history to measure our lives in relation to it, to succeed where others have faltered, to run the race that others ran, to try to keep the wheels of history moving in a positive direction. The past teaches us, most importantly, that the movement of history in the direction of good can never, ever be taken for granted.

The founding of America is not a tale drawn from one-dimensional lives. Jefferson, Washington, Franklin, Madison, Hamilton, Adams, and Paine were very real people—nothing in their day like the formal and official portraits of them that now hang in polite museums. The same is true of their successors— the great American statesmen, political thinkers, social reformers, philosophers, writers, and artists who have helped us re-found ourselves from that day to our own time.

We have made wooden characters of very juicy people. Jefferson almost did not emerge from his grief over the death of his wife, and years later wrote love letters to Maria Cosway that make *The Bridges of Madison County* look tame; Lincoln would bury his head in his hands each time news reports reached him of massive casualties in the Civil War, sobbing, "I cannot bear it, I cannot bear it"; polio victim Franklin D. Roosevelt clung to the arm of his son in a heroic effort to appear to walk on his own to the podium at the 1932 Democratic Convention, knowing that if Americans thought he could not walk then they would never elect him. He succeeded, and was then described as having been "cleansed, illumined and transformed by his pain."

They were so much more interesting than the characters on most TV sitcoms. All Americans should introduce ourselves to our great historical figures, and bring them to life in our hearts and minds. Things they said and did affect each of us in a practical manner, every day of our lives.

The principles that our Founders elucidated in the Declaration of Independence, our Constitution, and our Bill of Rights —what the Revolutionary generation called our "first principles"—continue to keep us together despite the many forces that would pull us apart. They can handle any assault except the people's diminished commitment to them. It is seriously detrimental to our individual and collective good that the average American citizen does not know what those principles are.

## A Nation So Conceived

Our Founders were acutely aware that generations of Americans would be living under the influence of the principles they set down. They poured all of their prodigious talents into defining these principles. As the architects of the American experiment, they eagerly scoured history for the best ideas to draw from, from republics ancient and modern, to English common law constitutionalism and state constitutions, to the writings of Renaissance and Enlightenment philosophies. No body of knowledge or experience was irrelevant to their quest.

These were also religious men, though of a kind that modern fundamentalists might not recognize. They saw no hostility between religion and science; John Adams described God as the Great Legislator of the Universe. Theirs was a reasonable religion, and the total and complete freedom to worship—or not, and to whom—was central to their conception of American liberty.

America's first principles are not partisan issues. They are the things on which we have agreed to agree. We agree that all people should be equal before the law. We agree that power in America shall stem not from the government into the people but rather from the people into the government. We agree to seek to balance individual rights with protection of the general welfare. And we agree that people shall have the right to freely practice and share their religious, social, and political beliefs without threat of external tyranny.

A nation "so conceived," in the words of Lincoln, is so radical in its inspired authority that there have been times in our history when the critical mass of American sentiment has not measured up to our own first principles. The Civil War, for instance, was a contest pitting those who chose to hold the nation to its principle of equality for all against those who tried to secede from the Union rather than give up slavery and comply.

In other words, our governmental principles are often more advanced than we are, owing to the extraordinary prescience and genius of our Founders. In 1801, the newly elected President Jefferson admonished the nation to make "periodic recourse to first principles," relying on their power and the power of our collective agreement to adhere to them, to guide us as beacons through darkened times. The fact that Jefferson himself, as an owner of slaves, did not fully live up to those ideals does not mean the ideals themselves mean less. It means that he began a process he did not complete, one that we have still not completed, yet which every generation of Americans must try its best to further.

Our founding principles are important not just because they are encoded in American law. They are important also because they are impressive reflections of a higher law. That is why they have been such a compelling force to so many millions of human beings throughout the world. It is why they continue to inspire. It is why we forget them or ignore them at our peril.

The fundamental ideals of American society are just that—

*ideals.* They are transcendent archetypes that stand over and above the material realities of life. It is not our role to merely complain if our reality doesn't match the ideal; rather, we should further the process by which the reality will some day, for some generation of Americans, completely reflect the ideal. To do that, we must ourselves embrace the principles. We must taste our first principles, understand them, and hopefully come to love them. They must remain alive in us if they are to remain alive in the world.

It is extremely rare that an issue comes up in American society that does not have light cast upon it by our first principles. They form America's political bedrock. Today, our problem is that most Americans do not know what those principles are. We were either taught them in school and have forgotten them, or we actually never learned them. We therefore tend to think of political negotiation as a fight between competing opinions, rather than a process by which we all work toward a higher realization of principles on which we already agree.

Freedom does not mean that we all agree on a particular issue. Quite to the contrary, it means that we are free to disagree. Our Founders did not presume to provide answers to future generations; what they provided was a creative framework for arriving at answers. Our first principles form the core of that framework, guaranteeing not the content but the process of democracy. Every generation is a guardian of the process. America is not a particle but a wave.

None of us has all the answers. But there must be a common understanding that underlies our disagreements—a sense that we are all involved in a common work. Every generation is challenged to manifest America's first principles at the highest possible level. Because these principles have roots not in trend or opinion but in higher truth, they have the power to sustain us as long as enough of us genuinely embrace them.

Our first principles stand outside of time, providing a stillness that keeps our nation centered through the centrifugal tides of historical change. To refer back to them at this time is vitally important.

Too few of us are passionate about these principles anymore. Citizenship means more than voting, paying taxes, or obeying laws. It is a powerful expression of self, the absence of which makes it easy to steal from us the powers we have been granted. In fact, much of our power as citizens has already been drastically diminished through the influence of money in the electoral process. That lessening of our collective strength, for those who wished it, was relatively easy to accomplish, for most of us have been too busy thinking about other things, or simply not thinking at all.

America's first principles are simple and basic. They are undergirded by an even more basic idea: that we are a democracy, and thus govern ourselves. These principles are guideposts for the process of doing so. They are the keys to our freedom and the freedom of our children. They are:

- *Equality of Rights and Opportunity:* that all of us are equal before God and should be treated that way by the American government;
- *E Pluribus Unum:* that within our diversity lies a national unity—that we are at the same time a people who reflect and embody diversity, yet are united by fealty to these treasured first principles;
- *Balance of Individual Liberty and Protection of the Common Good:* that it is the responsibility of government to protect the general welfare, yet with enough checks and balances to ensure that it remains limited enough to guarantee our individual liberties;
- *Religious Freedom:* that every American shall worship how he

or she wishes, if he or she wishes, according to the individual's own conscience and with no governmental interference in that right.

Only when we can say that these first principles are at home within us can we honestly say that we embrace the American ideal.

Lincoln said we must preserve the Union through the purity of its principles. The purpose of political progress is to make worldly conditions reflect more and more perfectly the principles on which we are based. Ideals are perfect; the world is not. It is our responsibility as citizens to actively promote an alignment of the two. *That* is politics.

You don't have to be a lawyer to understand the basic principles. James Madison was the leading spirit among those who *wrote* the U.S. Constitution, and he was not a lawyer. You don't have to be a theologian to care passionately about God; you don't have to be a politician to care passionately about America; and you don't have to be a scholar to understand the basic first principles of American democracy. As important as experts are at times, you don't have to be one to have a valuable opinion. The "myth of the experts"—the notion that only certain people are "qualified" to hold forth on subjects that affect us all—is an antidemocratic sentiment. Homemakers, surely some of our most naturally wise Americans, are apt to be particularly frightened off by that kind of elitist prejudice.

You can read a book wherever you are. Lincoln studied law in a town of three hundred people. The notion of a collective wisdom arising from reasoned debate, deliberation, and consensus building was our Founders' vision of the democratic process. Such collective wisdom cannot emerge if the average citizen lacks basic understanding of what is being debated. If you don't know the rules of a game, then how can you know to yell when someone is breaking them?

## Principle 1: All Are Equal and Shall Be Treated Equally Before the Law

The wording of the Declaration of Independence is as follows: "We hold these truths to be self-evident, that all men are created equal, that they are endowed by their Creator with certain inalienable rights, that among these are life, liberty and the pursuit of happiness. That to secure these rights, governments are instituted among men, deriving their just powers from the consent of the governed."

This principle is easy to take for granted until we remember how essentially radical it is. It means that in this country, it is not the circumstances of our birth, but the fact that we are American, that determines our rights and opportunities to pursue happiness. Note that the Declaration says that it is the responsibility of government to *secure* those rights.

The ideal of equality, and the reality through time of our progress toward it, is central to American democracy. Without that, the political treasure that is our system of government is little more than words.

Regarding both rights and opportunities, equality as a first principle is threatened in America today. But this threat is largely underestimated. It is couched in words that imply we take equality for granted here, that *of course* we all believe in it, and therefore we *need not be vigilant* on its behalf. That is a dangerous falsehood.

Every time we take support away from nutritional, medical, educational, or job training and creation programs that benefit those who need them most—then give tax cuts to the far more privileged—we are attacking the first principle of equality.

Thomas Jefferson said that we must endlessly struggle for, and never be complacent until we have achieved, equal opportunity for modest prosperity and equal treatment before the law *of every American* citizen. That is central to the notion of liberty in America.

We sometimes have a tendency to make our first principles stand second and third in line.

When some of our congresspeople say, as they so often do these days, that we must balance the budget because the deficit means we are not taking care of our children, what they really mean is that we are not taking care of *their* children. *Their* children stand to receive Social Security and Medicare payments fifty years from now, and *their* children do not need Head-Start or nutrition programs *today*. The American public is being asked to acquiesce in an unethical arrangement whereby we steal from poor children today to make sure that children of parents more well off are presumably taken care of in the future. If we believe in the principle of equality, then the rich should not be granted greater opportunity than the poor.

Where there is little adequate education—as in the inner cities of America—there is no equality of opportunity. Where there is little adequate health care—as among America's poor —there is no equality of opportunity. Where there are very few opportunities for true professional advancement—as is also true among America's poor—there is no equality of opportunity.

Many issues look different when seen through the lens of the first principle of equality—universal health care, education, and criminal justice, to name a few. The political question, for instance, should not be, "What do you think of homosexuals?" but rather, "Do we or do we not remain committed to the principle of equality for all, and how does that principle apply to the quest for homosexual rights?" Whether someone in America *likes* someone else in America is irrelevant to what both of their rights should be before the law.

Martin Luther King, Jr., used to say that he was not going to Washington to *ask* for rights for black Americans but to *demand* the rights they had been given already. Equal opportunity is not a principle that someone gets to bring up for a vote. It is a sacred first principle already established; to threaten it is to threaten our liberty. As my father used to say, "What they can do to anyone, they can one day do to you."

In the words of Martin Niemoller, a Lutheran pastor who was imprisoned by the Nazis for eight years because he spoke out against Hitler, "First, they came for the socialists, and I did not speak out because I was not a socialist. Then they came for the trade unionists, and I did not speak out because I was not a trade unionist. Then they came for the Jews, and I did not speak out because I was not a Jew. Then they came for me, and there was no one left to speak for me."

## Principle 2: Unity in Diversity

Our Founders were wide-ranging thinkers and students; they learned, directly or indirectly, from every body of ideas and information available to them. Both Benjamin Franklin and Thomas Jefferson were careful and respectful students of the government and politics of the Iroquois Confederation and other Native American peoples.

In the Iroquois Indian Confederacy, different Native American Indian tribes retained their individuality yet created a common network for the sake of progress and mutual protection. Echoes of that governmental philosophy, among others, can be found in America's first principle, *E Pluribus Unum*, or Unity in Diversity.

There are people in America who overemphasize our unity yet fail to appreciate the importance of our diversity, just as there are those who emphasize our diversity yet fail to appreciate the importance of our unity. It is imperative that we honor both. It is our unity *and* our diversity that matter, and their relationship to each other reflects a philosophical and political truth outside of which we cannot thrive.

Unity and diversity are not adversarial but, rather, complementary parts of a unified whole. They are, at their best, synergistic partners in the creation of a more highly evolved culture. We are woven from many diverse threads, yet we make one piece of fabric. We are one and many at the same time; you're a Catholic *and* you're an American; you're gay *and* you're an American; you're black *and* you're an American.

When our country was founded, our diversity was determined mainly by a geographical dimension. Massachusetts was very different from the Carolinas; they remained true to their individual identities while at the same time forging one American culture. Our statehood now is a less critical geographical concept than an ideological one; our ethnicity, beliefs, and economics define our differing "states" today. We are different colors, different religions, different beliefs, and different cultures. Yet we must agree, as adherents of basic American democratic principles, on the sanctity of our commonality, as well. We are all Americans, and we are involved in a great experiment *together*. No group of Americans are the "normal" Americans, no group of Americans monopolize truth or wisdom or righteousness, and no group of Americans deserve more or less protection or opportunity from the American government.

It is when we have a healthy experience of our individual identity that we can most easily accept sharing a larger one. But the former step cannot be skipped; it is wrong to expect someone to play down his or her religious or racial or cultural identity in service to a larger identity until he or she has first been shown honor for what that individual identity is. At that point—once we have all been acknowledged as individually significant—it is important for us to then turn our attention to how we might together serve a greater whole.

There are many times when conservatives act as if white middle-class Americans were the *real* America and everyone else's values are given lip service, at best. There are just as many times, however, when liberals take part in an election and then say, "Look, we delivered *our* vote, so *we* should get *this*," as though all of us are separate islands in a meaningless sea. Those viewpoints show equal dishonor to this first principle.

Unity in diversity is a principle that demands of us personal maturity. We must develop the ability to tolerate the creative chaos of many voices and opinions all expressing themselves at once; to not seek control over the thoughts or behaviors of others just because they are different from us; and to listen with respect and recognize the dignity of those with whom we disagree. It is not a first principle in America that any one group gets to be *right*. It is a first principle that each of us, and each of our many cultures, has valuable things to say and to contribute. Allowing everyone to do so is central to our liberty, our genius, and our evolution toward greater good.

Wrote St. Thomas Aquinas, "We must love them both, those whose opinions we share and those whose opinions we reject. For both have labored in the search for truth and both have helped us in the finding of it."

This principle, as well as the freedom of religion, demands that we go much further than mere tolerance. There are people in America who "tolerate" through clenched teeth, who "respectfully disagree" with a look that is chilling. Liberty depends on our understanding that America *belongs to all of us.* Equality means that none of us is inherently better than anyone else. Freedom means that we actually like it that way.

## *Principle 3: The Federal Government Shall Secure the Collective Welfare, Yet with Enough Checks and Balances to Ensure Individual Liberty*

This principle is at the center of our greatest achievements, as well as our greatest political battles. America ideally seeks to balance the needs of the individual with the needs of the collective.

This first principle demands our very best thinking and action. Yes, it is true that we must protect the environment and the children—but yes, it is also true that the individual should be as free as possible to pursue personal economic goals without interference or obstruction. Yes, it is true that we must protect the rights of the citizen from too much police or government involvement in our personal affairs—but yes, it is also true that law enforcement officials must have the means they need to protect us. Very few of us can honestly say that we do not get carried away sometimes, overemphasizing either individual rights or collective welfare. Depending on whether we're liberal or conservative—and what particular issue we're discussing— it's amazing how revved up we can get about one side of the equation or the other. What we need at this time is a passion for creating balance between the two.

President Eisenhower once said that the American mind at its best is both liberal and conservative. We must seek to conserve those things that are eternally true, while retaining the ability to respond liberally and spontaneously to the immediate demands of our time.

A true liberal doesn't think government can fix all our problems, any more than a true conservative believes that what's good for General Motors is always good for America. But in fact, it is the purest liberals as well as the purest conservatives who are having a hard time being heard in America today. The best of American political thinking is not somewhere in the middle, but rather liberal *and* conservative. The highest political truth emerges from a synergistic relationship between the two. After the hardest fought Presidential election of his time, Thomas Jefferson reminded his countrymen, "We are all Republicans, We are all Federalists."

Civic life in America *should* include vigorous debate between liberals and conservatives: that is democracy in action. But the debate must remain within the bounds of mutual respect and dignity or our civil life is no longer civil. Those who couch political debate as merely "your needs and desires vs. my needs and desires"—with no respect for America's need to balance individual liberty with the common good—bring down the political process.

## Principle 4: All Americans Shall Be Free to Find God, or Not Find God, However Their Conscience Permits

The separation of church and state was not meant to religiously constrict us, but rather to religiously free us. A thick line between the state and religion allows the religious world to go forward untethered by state interference, and it allows the state to go forward untethered by religious interference. It is an enlightened concept.

---

But separating the state from the undue influence of religious institutions should not be an impediment to the search for higher truth within the political arena. Spiritual understanding is a human need, not just a religious issue. Without it, the world does not make sense and any human endeavor that leaves it out of consideration will not end up making sense, either.

The genuine religious impulse is an internal phenomenon, and civilization has always suffered when any particular dogma or doctrine has sought to impose itself upon the peoples of the world. The highest, most spirit-filled religious consciousness is a living water. The container through which that water is poured into the world is not the organization of a religion but the human heart. Love *is* the religious experience. No religion has a monopoly on God. Religion itself has no monopoly on God. Ecclesiastical, orthodox religious systems are not the only arbiters of spiritual force. We will not be renewed by a worldly religious authority; we will be renewed by God Himself.

Religion can be a confusing concept. The word itself comes from a root that means "to bind back." The actual religious experience is an internal phenomenon, a "binding back" of our hearts to the truth within. An example of a spiritually based political force in America was the Civil Rights movement of the 1950s and 1960s. Although emanating from Martin Luther King's Southern Christian Leadership Conference, its call reached not only Christians but also all other people of good will, for its message was one of universal harmony and brotherhood. That's what made it so radical and also so purely religious. King's goal of achieving the "beloved community" is a vision at the heart of not one but all religious faiths.

There is an important distinction to be made between a religiously based and a spiritually based political impulse. While religion is a force that either creatively or noncreatively separates us, spirituality is a force that unites us by reminding us of our fundamental oneness. The religionization of American politics is dangerous; the spiritualization of our political consciousness is imperative.

When violence erupted in Israel in September of 1996 over the Israeli opening of a tunnel near the Dome of the Rock in Jerusalem, the clear difference between religious dogma and spiritual passion was obvious. For three of the great religions of the world, this particular piece of land is holy: Muslims believe that Mohammed ascended to heaven from there, the Jews believe that it is the spot from which God created the universe, and the Christians hold that Christ walked past there on his way to the cross. While a strictly exoteric religious perspective tempts us to compete for land, a genuine spiritual experience joins our hearts.

The authentic teachings of all the great religious perspectives reveal that it is not land that matters, but love itself. God's call is not that we build His temple on a particular piece of land, but in our hearts. That is where the Rock is.

Many people in the world today use religion to divide us. They cite a particular book, whether the Bible, the Koran, or any other religious text, and claim that herein lies a universal prescription for all human behavior. Such fundamentalist mentality is more *about* God than *of* God, and the distinction between the two is one of the most important issues in world affairs today.

In *Notes on the State of Virginia*, Thomas Jefferson wrote, "[I]t does me no injury for my neighbor to say there are twenty gods, or no god. It neither picks my pocket nor breaks my leg."

In the summer of 1996, the public library in Seabrook, New Hampshire, was forced to cancel two lecture programs, titled "The History and Use of Tarot Cards" and "Numerology and Dream Analysis." Some local church members threatened to force the closing of the library, if need be, to keep the lectures from happening. A minister from a local congregation said that these "occult" talks were "inviting all who would participate to unleash a literal 'hornet's nest' of destructive spiritual entities into their lives." The leader of his church choir said that "there is a power at work in these tarot readings and the like, but it's not the power of God."

Religious freedom, as an American first principle, means no one in America has a right to monopolize the religious discussion. We must cultivate more than tolerance; we must cultivate respect. Jefferson wrote, "Toleration is not enough. What we need is liberty, fully protected by the law, to believe or not believe as you see fit." America was not founded to protect the definition of God as proposed by any one group or individual; it was founded to protect our liberty to think however we wish to think.

I once said to my six-year-old daughter, an avid Barbie fan, "Darling, Barbie looks anorexic. Someone with a body like that would be in the hospital with a very bad disease. Her hair is stupid and her values are questionable. Do you think she ever does any charity work?" My daughter looked me squarely in the eye and said, "Mommy, I love who I love. I'm not going to change my thoughts." I gulped. I didn't agree with my child's opinion, but I was glad she was so quick to defend her right to have one.

And that is exactly the issue here. As Teresa Amato, a citizen of Seabrook who circulated an anticensorship petition regarding the library incident, was quoted in *The New York Times,* "The library is a place for controversy. Democracy depends on it, and on the free flow of information, not denying people the right to make their own choices."

We must not indulge any group of Americans who seek to ban other people's conception of spirituality from the public sphere on the basis that "it is not of God," when in fact it simply isn't in line with their conception of God. We are *not* a Christian nation. We are not a Jewish, Muslim, or Hindu nation. We are not a Buddhist, Sufi, Baha'i, or any other officially religious nation. We are not an atheistic nation. We are a nation where religious freedom, including the freedom to not believe, and religious pluralism are sacred first principles. No one is free unless all of us are free.

There are those in America today who seem to distrust the mechanics of liberty. Democracy is indeed a radical proposition. It is posited on the notion that each of us, from the depth of our own wisdom, brings to society the unique and precious gift of our own viewpoint and experience. We do not, and will not, always see things the same way. This is not a bad thing; it is a good thing. Nowhere does this hold true more than in the area of religion.

Religious freedom doesn't ban God from our midst; it gives Him more room to breathe among us. It makes more space for the various facets of His light. And all those facets are divine emanations.

If Americans cherish liberty, both here and around the world, then one of the most significant ways we can promote it is to learn of other people's religions. Throughout the world, from Ireland to Bosnia to the Middle East, and increasingly in the United States, violence comes from fear born of ignorance of another's religious viewpoint. There is one God, and one God only. He pours Himself into many vessels, expressing His Truth in many ways, but still His Truth is one. In making a basic study of comparative religion—reading such books, for instance, as Huston Smith's *The World's Religions*—we see the universality of basic religious themes.

Our Founders did not wish to keep God out of the public sphere, but merely to make our society a place where He—or She, by the way—could be freely sought or not sought according to an individual's proclivity. Indeed, religious pluralism is a most crucial issue in the world today. We should not be banning spiritual lectures; we should be attending them in droves. We should be learning more about our own religious traditions *and* the traditions of our fellows. In this way we will come to know the unity in our religious diversity, without which we cannot appreciate the full genius of our American system of government or the greater glory of God.

## Doing Our Own Thinking

Our first principles should be the stuff of popular conversation. If someone says, "By what authority do you hold forth on these topics?" you might say, "By authority of the fact that *I am an American.*"

Democracy cannot thrive if the Supreme Court refers to the Constitution, the media refer to the Constitution, Congress and the president refer to the Constitution, but not enough of *us* refer to the Constitution. In the spring of 1997, some Congressmen suggested the impeachment and removal from the bench of federal judges *only* because those judges voiced opinions about the Constitution and the law that those Congressmen disagreed with. Our nation learned long ago that we needed an independent judiciary to safeguard the Constitution—the formal expression of the will of We the People of the United States—from government officials and short-term majorities who claim to act in the name of We the People of the United States. A key component of that lesson we learned is that we should *only* remove judges from office for treason, bribery, or other high crimes and misdemeanors—not merely because we disagree with them. Without a free judiciary, there is, for all practical purposes, no freedom at all. Apparently, even some of our elected representatives seem woefully ignorant of the Constitutional principles on which our government rests.

I heard a Senator speaking on television recently about what he perceived as our need for a Balanced Budget Amendment. He said that balancing the budget is a fundamental role of government, and that we need this Amendment so that anyone sworn into office would have to swear on a Bible that, as part of the duty to defend the Constitution, he or she would be sworn to balance the budget.

But our government has something even more important to protect than our money: the principles for which we stand.

America has been slowly unraveling our commitment to the values at the heart of democracy, allowing the demands of the market to diminish our insistence on equality and justice for all Americans. In order to right ourselves, we need not so much to convert to a new organizing principle as to reclaim the one in which we are supposedly already grounded. Democracy works, if we work it.

Our political institutions have become more top-down and authoritarian, and our citizenship less participatory. Money seems to practically control the democratic process, and neither party has yet to genuinely press for change; our societal commitment to social equality seems to diminish daily, our schools even heading back to "separate but equal" status; lobbyists have actually come into Congressional offices and written the bills from there; we read of young people being shot in the back by policemen; the Air Force unveils new stealth bombers in ceremonies that look like a cross between a Disney press conference and a military parade through Red Square; and the CIA says to ailing Gulf War vets, "Ooops—we forgot to *tell* you about those chemical weapons sites before you bombed them!"

This is not a good time to fall asleep in America.

Although America ushered democracy into the modern

world, in the last few decades—while other societies have rushed to democratize—we have been slowly and insidiously retreating from our own democratic commitments. Americans have for the most part stood idly by while a wave of authoritarian forces has sought, and still seeks, to remove from our laws the most solid bulwarks of democracy. Big business has become our new aristocracy, while the average citizen is a new brand of serf.

Democracy was not established by our Founders so that any one group could triumph over another. It was established so that the people as a whole could triumph. Democracy carries within itself an understanding and commitment to the notion that when the greater good of all is not served, then the good of the few will not last.

In an interview for *The New York Times* in April 1997, former President Jimmy Carter said,

> The Government has changed dramatically since I was in the White House. I was with Presidents Bush and Ford early last week and we all agreed that since all of us left office, there has been a hardening of concern in the Federal Government and the other levels of government, a sternness about people who are unfortunate, a condemnation of people who are different from ourselves, a discrimination against people who are poor and deprived that is quite traumatic in its impact.

According to the newspaper account, Mr. Carter cited inequities in the criminal justice system that often penalize blacks and other minority groups more than whites. He said that as a young governor of Georgia, he and contemporaries like Reubin Askew in Florida and Dale Bumpers in Arkansas had "an intense competition" over who had the smallest prison population.

"Now it's totally opposite," Mr. Carter added. "Now the governors brag on how many prisons they've built and how many people they can keep in jail and for how long."

Are American children truly inspired to understand and cherish anymore the principles by which we are called to live? That all men are created equal and deserve the same rights and opportunities, and that the responsibility of every generation is to try to make that creed a living truth for an entire nation? The purpose of education is for something more important than getting and keeping a job; even citizens of a fascist state have jobs. The purpose of education is that we might come to understand the world and our place in it, that we might be fueled in our actions by our own resources of depth and intelligence. We should be educated not to serve the system but to *run* the system. In a democracy, we must all be leaders, and we cannot lead what we are ignorant of.

America's most fundamental problem is a crisis of our democratic process. We are being asked, as we were asked over two hundred years ago, to decide for ourselves and our children what it is worth to us to govern ourselves. While it appears that we have problems very different from those faced by earlier generations, it is in fact not the complexity of our current affairs but the simple drama behind them that Americans most need to consider. What we call the issues are not the issues. The great issue of this particular moment in history is not taxes, balancing the budget, Social Security, or Medicare. Those items are rather elaborate red herrings. The great issue that confronts us, as it confronted Jefferson's generation and Lincoln's generation and every generation to some degree, is this: Is America to be ruled *by* all of us and *for* all of us—or has the American government in fact become a government *of, by, and for a relative few?*

Americans love to think that we are a classless society, but perhaps we should take a closer look. Economic disparity creates class distinctions. We have already become, for all intents and purposes, a society made up of three classes: very poor servants to the system, middle-class servants to the system, and an ever-richer aristocracy. The economic, political, and social policies of the last thirty years have succeeded in tilting the balance of opportunity so far in the direction of the already privileged that our cornerstone principles of equality and democracy have become—in dangerous ways—little more than words. In the late 1980s, one of the richest men in America said to me, "It's obscene how low my taxes are."

Lincoln declared at Gettysburg that "this nation, under God, shall have a new birth of freedom; and that government of the people, by the people, and for the people, shall not perish from the earth." We must take a very good look at that sentence—especially the part that reads "for the people"—and ask ourselves if we have decided to be the generation to repudiate Lincoln's words.

If ours were a government *for the people,* wouldn't our children receive the best education in the world? If ours were a government *for the people,* wouldn't we have universal health insurance? If ours were a government *for the people,* wouldn't we have massively committed to "clean" energy sources by now?

A mean group of selfish people did not decide to steal America. What happened is that we gave her away. We have failed to be vigilant on behalf of our own good. We have failed to make periodic recourse to first democratic principles, settling for the disempowerment of ignorance and distraction. We have turned our eyes away from things that, in a free and democratic society, the average citizen cannot afford to turn his or her eyes away from.

We must turn them back.

## Choosing Democracy

A renewed dedication to democracy is the perfect antidote to the current dissolution of American culture. True democracy, as a context for the release of individual units of creative power, is a much more powerful corrective to our problems than any bolstering of authoritarian strength. There is a deep populism inherent in American democracy—the claim that there is within each of us a wisdom and intelligence that makes us capable of governing ourselves. The diminution of our political rights is a direct reflection of our diminished commitment to them.

There is a spurious patriotism in America today, a "rah-rah" mentality regarding American liberty that is used to mask the systematic dismantling of our freedoms. Reflexively increasing the powers of law enforcement and security agencies is hardly something that lovers of democracy should be excited about. Economic deference to the preferences of big business, as opposed to the needs of ordinary people, is hardly something that lovers of democracy should be excited about. Institutionalized demonization of anyone not considered "normal" by a narrowly defined status quo is hardly something that lovers of democracy should be excited about.

It is important to understand what our Founders envisioned for this country, so that we might effectively cry "Foul!" when people work to undermine that vision. The original vision for American democracy is radical, indeed. Our Founders had the audacity to posit the notion that all American citizens should have equal access to opportunity and power, and that we contain within ourselves the inherent intelligence, through deliberation and consensus, to run our own affairs.

The promises of American democracy, and the personal dreams and creativity they make room for, are central to who we are as a nation. Our responsibility is to cherish and protect those promises, handed down to us by our Founders, that no one group of people has the right to dream at the expense of others. There is a radical equality at the heart of the American ideal. Our government—because it is of, by, and for the people— should be the primary defender of that equality. The last thing it should ever be is the protector of the rights of a privileged few —whoever they are and whatever might be the means of their power. No one has the right to keep solely for themselves the ingredients needed for an existence in which dreams have the best chance to flourish.

Democracy is a living, breathing thing. You don't just set yourself up as a democracy and then say, "Okay, we're a democracy now," and that's that. Democracy isn't a *given;* if it isn't practiced, it doesn't really exist. There is no greater undermining of democracy than all the millions of Americans now sitting out the democratic process. It's not enough to just be disgusted with it; we must remember who it's supposed to belong to, and take it back.

## Rebellion as a Mature Act

A complete cycle of growth always includes rebellion: the teenager who does *not* rebel in some way, for instance, misses a critical piece of personal development. The rebellion is necessary in order to separate from the parent, to individuate into one's own being.

After rebellion, however, must come a unique contribution. Our founding generation did not just fight a revolutionary war; they wrote and maintained the U.S. Constitution as well. While a teenager must rebel in order to mature, so she then must mature beyond the rebellion and initiate life at a higher level than the one she rebelled against.

Thomas Jefferson wrote to John Adams in 1787, "I hold it, that a little rebellion now and then, is a good thing, and as necessary in the political world as storms in the physical." And to Adams's wife, Abigail, Jefferson wrote, "The spirit of resistance to government is so valuable on certain occasions, that I wish it to be always kept alive. It will often be exercised when wrong, but better so than not to be exercised at all."

In a world where selfishness is the accepted ethos, a commitment to social justice is a rebellious mode of being.

Influenced by the philosophers of the Enlightenment, Jefferson believed there is a spirit of goodness in all people. He felt a government could be created that would tap into the capacity for goodness within us and harness it for the purposes of good. That is a high and noble evolutionary precept.

Our Founders strove to overthrow the very notion of aristocracy, creating a system in which anyone could rise according to his or her own abilities, talents, and efforts. Jefferson thought democracy was humankind's best antidote to what he referred to as the "general prey of the rich on the poor"—*rebellion against which he considered natural and good.*

What is happening in America today is that there is not enough spirit of true rebellion. While a market-obsessed corporate mentality lords over us like a new ruling class, we act more like royalists than like our own Revolutionary forebears. This time we are not being assaulted directly, as the colonists were by the English through endless taxes and other burdens, but rather through an endless dripping stream of pleasure that the system is able to provide us, much like a low-grade morphine pump pushed into our veins, making us think we can't live without it. Pleasure can be used to enslave a person as effectively as pain.

---

And so, while we are not happy, perhaps we are having fun in some peculiar way or are so addicted to the pure adrenaline rush of contemporary culture that we no longer question the pain of it all. If this continues, we will lose America. Our national life force is already seeping out. A choice to become culturally sober, and the spiritual experience required to make that happen, is the miracle we need.

The most creative living entails a balance between deep respect for the things that came before, and total disrespect for the power of things past to hold us back. The difference in temperament between the European and the American is interesting in this respect. We, after all, are the children of those who left the Old World, while our European counterparts are the children of those who stayed. Today, Europeans have a civilized understanding and respect for their history that puts Americans to shame, while Americans have a capacity to just go for it, regardless of how things had been done in the past, in a way that makes for awesome creativity.

There is an evolved and an unevolved aspect, then, to both positions. America has spunk, but we are also immature. We are often perceived by the rest of the world, and with good reason, as a brilliant, obnoxious teenager. Our challenge is to retain our sense of optimism and vitality, yet drop our mantle of childish inconsideration for anything and anyone but ourselves.

Our Founders were anything but immature. At the end of the Declaration of Independence Jefferson wrote, "And for the support of this declaration, with a firm Reliance on the Protection of divine Providence, we mutually pledge to each other our lives, our Fortunes, and our sacred Honor." I doubt that too many people today have asked themselves what that means. The signers of the Declaration of Independence were, by so signing, committing treason against the King of England. Had they lost the war and been captured, they would have faced the most horrific penalty under English law—hanging, drawing and quartering, in which your major organs are removed from your body before you're actually dead, then burned in front of your eyes.

They did not just declare a war, then; they themselves would fight it. Though they were men of genius, they were also men of great personal courage. These are the things we must hearken back to.

Who in our generation can easily relate to the signing of a document at the risk of death? Who in our generation can easily relate to such heroic commitment for the sake of one's country? Most of us can't, but many of us would want to. For current generations of adult Americans would like nothing more than to fulfill some sense of historical destiny.

We can, and perhaps we will.

# 3

# THE
# RESURRECTION
# OF
# CONSCIENCE

"Agape *means nothing sentimental or basically affectionate; it means understanding, redeeming good will for all men, an overflowing love which seeks nothing in return. It is the love of God working in the lives of men. When we love on the agape level we love men not because we like them, not because their attitudes and ways appeal to us, but because God loves them. Here we rise to the position of loving the person who does the evil deed while hating the deed he does.*"

— MARTIN LUTHER KING, JR.

WHILE our Founders struck a balance between high ideals and politics, the last generation of Americans to create such a balance, then lose it, was the generation that came of age in the 1960s.

No progressive political vision has a profound hold on America's heart anymore. While millions of us would love to see societal ethics and a passion for social justice reemerge in America, these have all but disappeared as dominant political values. It's as though we blinked, and conscience became just another word. Brotherly love? A mere symbol. All men are created equal? Right. Government "of the people, by the people, and for the people?" Yeah, he had a way with words. This nation has become completely diverted from a path of social conscience.

When I was growing up, the hipper you were, the more politically progressive your vision tended to be. But not anymore. Our newest breed of hip and cool seem so tied to the money-making possibilities of America, so jaded at the thought of idealism, that they're often the first to roll their eyes when you mention something like, "Thirty-six million Americans live in poverty. Shouldn't we *do* something?"

"Oh, please," younger ones respond, as though everybody knows that there's nothing we could do, even if we wanted to.

Or, "Oh, please," older ones respond, bored. "Haven't we all gotten past that by now?" As though a sense of moral outrage is something you try out in college, then outgrow.

Still, I don't think that the last generation to devote real political capital to the cause of social justice actually outgrew its conscience or consciously closed its heart. I believe that what happened is that we, like the young son of Robert Kennedy who watched his father assassinated on television, have been traumatized and in shell shock ever since the sixties. Our heroes were shot in front of us, and our dreams, which they articulated for us, have seemed to lie dead in their graves.

## The Marriage of Body and Soul

In the 1960s, love and politics were uttered in the same breath. "All You Need Is Love" was a song that we sang at *political* rallies. Such slogans helped fuel the antiwar movement, certainly a major political force at the time and ultimately a successful one. But by the mid-seventies, love and politics took different paths. Many who stayed interested in politics would come to trivialize the consciousness movement, and many of those interested in consciousness would start to ignore politics. Both sides tended to smugly, self-righteously dismiss the other as ultimately irrelevant, thinking that they and they alone knew what it takes to change the world.

The consciousness movement concerns itself with addressing the causal level of events. All things in the outer world are sourced from consciousness, and thus merely changing external conditions is seen as a temporary palliative, at best, for the problems of the world. Enlightened laws can be passed, but then repealed. The search for higher consciousness is the effort to attain the level of mind from whence only peace can flow and in the presence of which only peace can exist.

Those interested in traditional politics, on the other hand, are primarily focused on the world of effects. They argue that we cannot afford to just sit around meditating while human suffering goes unchecked. They wish to use the means of the material world to solve the problems of the material world, and tend to see transcendent vision as airy-fairy when applied to politics.

But we cannot give what we do not have—everything we do is infused with the energy with which we do it—and an angry generation will not bring peace to the world.

Upon meeting the Dalai Lama in India in 1996, I asked him: "Your Holiness, if enough of us meditate, will that save the world?"

He leaned toward me and said, "I would answer you in reverse. If we want to save the world, we must have a plan. But no plan will work unless we meditate."

To fundamentally change America we must be equally committed to our spiritual *and* our political goals. We must reconnect the earth and sky, and blend again the two realms of our being. A combination of body and soul infuses both with greater importance. Soul without body is ineffective and body without soul is dangerous. Our political consciousness can mature into a soulful place, where it has been before and can be again. The combination of spirituality and politics is, in fact, a distinctly American philosophical through line, and the value of their marriage is as applicable to the world today as it was to any other time.

## Transcendent Power

The thought that spiritual power can transform social and political conditions is nothing new; indeed, it is a well-established political tradition. From the Quakers of early America to Mahatma Gandhi to Martin Luther King, Jr., there have been those who used spiritual principle to foster outer as well as inner change. It is not external but internal power that most deeply transforms our thoughts and feelings.

Transcendental power, with its emphasis on internal rather than external religious experience, has deep and penetrating roots in American history. The Quakers, who founded Pennsylvania, are an example of people who place spiritual experience above the religious dogma. As historian Daniel Boorstin wrote in his *Landmark History of the American People:*

> The Quakers, like other Puritans, wanted to "purify." But they went much further than the Puritans of New England. They were afraid of any rules. Even those rules copied from the Bible, they said, would destroy the true religious spirit. Then people would take their religion for granted. God, they said, did not limit his Chosen People only to those who knew the Bible or to those who could read and write. That is why Quakers had no ministers. They believed in the "universal priesthood of all believers." They believed God had put his spirit into every man, woman and child. They overflowed with God's spirit. But they were suspicious of anyone who said he knew God's plan.
>
> Just as the Puritans were enthusiastic pessimists, so the Quakers were fanatics about their consciences. Keep looking inward, they said. Let your conscience be your guide. They were afraid of any scheme that was cut and dried, even if some people thought it came from God Himself. God, they said, did not re-

ally communicate with man from any printed page. He spoke to each man from within, brightening each man with an Inner Light.

During the 1800s, Transcendentalism, which was inspired by the Quaker notion of "inner light," became an important philosophical and spiritual movement in America. Its main thrust was the exaltation of the role of intuition in connecting the individual to ultimate truth. Major American writers, from Ralph Waldo Emerson to Henry David Thoreau to Walt Whitman, devised and embraced Transcendental philosophy. They formed a counterforce to the materialistic worldview of the approaching industrial era, seeking to preserve the power of the soul in the consciousness of Western humanity.

In his essay "Civil Disobedience," Thoreau claimed that following the dictates of one's conscience is more important than following the dictates of a government. At the time, such a philosophical assertion was groundbreaking; with the prosecution of Nazi war criminals on those grounds at the Nuremberg Trials following World War II, the Western world solidified its adherence to the notion of the primacy of conscience.

In India in 1929, Mahatma Gandhi had written to a friend of the "deep impression" that Thoreau's essay had left upon him. Inspired in part by Thoreau's message, Gandhi organized a massive resistance to the British colonial occupation of India, developing an entire political philosophy—the philosophy of nonviolence—to harness the energies of the Indian people.

Gandhi believed in a universal spiritual Truth, reflected in all the religions of the world. He did not seek to use spirituality to achieve a political end, so much as to exalt spirituality as a state of being in which political healing naturally results. He was the first major figure of the modern era to introduce into politics the power of spiritual wisdom.

The restoration of India's independence was secondary to Gandhi; what he wanted most was the restoration of India's soul. The British rejection of and contempt for the Indian people—much like White European treatment of Native Americans and Africans in the United States—resulted from a terrible dissociation of the Westerner from the most vital elements within himself. Having turned away from his own soul, the European grew vicious in the face of those who preserved and lived from theirs. Gandhi, and later Martin Luther King, Jr., sought first to heal the battered spirit of their people and then to treat the external wounds that the battering had produced.

Gandhi said that he would have the greatest effect on the world by trying to "reduce himself to zero." He gave this counsel to others:

> I will give you a talisman. Whenever you are in doubt, or when the self becomes too much with you, apply the following test.
>
> Recall the face of the poorest and the weakest man whom you may have seen, and ask yourself if the step you contemplate taking is going to be of any use to him. Will he gain anything by it? Will it restore him to a control over his own life and destiny? Will it lead to deliverance for the hungry and starving millions?
>
> Then you will find your doubt and your self melting away.

Gandhi believed the soul has the power to restore society. He promulgated the notions of *sarvodaya*, or socializing relationships through the strength of spirit; and *satyagraha*, or holding to truth and nonviolence as a political force. *Sarvodaya* is composed of three main themes: spirit working through matter and making it harmonious; the total blossoming of the individual, physically, mentally, and spiritually; and dedication to the welfare of all. *Satyagraha* is the notion that the force of spiritual truth, as revealed by all the major religions of the world, is more powerful than any army, weapons of destruction, or political authority. Gandhi felt the public realm was not secular, but sacred.

Gandhi on nonviolence:

> Non-violence is the law of our species as violence is the law of the brute. The spirit lies dormant in the brute and it knows no law but that of physical might. The dignity of man requires obedience to a higher law, to the strength of the spirit.
>
> Non-violence is a power which can be wielded equally by all children, young men and women or grown-up people, provided they have a living faith in the God of Love and have therefore equal Love for all mankind. When non-violence is accepted as the law of life, it must pervade the whole being and not be applied to isolated acts.
>
> The very first step in non-violence is that we cultivate in our daily life, as between ourselves, truthfulness, humility, tolerance, loving kindness.
>
> Non-violence is an unchangeable creed. It has to be pursued in face of violence raging around you. The path of true non-violence requires much more courage than violence.

As Gandhi was influenced by Thoreau, Martin Luther King, Jr., would then be influenced by Gandhi. Dr. King found great inspiration in the Mahatma, enthusiastically studying and applying the principles of nonviolence to the crusade for civil rights in America. He believed, as did Gandhi, that only the universal awakening of conscience could cast out institutionalized systems of injustice.

Dr. King traveled to India, and said about Gandhi, "He was probably the first person in history to lift the love ethic of Jesus above mere interaction between individuals to a powerful effective social force on a large scale." Gandhi argued the notion —and both men displayed it—that "soul force is more powerful than brute force." Dr. King and Gandhi believed in a God who concerns Himself with the problems of the world, and they believed His power is a spirit we can personally access. The Quakers sought to experience this power, the Transcendentalists sought to exalt it, and Gandhi and King both sought to use it to heal a broken world.

O N the last Sunday of January 1960, Dr. King resigned from his job as pastor of his Montgomery church. "On that day," wrote his biographer Stephen Oates, "King went from being a preacher with an interest in civil rights to a movement leader with a deep and abiding religious faith." For years, King had struggled with the question of how far the religious person should go, entering into worldly affairs and political dialogue. Ultimately, Dr. King felt he could not be true to his religious calling *unless* he were to make a stand for political change, for what he saw around him was unjustified and unnecessary human suffering.

Dr. King said,

> The gospel at its best deals with the whole man, not only his soul but his body, not only his spiritual well-being, but his material well-being. Any religion that professes to be concerned about the souls of men and is not concerned about the slums that damn them, the economic conditions that strangle them and the social conditions that cripple them is a spiritually moribund religion awaiting burial.

When asked how a religious purist could be involved in politics, Gandhi had said, "Is not politics a part of *dharma* too?"

Plato said that "to philosophize and concern oneself with politics is one and the same thing." The philosophy of non-violence is the bridge from a love which stays on the political sidelines to a love which engages the larger world.

# The Power of Nonviolence

The power of nonviolence is the love of God expressed through human beings. It results from human dedication to love, and devotion to the effort to remove all fear and hatred from our hearts. Nonviolence lifts the human consciousness to realms of divine authority, as it provides spiritual power to our words and deeds.

The powers of the world are often contemptuous of the powers of spirit. But the meek shall inherit the earth because their ways are more fit for ultimate survival. The meek display a gentleness more adaptive to change than is an attitude of harsh resistance. This gentleness is not weakness, but strength. It brings a mildness and openheartedness that provide optimal opportunity for healing, forgiveness and love. Ultimately, it is these things—the powers of the soul—that will heal our hearts and save the world.

Tenderness and mercy are the vessels through which God extends His miraculous power. It is in our softening that we experience the power of nonviolence. When our hearts are hard we cannot receive Him—no matter what we profess—for love is His only conduit.

In softening our hearts, however, we must not soften our minds. It is in the lion lying down with the lamb—the fusion of our strength with our gentleness—that we experience the miraculous. Very few of us can honestly say that the brilliant combination of tough mind and tender heart is yet perfected within us, but the examples of both Gandhi and Dr. King serve as powerful inspiration.

Nonviolence carries the power to interrupt and supersede entrenched patterns in human affairs. How spiritually intoxicating is the thought that perhaps we could learn to love as God does. The awesome power of both Gandhi and Dr. King emanated from a deeper, more spiritual level than did their mere political actions. Both men saw the transformation of their own hearts as a necessary prelude to touching anyone else's. Both of them brought about historic social changes. Their faith indeed moved mountains.

## Miracles and Politics

Those who love are God's miracle workers, and both Gandhi and King are examples. They prayed continuously for the power to not hate those who hated them, for hatred cannot contain the miraculous. If we desire access to the power of God's nonviolent authority, we must refuse to hate those who disagree with us. Otherwise, we lack the capacity to triumph over the effects of their ill-will. To learn to love effectively is the highest form of political training.

As both Gandhi and Dr. King stressed to the world, those who practice nonviolence are hardly cowards; their ability to strike back if they so chose is presupposed. It is not passivity but restraint that guides their actions; meekness reflects not a lack of power but the presence of a *higher* power.

In his book, *Stride Toward Freedom: The Montgomery Story,* Martin Luther King, Jr., wrote the following about nonviolence:

> Non-violence in the truest sense is not a strategy that one uses simply because it is expedient at the moment; non-violence is ultimately a way of life that men live by because of the sheer morality of its claim. . . .
>
> It is not a method of stagnant passivity. The phrase "passive resistance" often gives the false impression that this is a "do-nothing method" in which the resister quietly and passively ac-

cepts evil. But nothing is further from the truth. For while the non-violent resister is passive in the sense that he is not physically aggressive toward his opponent, his mind and emotions are always active, constantly seeking to persuade his opponent that he is wrong. The method is passive physically but strongly active spiritually. It is not passive non-resistance to evil, it is active non-violent resistance to evil.

Both Gandhi and Dr. King believed that the purest, ultimately most powerful form of struggle against social injustice is to awaken the conscience of the oppressor. As conscience awakens in anyone, the conscience in everyone sleeps less soundly. "Are you prepared to go to jail?" King asked his followers. "Are you prepared to be beaten without fighting back?" If they were not, he said, then they were not prepared to take part in his nonviolent crusade for civil rights. The political strategy of the movement was to awaken the conscience of America, and that would not happen, King knew, if white America saw African Americans reacting violently to their oppressors. Violence undertaken by the few will always be used by repressive forces to justify further suppression of the many. Crusaders for civil rights, like all those who seek to usher in new orders, suffered great humiliation at the hands of the defenders of the status quo.

But faith brings forth divine compensation; there is, King claimed, "a redemptive power in unearned suffering." Love does not always *immediately* triumph; it does, however, always *ultimately* triumph. That is the message of the resurrection, echoed in various ways by every great religious system. Goodness, claimed King, would prevail over the hatred and bigotry lodged in men's hearts. Thus his prophetic vision: "We shall overcome."

King saw Gandhi's concept of *satyagraha*—holding to truth as a political tool—as a vehicle for removing not only the evil of racism from American society but also all injustice anywhere.

His goal was larger than the passage of civil rights legislation; the end of segregation was merely its political externalization. His ultimate dream, as he often said, was the attainment of a redeemed world. Tyranny will ultimately be eradicated from the earth not by worldly maneuver alone, but through enlightened understanding.

Only with the removal of hatred is the soul restored to its triumphant power. With hatred we can resist the ways of the world, but with love we can overcome the world. According to the philosophy of nonviolence, we must seek a way to love our opponents, not just our friends. This would not be a "personal love," King said, but an "impersonal" love. He often mentioned how grateful he was that God didn't say we have to *like* our enemies!

In ancient Greek philosophy, Dr. King found ideas about the varieties of love that resonated with his nonviolent political goals. He pointed out that the ancient Greeks described three kinds of love: *eros, philia,* and *agape.* Eros, or romantic sexual love, obviously won't save the world. Even philia, or love among friends, lacks the spiritual power to counter the world's decline. But agape, our capacity to love even those whom we do not like, is a love that restores the world to its native grace.

## The Coherence of Ends and Means

The love that we would seek to inject into civilization, must first run through our own veins. Activism along a lateral axis, in which we seek to change the world by addressing conditions outside us, is not the highest medium of political transformation. The spiritual, or vertical axis, along which we seek the transformation of conditions inside ourselves, carries the highest potential for transforming the world. We need less to get the message out than to get the message in. Gandhi said, "My life is my message."

Emotionally violent people—and emotional violence is violence, indeed, the root of all violence in the world—will not bring forth peace. We must see our own personal development as part and parcel of our social and political training. It is ultimately not just what we do but who we are that makes a permanent stamp on world affairs, however visible or invisible the effects of our being might be to the outer eye.

The most powerful medium for change is the presence of a superior personality, for a spiritually awakened person has subtle, invisible effects on the world. On the deepest level, we are all one, and our own transformation is a means to a political end.

Dr. King said, "The first principle of this movement is that the means must be as pure as the end. This movement is based on the philosophy that the ends and the means must cohere.... For in the long run, the end represents the means in process and the ideal in the making...the end is preexistent in the means. ...The means must be as pure as the end, for in the long run of history, immoral destructive means cannot bring about moral and constructive ends."

Turning spiritual conviction into a political force, as Gandhi did in India and King did in the United States, is a divinely rather than politically inspired process. Paradoxically, it necessitates complete investment in an effort in which we also withdraw all attachment to result. The only political vantage point that can fundamentally contribute to America's healing is one in which the dedication of its adherents is to the demonstration of principle in action, rather than to getting a candidate elected. Only in this way will we stand a chance of transforming politics from a corrupt contest for material power to a dedicated instrument of transcendent authority.

Nonviolence is a co-creation between the knowledge of the

mind and the wisdom of the heart. Spiritual surrender is not an anti-intellectual stance, but rather the leap of faith we take when facts are gathered and analyzed by the rational mind, then delivered prayerfully into the hands of God. True faith does not close the mind; it expands the mind.

Gandhi said that the leader of the Indian Independence Movement was not him, but rather the "small still voice within." The more we pray and meditate, the more we develop a divinely inspired intuition. Nothing produces more tragic consequences than thinking we're so smart that we don't have to ask God what to do. There is a silence, a not-knowing out of which all wisdom flows. The entire planet will one day have the feeling, during certain times, of a Quaker meeting. Power will come mainly from our silence, listening and sharing.

People are beginning to understand quite clearly that, as Sigmund Freud said, "Intelligence will be used in the service of the neurosis." Someone's being able to score well on Western academic tests, or even graduate from Harvard, may or may not mean that the person has the wisdom or strength of spirit it takes to bring healing to the world.

## Love Endureth

Since King's death, nonviolence as a serious political option in America has been all but dead as well. King's death remains an inestimable loss for America and the world. He presumably would not have stopped his message at civil rights; just as he was already doing in speaking out against the Vietnam War, it is reasonable to assume he would have continued his crusade for heaven on earth with a passionate strike against injustice wherever he perceived it.

There are many today who would call nonviolence a defunct

political philosophy. But nonviolence is not just a political philosophy; it is a philosophical truth. It lives outside of time in the realm of absolutes. Truth can never be defunct but merely unexpressed. If nonviolence is an ineffective political force today, it is only because it is not being used.

Nonviolence is spiritual *force*. It is content, not form, and like the spirit of God of which it is part, it can be killed but it cannot die. When there is no container to hold its living water, it turns to steam until new containers present themselves. They always do. From Dr. Bernice King reading to audiences from her father's "Letter from a Birmingham Jail" to the millions of people throughout the world now rediscovering the works of both Gandhi and King, the power of good as reflected in those two great human beings continues to flow forth from the mind of God to the mind of humanity. In subtle and not-so-subtle ways, the world is moving in their direction.

Neither Gandhi nor Dr. King saw politics as an end in itself, but merely a means to an end. Neither saw politics as a realm of first cause, or ultimate reality, but rather as a worldly means through which we might effectively address the suffering of humankind. Neither of them—two of the greatest political lights in human history—ever ran for nor held elective office. True political power means more than the power to get elected, stay in office, and pass or repeal legislation. The power to invoke renaissance—and that should be the highest goal of politics—is the power to move human hearts.

We should not be overimpressed by the vicissitudes of worldly change; we best contemplate eternal things. For there are no statistics or traditional political tomes that can help us where our hearts are stuck, and that is the problem of humankind. The problem of the world, said Gandhi, is that "we are not in our right minds." We must reawaken our capacity to hope, our willingness to forgive, and our commitment to love as a mode of

—

cultural and social renewal. We must put together, Dr. King said, "coalitions of conscience" to bring forth a new society.

The only real death is an unaware mind. If we ignore the laws of love and the reality of spirit, then we are dead although we live. If we remember and demonstrate the spiritual authority brought into the world through the likes of Dr. King and Gandhi, then they remain alive although they are dead. Any human being can be a womb for the rebirth of the spirit of nonviolence. Death can make love stumble, but it cannot make it die.

## That Was Then; This Is Now

And what is our task, in these still unjust, yet infinitely more complicated times? Although it could hardly be argued that the challenge before us is harder than those before Dr. King and Gandhi, it could indeed be argued that our work is less simple and clear-cut. Evil wears business suits in the world today, hiding behind pinstripes, smiling away.

Today's darkness is like an inoperable tumor, a hidden cancer. It's always lurking *behind* this or that, or like a spider tumor— sort of *everywhere*. There is cancer underlying our cancers; it is spiritual and systemic; it cannot be treated effectively through any traditional means.

The power of nonviolence is not circumstance-specific. It is as applicable to the problems that confront us now, as to problems that confronted generations in the past. It is not a medicine or a solution so much as a healing process. It is the active spiritual immune system of humanity.

Our disease is a web of falsehoods. A big lie meanders somewhere near the center of things in America, like a slow-acting poison. From illegal CIA interference in the domestic politics of other nations, to the democracy-threatening influence of big money on the electoral process, to increased secrecy in our military and intelligence agencies and economic injustice, it reveals itself in sickening ways. People feel it on the Left and on the Right. Polls indicate that Americans feel good about their lives but cynical about the country. It feels like light is pouring through us as individuals, but some darkness infests the nation.

Today's darkness is a *negative* darkness. It is not an active, aggressive evil force so much as a vast spiritual emptiness, the nothingness of which has formed a black hole in the consciousness of the human race. Darkness is merely the absence of light. Our enemy is not an evil consciousness in charge of things; it is the fact that no particularly light-filled consciousness is in charge of things. The worst danger is not that a room full of people are trying to figure out how to destroy the world, but that not *enough* people are trying to figure out how to heal it. We're so consumed with consumerism that we're on the brink of being consumed.

We have allowed ourselves, in the last fifty years, to become intoxicated by money at the expense of things that matter most. As a society we have made money our bottom line, when our bottom line should be love. The perennial American drama repeats itself, as once again we have before us the choice between our nobler or most selfish selves. At the moment, we need to look very carefully at the choices we're making. As a society, we are in a collective backslide of conscience. A terrible economic injustice has set in as a result, leaving millions of lives displaced or ruined by our collective willingness to make human life less important than the dollar.

This is not a problem that applies so much to the consciousness of the average American. The American people know—and act like—money isn't everything. But our collective behavior and social policies do not reflect that knowing. The next step in America's progress is to reclaim the public sphere for what is best about America. We were brought to this earth for something much more important than feeding a gargantuan money machine at the expense of our children and the expense of our souls.

## America's Mission

America has always been a land of pioneers, not just geographically but also ideally. The American ideal is like a mark on our foreheads. It is emblazoned onto our national psyche that this is a land that should seek remedy to institutionalized oppression. What history has proved, of course, is that some of humanity's worst afflictions have emanated from America—from our treatment of Native Americans to our practice of slavery and systemic racism—yet this has not changed our mission or our destiny. It has increased our pain to know that we are as capable as anyone else of atrocities directed toward others of our species. Yet it is in our shame, as well as our well-deserved pride, that we are prodded by something larger than ourselves to become a nation that helps enlighten the world. We started that way, then stumbled and fell. But a great nation, like a great individual, is not one who has never fallen. The great are those who have gotten back up. Our Founders blazed a trail not only for us but also for the rest of the world. The blazing fire we presented to the world was the ennobling power of a great idea—the democratic ideal.

Like the children of great parents who fail to live up to their legacy yet never can erase it, we have failed to carry forward in our time the fire at the center of democracy's ideal. Now, though it is the eleventh hour and our streets are riddled with social cancers, there is a stirring, an awakening, itself a part of a greater planetary awakening that says to this nation, "Return to your purpose." It leads now not to more outer geographical states but to inner states of being.

As we consciously return to our enlightened collective purpose, the unenlightened energies that surround us now will begin to wane. We don't need to fight the darkness so much as we need to turn on the light.

It is our nature and our destiny to pioneer new ground. What we must pioneer now is an effort that we ourselves have been running from: the search for oneness of mind and heart.

Our challenge is to speak up *for* heart, *with* heart. The greatest contribution a liberal can make to a political renaissance in America is to surrender his or her contempt for a conservative viewpoint, just as the greatest contribution a conservative can make is to surrender his or her contempt for a liberal viewpoint. Judgment undercuts our personal power, diminishing our capacity for insight and destroying the emotional connection without which true communication is impossible. Contempt is a low-level emotion, and nothing low level will serve us now. We will find our way to renaissance through heading upward, not downward, in our use of personal energy.

It takes spiritual effort to withhold judgment of those whose attitudes and behavior we oppose. It is a social and spiritual art form to hate injustice while retaining love for and refusing to denigrate its agents. Such work is necessary, however, for we can have no power as moral persuaders with people who can feel on some level the contempt we feel for them.

Such effort takes rigorous discipline. We must always remember that God has asked us not to judge each other. If we wish a return to civil society, we must learn to debate, indeed to disagree, without withholding love or respect from our opponent.

Just as there is a so-called art of waging war, so there is an art of waging peace. "True peace," said Dr. King, "is not merely the absence of some negative force—tension, confusion, or war; it is the presence of some positive force—justice, good will, and brotherhood."

The next great political unfolding for our age is a broad-based commitment to wage peace, to declare it with as much serious intent and effort as we have ever employed in the waging of war. Merely managing the effects of a war mentality—and fear-based consciousness is at heart a war mentality—is an inadequate response to the dangers of our age. The new politics is a kind of shamanic power that seeks to influence the world around us by *becoming* the change we want to see happen. Gandhi said, "We must *be* the change." This does not mean that we must become enlightened masters before we can have a positive effect on the world. It means, however, that our every effort to live lives of righteousness and purity as we understand it is supported by the power of God. It is in forgiving people that we release them from the darkness we might judge them for; it is in refusing to judge people that we have the most power to affect them; and it is in loving people that we heal them of the wounds that have hardened their minds and hearts. That is why a new politics is one in which *our* own whole person must be the world we work on first. *Our* meditations, *our* personal growth work, *our* prayers, *our* healing, and *our* need to forgive and withhold judgment are the things we must concentrate on first in seeking to transform the world.

Otherwise, we remain stuck in a Newtonian paradigm, keeping ourselves separate from the thing we wish to change and therefore unable to do so. People have said things to me like, "How can I bring love into the corporate system, when all the executives are just crass capitalists who think about nothing but the bottom line?" Note the insidious way the negative ego works: that question begins with an obvious judgment about someone else, and an assumption of their guilt. Judgment is an attack that has no place in a new politics.

—

The truth is that in business, as well as in government, there are important efforts being made to usher higher consciousness into the world. There is a difference between holding people accountable and personally demonizing them. The former guarantees the survival of democracy; the latter guarantees its demise. A conscience-based political question is, "How can I support executives in seeing the value, to themselves and society, of shifting the bottom line from economic to humanitarian values? How can I demonstrate that in fact we'll all make more money when more of us have a chance to? How can I help demonstrate in the world that a shift from a fear-motivated to a love-motivated economy will be the salvation of our economic system as well as of our souls?"

There are those who believe that where there is no anger at something, there is no motivation to change it. But violence only leads to violence. Anger, like money and white sugar, is a temporary motivator of lower human energies. It is love that calls up the divine within us, and love that gives us divinely inspired power.

## *Transforming Anger into Love*

Transforming anger into love can be a very difficult personal assignment for formerly disempowered people. For women, people of color, and others formerly disenfranchised from the mainstream, there can be a great temptation, the first time we're invited to sit at power's table, to let loose on its agents with all the anger and frustration borne of years sitting crouched beneath the table. This won't work, however, because it frightens people. Style is critical. To be effective, moral outrage must express itself in a nonoutrageous way.

We must make part of our personal devotion our efforts to

forgive and love all people, for until we have applied due diligence to that task we will not be the agents of a renaissance or hope. The issue in America today is not how to defeat the *opponents* of a love-based, humanitarian politics; there are actually not as many of those people as one might think. The most significant political question today is not how to fight those whose minds are attached to fear-laden patterns. Rather, it is how to harness the tremendous power of all those who are already committing themselves to lives of greater love. Our political challenge is not to create a love-based impulse in America, but rather how to harness the energy of one that already exists.

I am not naive regarding the huge amounts of money spent in America each year to protect and support conscienceless, entrenched economic interests. But the power in our hearts can make all that money look useless by comparison. If we play the game on the ego's terms, we will lose; only spiritual power can triumph over material power. If we articulate a loving alternative for human society, and witness to our desire for it without timidity or apology, then we will triumph. We will fly above the regions of limitation and demonstrate for all to see the power of love to change the world.

We must look at what is wrong in America, but not dwell on what is wrong. We must allow our righteous anger to be aroused, but only so we might then transform it into constructive energy in the service of social change.

With anger, we gain the power to agitate, but with love we gain the power to persuade. Anger can make us active, but love makes us insightful. With anger, we can move armies, but with love we can move hearts. With anger we can fight war, but with love we can obliterate war. With anger, we might end the world, but with love we can recreate it.

We must be morally aroused by divine love and commit ourselves fully and without reservation to the struggle for universal social justice. That is our imperative as American citizens and as children of God. But moral conviction can also tempt us to become proud and arrogant, rendering us incapable of the very power we seek. What we judge we have no power to change and we are no better than. Nonviolence as a political philosophy insists on respect for the dignity and soul of everyone. Our task is to speak from our good to the good in others. We must point out the darkness, and in some cases explain it, but our major task is to exalt the light in everyone. Particularly in those with whom we disagree.

Only one thing can truly eliminate institutionalized corruption, and that is a genuine awakening of collective conscience. Only one thing can undermine hatred, and that is true forgiveness. Only one thing now can recreate the world, and that is unconditional love.

A conscience-based politics will not rise among us because a particular candidate or organization creates it, but because it is our next evolutionary impulse. Deep in our hearts, Americans know better than to let our country be devastated because of the lack of values in our political system. From the Left and from the Right, a new politics is already emerging and a new kind of activism is beginning to appear.

## The Moral Debate

The Material Age is over, and its most compelling notions are losing their emotional force. People are not going to respond in truly large numbers anymore to a message that lacks a spiritual dimension. The winners in any political game—and this can be seen, by the way, throughout the world—shall be those who do their work in the name of God. This shift is as potentially dangerous as it is potentially liberating, for the contest now is between an open-hearted spiritualization that transforms the world by transforming consciousness and a repressive and authoritarian pseudo-religious force that injects itself into politics.

When the genuine spiritual impulse within a culture is denied or suppressed, the shadow side of that impulse will inevitably arise. People with a progressive political vision cannot afford to ignore a moral debate. If a discussion of ethics is not given its proper place in the public domain, then society does not develop the habit of having that discussion in a sophisticated way. And *that* is a danger. When such discussion is denied its proper place in the public sphere, a bastardized version of the conversation will appear to assuage the desires of those who do not know what such a discussion should sound like, yet feel its absence in their bones.

Any society, if it is to survive and thrive, must have a moral anchor. American conservatives are correct to insist on this. In direct opposition to some of its own most shining lights, the American Left has in the last thirty years abdicated the moral debate to the other side of the political spectrum. But ethical questioning is a domain that belongs to all of us and that rightly belongs in politics. Pushing ethical and moral dialogue out of the political discussion in the name of the separation of church and state has done much to devastate the popular appeal of a progressive political vision.

Leaving the ethical debate to the private domain deprives society of collective meaning. Our diversity—both cultural and religious—must have an underlying unity, and common ethical assumptions are part of it. We must have common spaces, common experiences, and common conversations. Without those things, we become one nation in name only.

America's ethical questioning is made richer and more significant by our religious freedom: it is a constitutional first principle that there is deemed in America no one right way to find

God, no one official moral or religious dogma, no one religious viewpoint that monopolizes divine truth. This principle does not diminish the rich potential for ethical questioning in America; in fact, it increases it. But everyone must take part, not just one segment of the American people.

The experience of deep listening to others, in charity and humility, is part of what makes the public realm a potential reflection of the sacred. Anything that serves our coming together as brothers and sisters serves the will of God. And that is the opportunity afforded us by freedom: to say what we think with depth and clarity, to listen to the thoughts of others with humility and open-mindedness, and to bring together our diversity of viewpoints in such a way as to increase the common good.

The Left has little permission to say, "This or that public policy is immoral," if for years it has denied the validity of morality as a political issue. As long as progressive politics tiptoes around the word *God*, it will fail to resonate with the American public. As long as it refuses to debate the larger moral questions, it avoids its responsibility to call Americans to energetic action. As long as it remains frozen in its oversecularized political correctness, it will continue to wither on the electoral vine.

Charisma is not a bad thing; the word literally means, "of the spirit." Progressive politics lacks charisma today because it is literally dispirited. It does not even know how to say to America that we must address the extreme disparity between rich and poor, not just because it is financially unsustainable (which it is), and not just because it limits our freedom (which it does), but because it is *morally wrong*.

Black Americans have never severed the bond between a genuinely religious consciousness and left-wing politics, but white liberals have basically torn the two asunder. The last great white liberal in America to couch political issues in moral terms was

Robert F. Kennedy, and it is not an accident that he was the last American liberal to truly own a piece of America's heart.

## Not Dead, Merely Sleeping

The generation that lost the Kennedys and King has never totally gotten over it.

The invisible order that shot our heroes did not keep shooting, but began providing goods and services as quickly as possible to distract a grieving generation from our psychic pain. They did not leave us out of their conception of what America should be; quite to the contrary, they used us as their fodder, luring us into their planned environment of endless material consumption. We have been relatively quiet about anything meaningful ever since. Our leaders assassinated, our ranks dispersed, our generation received instructions: go home now, scatter, go to your rooms, and enjoy yourselves with all the toys we sell you.

Are we not now a class of rich slaves? Fear that what happened to our slain leaders might happen to us, our naive and immature relationship to drugs, and ultimately our complete seduction by consumer society conspired to turn us into the greatest fuel source for the status quo that America has ever seen. Given our previous repudiation of the downside of American materialism, the irony here is stunning. We who sought to heal America once before, have helped to run it into the ground.

Because the sixties generation was not well versed in its historical past, we believed that the loss of our heroes' vision was a loss for all time. We were not aware enough of the rhythms of history, of the myth of the eternal return, of the cyclical nature of humanity's march through time. In pain, we turned away from politics, abdicating the field to those who wanted it in the first place.

But perhaps the generation that froze in the sixties is slowly beginning to thaw, our disgust with ourselves for not participating in the march of history beginning to overrule our fear that if we do, they'll kill us, too. That fear has been very real, and we have cowered before it. Our deeper creativity lies fallow as we have reached for no higher collective purpose than to get rich fast and then get richer. We have been all but sapped of our moral genius. Something psychically died in all of us when the bullets struck down our heroes.

We have countenanced the undermining of our political system; we have tolerated the widening gap between rich and poor in America to levels deemed unsustainable by serious economic indicators; we have sold the health and welfare of our children, and our environment, to the highest bidders. Like Esau in the Book of Genesis, we have sold our birthright for a mess of pottage. Even more important, perhaps, we're so stoned on our very way of life, so distanced from our own authentic human knowing, that we hardly seem to realize what a black hole these things are forming.

The baby-boom generation has huge size and potency. Our woundings are as a logjam beyond which the river of American genius can flow but in a trickle compared to its potential. Yet all generations now converge at a watershed moment. While the sixties fervor for the creation of a better world was shot down like a bird from the skies above us, it has been thirty years since that time. Historian Arthur Schlesinger has pointed out that Americans become involved in politics again every thirty years.

No political power can bring the dead back to life—only spiritual power can do that. Resurrection is not of the body, but of the mind. We so mourned the passing of great personalities who were taken from us, that we mistakenly believed their principles died with them. But that is only true if those principles pass from our minds. The highest possibilities for American democracy are never dead; they merely fall asleep sometimes. They are a permanent part of our potential as a nation, as long as even one of us remembers them. It is time for us to remember, that an essential part of ourselves now sleeping will awaken, before it is too late.

## Behind the Mask

These words of Robert Kennedy resonate today:

> I urge you to learn the harsh facts that lurk behind the mask of official illusion with which we have concealed our true circumstances, even from ourselves. Our country is in danger: Not just from foreign enemies; but above all, from our own misguided policies, and what they can do to this country. There is a contest, not for the rule of America, but for the heart of America.

The ideas that Dr. King and Kennedy stood for in America thirty years ago are as meaningful now as they were then. And just as desperately needed. It is an internal wounding of the American psyche that we must address: our economic obsessiveness and moral paralysis in the face of huge amounts of human suffering.

Thirty-six million Americans now live below the poverty line —enough men, women, and children to fill the twenty-five largest cities in America. From the deterioration of the American city to the horrors of racial tension, the immorality of economic injustice to the devastation of our environment and the virtual abandonment of America's children, this country awaits our awakening to the power to heal them all.

America is plagued today by economic injustice, but even more so by our inability to meaningfully discuss it. We're not comfortable anymore with words like *poverty*, however; instead, we use value-neutral terms like *economic disparity*. There was a time in America when we would have discussed this issue in terms of right and wrong. After President Kennedy's death, his brother Robert, Dr. King, and Lyndon Johnson put the issue of poverty in America at the center of America's political agenda. While the welfare system that arose from Johnson's War on Poverty certainly had its faults, its moral foundations were correct.

Both Robert Kennedy and Martin Luther King, Jr., said things that major political candidates rarely say anymore, not because the issues are any less relevant now than they were then but because the listening they spoke to has all but stopped. The call for social justice has been trivialized in America, made to seem like just the frantic swoonings of a special-interest group here or there. Most people who suffer are portrayed as mere whiners, and if you're interested in defending them, then you're a whiner, too.

Our current gap between rich and poor—the largest since 1926—is morally indefensible and economically unsustainable.

The backlash against welfare in America today is not really a backlash against welfare abuse, so much as it is a backlash against compassion in the public sphere. While America is full of those who would police our private morals, there is far too little questioning of our societal morals. We are among the richest nations on earth, yet we spend a trivial amount on our poor compared to that spent by every other Western industrialized nation. One-fifth of America's children live in poverty. Half of our African-American children live in poverty. We are the only industrialized Western nation that does not have universal health care. For us to call our economy "good" is like saying, "Except for my cancer, I feel fine."

A theologian once said that it is the role of religion to comfort the afflicted and afflict the comfortable. Such is good advice today, for many of our most powerful institutions seem systemically devoted to comforting the comfortable and afflicting the afflicted.

It is important to emphasize the positive, but not at the expense of truth. We must acknowledge the sorrows of the earth before we can fully activate our capacity to overcome them. It is not transcendence but, rather, denial to merely point at all that is right in America and use that as an excuse to avoid or ignore what is wrong.

The enemy is not capitalism, but greed. Capitalism is an economic system that reflects whatever integrity and compassion we choose to express within it. The problem in America is one of values, not of one or another economic system: if we choose the value of the market over the value of human life, we are violating the laws of God.

In the long term, this diminishes us all. We are, as Martin Luther King, Jr., used to say, "all woven from a single garment of destiny." A nation, like an individual, will reap what it sows. Spiritual law is inescapable and impersonal. Those who would have us ignore our spiritual obligations as a society lead us toward ultimate tragedy.

## We're All Too Hip to Make Noise

Some would argue that practically everyone who suffers in America is totally responsible for that condition. While this might be true on some larger metaphysical level, it is not true in terms of practical circumstances, particularly for children. And even if some people "choose" their suffering as part of a larger spiritual lesson, the lesson for *us* is to help them! There is no valid psychological, metaphysical, or spiritual justification for turning our backs on human suffering.

The plight of the poor in America today, and the desperate conditions of life in our inner cities, form a tinderbox just waiting for a match. Our political leaders, many of whom are aware themselves that the tinderbox exists, seem to think they won't be reelected if they mention it. They spend more time and money investigating one another than on addressing the critical social and economic injustices that rage among us and threaten our children.

Many of those leaders would say that this is irresponsible, incendiary talk: our children will *not* be threatened by all this injustice and suffering, because our fine responsible civil servants are working night and day to make sure we build enough prisons, fast enough, to lock up anyone who has even the slightest urge to act out their desperation. Prison-building is the single largest urban industry in America, prisons are half of all public housing built in this country in the last ten years, and we already have a greater portion of our citizens behind bars than any other nation in the world. We could call this our "Bastille policy."

We are saying to people who are as afraid of the police as they are of the criminals, whose children do not have safe schools, whose children are at risk even walking to school, whose children do not even have working toilets in their schools, and whose children have practically no chance of finding a job in the neighborhood even if they do by some miracle muster the courage and the inner strength to make it through that dangerous maze and graduate from high school, that you'd better fly right now and not make a single false step from here on out, *because we've had it up to here with helping you.*

In one of his songs, Bob Dylan sings, "Sometimes I can't help wondering what's happening to my companions." What has happened to America that so many of us think—and act—as if there's nothing we can do to change things? That's when you know they've got you: when you're too cynical or too tired to dissent. When the established order lacks universal justice and inclusive love, then the person of conscience has a responsibility to energetically and passionately dissent. Jefferson said that we must keep the spirit of rebellion alive in America just to keep the forces of tyranny on notice that Americans are free and plan to remain so.

If I could take every person who has ever said to me, "You know that Faye Dunaway movie where the guy opens up the window and shouts, 'I'm mad as hell and I'm not going to take it anymore'?—that's my favorite movie!" and put them all together, we'd have a veritable political movement. But that's part of the problem: movies are not life. There is an important distinction between desperation in the movies and the desperation of real people on the other side of town, as well as between romanticized expression of outrage on the part of a character in a movie and genuine political resistance to an unjust worldly system. The problem is not fictional, and neither will its solution be.

In the 1960s, Robert Kennedy said,

> It is not enough to allow dissent. We must demand it. For there is much to dissent from.
>
> We dissent from the fact that millions are trapped in poverty while the nation grows rich.
>
> We dissent from the conditions and hatreds which deny a full life to our fellow citizens because of the color of their skin.
>
> We dissent from the monstrous absurdity of a world where nations stand poised to destroy one another, and men must kill their fellow men.
>
> We dissent from the sight of most of mankind living in poverty, stricken by disease, threatened by hunger, and doomed to any early death after a life of unremitting labor.
>
> We dissent from cities which blunt our senses, and turn the ordinary acts of daily life into a painful struggle.

We dissent from the willful, heedless destruction of natural pleasure and beauty.

We dissent from all those structures—of technology and of society itself—which strip from the individual the dignity and warmth of sharing in the common tasks of his community and his country.

Those comments are no less relevant today, but dissenters are relatively few. We're too *embarrassed* to speak up. If Jefferson were alive today, some would say, "Go back to Monticello, Thomas Jefferson. *You've* got a nice house! What are *you* complaining about?" Clearly, there is a critical need in America for the average citizen to risk the ridicule of pointing out what so many of us know but feel powerless to change. Just starting the conversation among ourselves will give others the emotional permission to do the same.

Most politicians in America today—Democrat as well as Republican—talk about America as though anyone who earns less than the middle class doesn't even exist except as a "problem," doesn't have citizenship as important as everyone else's, isn't part of the significant equation.

There are certainly leaders who *do* care and try very hard to change things. But some of them have merely said they care, as a substitute for making any serious effort to bring about fundamental change. This has done more to damage the cause of true progressivism in American politics than anything their opponents ever did. Those who actually attack the cause of social justice have a way of stirring us to action. Those who give it mere lip service have a way of lulling us to sleep.

## *The Noblest Virtue*

Many Americans are greatly disillusioned by our current state of affairs. But disillusionment is not so bad when you consider that it means you were laboring under illusions before.

A therapist brings up a subject to his or her client and often hears, "Do we really have to talk about that?" In other words, there are times when the dull ache of knowing something is wrong feels preferable to the pain of bringing it up for discussion. That is in some ways where America is now; we are not really sure we want to talk about what's wrong. We must find a way to face the terrible problems in our midst without being overwhelmed by either guilt or anger. Neither one serves the purpose of national healing.

It takes courage at times to look clearly at what is. A generation of tremendous potency, which for the last two decades has been busy tending only to our own gardens, has begun to think, however infrequently, about how it will feel to face death one day. Will we say on our deathbeds, "I went for it. I did what I could," or will we shudder to think of our missed opportunities to love and be loved? For those of a certain age, such thoughts are very real. Once we have outgrown our obsessions with sex and money, important things come rushing to mind.

Thomas Jefferson envisioned an America in which, after a certain age and a certain level of achievement, people would apply their energies to the welfare of the nation. We must do that with neither apology nor timidity. "The noblest virtue," wrote Virgil, "is the public good." To the ancient Greeks, *politics* referred to one's concern with a broader context of society than just one's own circle or family. American politics should be a context for service, not just to oneself or those like oneself, but to the entire nation, and ultimately the world.

Humanity in general, but particularly American society, is at a crossroads. We must decide whether our bottom line, our highest good, our power, is to be measured in economic or in humanitarian terms. Our own hypocrisy is becoming too obvious, not only to other nations, who have noted it for a while now, but also to our own citizens. Our young look with increasing disrespect at our government and other institutions of power. They are not stupid. There is such a lack of moral integrity at the center of how the United States politically organizes itself that we cannot expect people to pretend for much longer that America is all it cracks itself up to be.

It will take more than traditional politics to heal this country, or any other. "The spirit of democracy," wrote Gandhi, "is not a mechanical thing to be adjusted by abolition of forms. It requires changes of the heart." We must let go a social system based on fear and accept one based on love.

The attainment of our spiritual essence *is* our worldly salvation. As Einstein said, "We will not solve the problems of the world from the same level of thinking we were at when we created them." Inner peace, or nonviolence, is the Answer, simply placing us where we want to be rather than trying to figure out how to get us there.

But we must not use spiritual seeking as a form of escapism, using it to shield our eyes from the suffering of the world. Our challenge is both to reenvision the world and then to act upon the vision.

## If Love Came First

In business, for the most part, there is an inherent motivation to serve people. In government, owing to the extraordinary and pernicious influence of money on the electoral process, this is no longer necessarily true. The interests of "the people" are often secondary to the interests of major political contributors. Those who see economics as the defining issue of our "vital interests" aren't always looking for the loving solution to domestic or international problems. If love came first, we would use our financial resources to create jobs to help people live well, instead of building more prisons to punish them when they do not; if love came first, we would value human rights at least as much as economic rights; if love came first, we would seek to educate and help rather than to prosecute our children violently screaming out for attention.

It is a sociological truism that any old-guard system sees the coming order as "unrealistic." It is true that the political order in power now sees too much "love" talk as rather silly. But I have watched them as they make their decisions and heard them as they talk about their plans. The guys in suits who run the world are as emotionally vulnerable in their own way as anyone else. They just as easily could consider the world from an expansive, openhearted consciousness, but they do not do it for three basic reasons.

First, most of them actually do not know how. They have been trained to think along authoritarian, patriarchal thought patterns, and that's the box they're stuck in.

Second, they fear mockery by the mainstream press and cultural gatekeepers if they were to appear too "soft." We're particularly enamored of militaristic imagery these days—one of the sure signs, by the way, of a crumbling democracy. (Got a problem? Hell, just bring in a general! Talk in militaristic terms—it'll make people feel secure. Surely if he can fight a war...)

Third, they seem to think the public isn't looking, isn't thinking, and doesn't deeply care anymore about social justice. You suggest that maybe they could remind the people of such an important thing—you know, *lead*—and they look at you with empty eyes.

The leader with conscience must be willing to risk repudiation. The person with conscience must be willing to risk being considered a whiner by polite society. The person with conscience has a responsibility to be a thorn in the side of a complacent status quo. The person with conscience holds up a mirror to the world, which must include himself. The person with conscience is an agent of awakening in a world where there is a collective urge to sleep.

Why should news programs have daily reports on how Wall Street is doing but not on how our children are doing? Why are we to be more concerned, as a society, if the stock market is depressed than if our *people* are depressed? And who is going to change the conversation, and our bottom line, if not us? It is true that, in many environments, to bring up the unnecessary suffering of millions—and the policies that perpetuate that suffering —might get you quickly slapped with a label of "bleeding heart." But there's an answer to that: *Be slapped.* And take heart. All you need is one person in the room to say, "Actually, I agree with that," and we're starting to act like participants in broad-based social change.

I'm for work, family, local control wherever it's appropriate, responsibility, and accountability as much as anyone. I work hard, and I think others should work hard too. Show me a person who's got the tools, and I'm the first to say they should be up at dawn using them. But not enough people in America today have access to the tools—education, job training, child care, mass transit. We are told that these are things we cannot afford. That excuse is a lie. We are not providing those universal tools because we do not yet have a critical mass of the American electorate who are willing to stand for the notion that we should.

Just saying those things is not enough, of course; there is much more we need to do than just talk. But once those words have left your mouth, they tend to be more alive within you.

After World War II, the United States spent $12 billion over four years on the Marshall Plan, rebuilding the devastated economies of Western Europe. There is no reason why we should be less generous to the people of the United States.

We must not apologize for the moral basis of that argument. To those who complain that our Social Security system is threatened, let us say that our spiritual security is threatened even more. For according to every great religious tradition we shall reap what we sow. The sheer greed and selfishness behind American public policy at this time threatens the future of our children more strongly than any unbalanced budget ever could.

I do not believe that the average American would ever want to see a child living under oppressive and cruel conditions; I believe the average American does not realize how many millions of children in America today are literally dying beneath the yoke of our current social policies.

There is a power within us that we are not yet collectively using. We have in our hearts, said Dr. King, a "power more powerful than bullets." And it is time for us to use it.

If enough of us embrace the spirit of nonviolence and adopt a personal commitment to conscience, making what efforts each of us can to increase the power of good in this world, then we will achieve at this time of millennial shift as stunning a leap forward in human consciousness and world affairs as any generation has ever made. There is a door that we can open together, on the other side of which is a shining new world.

# 4

# EMERALD CITY

*"This country cannot afford to be materially rich and spiritually poor."*
— PRESIDENT JOHN F. KENNEDY

To place money before love is idolatry. That is true for an individual, and it is true for a nation. A nation of idol-worshippers always has been, and always shall be, struck down.

There can be no serious healing of America without looking deeply at the ways in which money runs this country any more than there can be any serious healing of a wound without treating it. It leads us into areas that are neither fun nor uplifting to consider. Until we do, however, we cannot be true healers of this nation.

## Tainted Billions

I used to think that maybe the rich knew something I didn't know: that *maybe* they considered the collective good of the nation in ways I didn't understand. But when I made some money, what I found out is the following. There are glamorous rituals you go through once your bank account reaches a certain level. You are ushered into very nice offices, given lots of coffee or tea or Evian water in crystal glasses, treated very nicely by people who are just as aware as you are that we're at a party that can't go on forever but wouldn't dare say so at the office, then given the message in various ways that the point of all your money is number one, to buy a nice house, and number two, to protect your investments.

It could work another way: once we have a certain amount of money, we could go through a ritual in which we commit within our hearts to do everything we can with our newfound material power, to ensure that those who do not have it yet might have the same opportunities to make it that we had. We could discuss *that* over crystal glasses. We could feel, as affluent people, that we carry a sacred responsibility to increase the good of our country and our world. This kind of thinking wouldn't decrease our wealth; it would increase it many times over, for it is thinking that carries spiritual power. The tainted billions brought forth by greed are peanuts compared to the wealth that will open up for all of us when we open our hearts to the next evolutionary step of universal love.

There are millions of people in America, rich and poor, who are more than ready to participate in a collective commitment to an ever-increasing societal good. But such an effort doesn't currently exist as a dominant social force, a sense of national purpose. We are rediscovering the importance of individual communities, but the *nation itself* should be a community as well. Helping each other shouldn't be seen as a radical, fringe idea.

At the moment, we place the needs of the market before our principles, our children, even ourselves.

There is a fundamental problem in the air, and just tinkering with details will not solve it. American society will not be healed until we shift our basic consciousness in relation to money: America needs to change its bottom line, from making money to improving the world.

Our current economic principles are spiritually barbaric. Money is not just a management issue, it is an ethical issue. Economics should not exist outside a moral context, any more than anything else should. First things have to come first in life. Second things should then come second. Your kids are first. Your money is second. Fairness is everything. End of story.

## The Business of Politics

Corporate interests—not the people of the United States—for all intents and purposes now own America.

Moneyed interests control the political process, routinely pouring so many millions of dollars into so many political campaigns as to have completely corrupted the process. This is not a secret anymore. The health and well-being of corporate structures is placed before the health and well-being of individuals and communities, no matter how many people are trapped in poverty by the process; no matter how much the preferred corporate policies widen the already alarming gap between rich and poor; no matter how much human havoc is wreaked among working people whose livelihoods are threatened by corporate restructuring and downsizing; no matter how many more known carcinogens are poured into our ground, our air, and our food; and no matter how many young people are sent to decrepit schools that cannot even afford textbooks, where teaching becomes by definition more like crowd control than education, in communities where real chances for young people making it in the world get smaller and smaller every day.

More and more, our political leaders are mere puppets dancing on corporate strings. To many of us, it used to feel as though one major political party acted like an abusive father while the other party was the mother always trying to protect us. But those days are over. Mommy's shadow self has now taken over and she colludes with Daddy—no matter how much she frets in the process, and *really* feels bad about it. We are on our own.

It could be argued, of course, that we should never have allowed ourselves to become like their children to begin with. But we did. We stopped participating and have now received a serious lesson in the dangers of looking away. We must go back into the political process now, with a lot more in mind than just voting, or even mere traditional political organizing. Traditional political action today is like a child petitioning a parental team that has already decided something else is more important than the needs of the child.

President Kennedy once said he was "an idealist without illusions." That is what we must be. We must not be naive, but we must not give in to anger either. The world will not be changed by happy people who are happy simply because they're not looking at the facts. Nor will it be changed by angry people who are angry because they *are* looking at the facts. It will be changed by those of us who have had the courage to look at the facts, have seen the extremely dark cloud looming on America's horizon, have worked through our personal anger with those who have created and now protect the new corporate aristocracy, and reached into the depths of our souls for the power it takes to create a movement of renewed social justice, conscience, and transformation for American society.

## Corporate Soul

The forces that drive the U.S. economy are drunk on power. They swagger, they deny, they justify, they intimidate. That's what drunks do. The American people must stop wimping out, and awaken from our co-dependent stupor. We must not allow the American political system to become little more than the servant of dominant economic interests. We must perform the political equivalent of an intervention.

Many people are doing extremely important work transforming the ethos of the American corporation. Just beneath the
surface, American business today runs on two separate tracks: one
of expanding heart and one of expanding greed. Are ethics more
important than money, or is money more important than ethics?

When business factors in the "costs" necessary to earn a profit,
those costs should include costs to our environment and costs to
human life and values. Profit and loss should mean more than
just money. We must, as a society, stop kowtowing to an old-
paradigm business philosophy that makes money more important than human lives. It does not have to be this way. There
is a new breed of "business philosopher"—Paul Hawken, Lance
Secratan, economist Hazel Henderson among them—now elu-
cidating the shifts we need in order to transform American business into a conscience-based structure. The slash-and-burn
mentality that permeates much of corporate America today, and
the government's greater commitment to serve the market rather
than protect people from its excesses, are at the heart of America's pain. Ultimately, it will do little good to have protected
people's jobs if they can no longer breathe the air, drink the
water, or survive the emotional and psychological pressures in
their lives. Most of America's social dysfunction is a symptom,
not a cause, of our deeper decay.

The top 5 percent of our population takes home half the
nation's income; huge and profitable companies lay off thousands
of employees for no other reason than to increase their short-
term stock prices and their already outrageous executive compensation packages; Congress grants huge subsidies and tax
breaks amounting to billions of dollars in "corporate welfare"—
and the life and safety of the average American are increasingly
crushed underneath it all.

Even our national security is threatened by our slavish devotion to the market. In 1995, for instance, we deregulated the sale

of supercomputers to the Chinese, a move that could dangerously increase their nuclear capacity. They have been buying
them up ever since. U.S. officials have said they believe that
civilian purchasers in China are making sure the equipment is
not diverted to military uses, but this opinion is based on no
hard evidence. Government sources admit that they received the
majority of their data *from the computer companies!* We have
attached our foreign policy to commerce to such an extent that
human values—even the security of our future—have become
secondary considerations.

Gargantuan economic concerns, whose financial interests are
unabashedly placed ahead of the collective good, pour through
the halls of our government like lava. We do not spend billions
upon billions of dollars more to support business than to support
our children for any other reason than that organized business
interests can afford highly paid lobbyists to make it happen.
None of this will change until a critical mass of Americans see
this game for what it is and lobby on behalf of our most noble
values—not in anger, but in absolute commitment to using all
our power as American citizens to making sure the situation
changes. Each of us must think about these things, read about
them, and pray about them. Out of that vortex of energy will
arise a new political constituency and the power to affect the
course of events.

THE influence of money on the political process is a fast-
growing cancer in America. It grows in small ways and big ways,
every day of the year. The average American citizen should
understand how it operates. There is an old French saying, "If
you don't do politics, politics will do you."

According to a May 17, 1997 *New York Times* article entitled

"Corporate Gifts Open Door to Governors' Inner Sanctum," a select group of 100 companies—among them Exxon, General Motors, and Phillip Morris—have given millions of tax-deductible dollars to the National Governors' Association in the past several years, including $786,000 in 1996 alone, in exchange for *intimate access to legislation that affects their businesses.*

For an annual membership of $12,000, a corporation can designate one or more of its employees to be members of the Center for Best Practices, a nonprofit branch of the Governors' Association that researches social and economic policies. According to the association's fact sheet, the so-called corporate fellows attend meetings, briefings, and are even offered private offices.

The corporations are courted by the Governors' Association as a resource to obtain the best information on the issues they legislate. However, because no labor organizations, policy-advocacy, or interest groups are invited to join, the plan clearly paves the way for the undue influence of big business on our government.

During a forum held to discuss electricity policy, environmental regulation by the federal government, and pending legislation on the cleanup of toxic waste dumps, Gregory Wetstone, the legislative director of the Natural Resources Defense Council, found himself head-to-head not only with the governors and state environmental officials but with lobbyists from the corporations that are members of the Center for Best Practices and opponents of tighter environmental standards!

Speaking to the *New York Times,* Mr. Wetstone said, "It is very troubling that corporations are able to buy a much greater level of access than the public in general or the public-interest community."

The *Times* article continues,

...senior lobbyists for the corporations rub shoulders with the governors and their staffs in a way that few others can match. The Governors' group describes the program as "an unparalleled opportunity to serve as catalysts to change." Ann McBride, President of Common Cause, the public affairs lobby, called the arrangement "just another permutation in the way that access is being purchased in the political process."

So much for our Founders' dream of disinterested leadership.

CORPORATIONS of themselves are not the problem, but only their undue influence. We don't want to turn *off* the system. There is nothing beautiful about what happens in a society where money stops circulating. Our challenge is not to destroy capitalism but to transform its dominant ethos; not to childishly and blindly demonize the corporation but to make a case for the importance—and ultimate benefit to all—of conscience within it.

The notion of a corporation existing for no other purpose than to increase the financial good of its shareholders, without thought of responsibility to workers or communities, must change and *is* changing. But it is not changing fast enough; we need a quantum shift. While I have every hope that within ten years the majority of American corporations will be run by people who feel conscience does indeed have a place in business, *we do not have ten years to wait.* There is already too much human desperation for the system to absorb, and all the volunteer summits in the world aren't going to make a serious dent in that situation.

We must do more than rally to serve all of America's underprivileged citizens; we must ask ourselves what is wrong in our society—including our public policies—that there are so many people living in desperate conditions to begin with.

President Kennedy said, "Those who make peaceful evolution impossible make violent revolution inevitable." We are moving people off welfare at the same time as we are decreasing the educational and vocational opportunities necessary to improve their own lives. There are disturbing facts behind a veil of government PR. On March 18, 1997, 4,000 people lined up for hours in mid-Manhattan in hopes of getting one of the 700 jobs being offered at a new hotel. And this kind of desperation has become common in America. Far too many other Americans are doing all right at the moment, but know that they are just a paycheck away from being in big trouble themselves. One of the sinister triumphs of radical conservatism in the last few years has been convincing the nearly poor that the very poor are to blame for their problems. Surely the American people will awaken to the game here. Millions upon millions of hardworking Americans slide further and further toward a financial abyss, while our laws do more to promote than to break their fall.

"The only thing necessary for the triumph of evil," said British statesman Edmund Burke, "is for good men to do nothing." In the final analysis, there is very little moral difference between actively hurting someone, and refusing to help them when someone else is doing so. The American people are *not* cruel, but we have naively acquiesced to a system that is.

People act as though *caring* is enough: I call it the "I really care, therefore I don't have to do anything" syndrome. Many people said after President Clinton's first election, "I finally feel we have a President who cares." But this poses an interesting moral question to our generation: if someone *cares* and they hurt you, do they get more or fewer points in heaven than the person who *doesn't* care and hurts you? Does the feeling of compassion itself count as a moral good, or must the feeling be expressed through action? And if we do nothing to stop injustice, does that not mean that we tacitly support it?

---

Caring and feeling are important—but they are often easy. They come relatively cheap. We live in a culture that exalts the verbal expression of compassion but often resists compassionate action. We use a syrupy concern for one hurt child or one lost soldier to mask the fact that life in America is hell for millions of others. When the dominant struggle of one's age is between property rights and human rights, fudging on our principles is often the path of least resistance. Good citizenship—and, clearly, good leadership—is not a popularity contest.

Outrage expressed at the prostitution of the American political system is liable to be termed "incendiary." That is much like saying there's a fire in the house but it's not polite to mention it. Nor do such opinions as those expressed here foster "class warfare" against the rich; class warfare is what is already being waged against America's poor and near-poor.

Someone pointed out to me recently that in Colin Powell's book, he writes that it *is* possible for the underprivileged to make it in America, to get past the obstacle course if they truly try. But in the richest nation in the history of the world, why should the basic material realities of life have to be an "obstacle course" for anyone?

## The Devil Often Poses as a Family Kinda Guy

American children are twelve times more likely to die of gun violence than in any other Western nation, five times more likely to be murdered, and twice as likely to commit suicide. If we're interested in family values, we will radically recommit to making this society safe for children, and we will stop creating red herrings to obfuscate the fact that we consistently protect business interests at the expense of our children's lives. Those who threaten the welfare of our children shouldn't be able to gain our trust simply by putting rosy filters on their political advertisements.

The people who are the most devoted to funneling public money away from children often do the most public relations work to show us how much they love their kids. That nails the issue. No one is doubting that they love *their* kids. But the exclusive love of *our* children, or even *some* children, is not the love that will save the world. I'm sure that many slave owners loved their own children. And there are numerous pictures of Nazi leaders pouring affection all over those beautiful little Aryan children with *lederhosen* and cute big bows in their hair. The children that matter now *are the children on the other side of town.* The moral and political shift that America most needs now is a switch from an exclusive to an inclusive sense of family and love.

American children are critically threatened with an array of forces stemming directly and indirectly from our societal neglect and injustice: lack of education, lack of health care and job training, and massive unemployment in the inner cities. Upon mentioning our responsibility to help millions of American children—who wake up each day and go to sleep each night in literally life-threatening conditions—we're liable to be met with the line, "But how are you going to pay for it?" When George Bush told us Kuwait was threatened, no one asked him that. Surely the problems of American children are much closer to home than Kuwait is.

Why should we consider it a serious pathology for one person to abandon one child, but not a serious pathology for a government to abandon millions of children? And why would we rush to rescue children from drowning in a flood, but not rescue children who are drowning in poverty and have been for years?

The mother of any advanced species becomes fiercely protective when her cubs are threatened. Perhaps there is a message here for the women of America. The children of the world *are* threatened, and our outrage is legitimate. We must not allow societal disapproval to dull our voices. A generation of Americans more sensitive to our own childhood issues than any generation on record has ever been are standing by and allowing millions of children to be denied what should be considered their basic human rights.

What we lack is not money but political will. It is a lie—a Big Lie—to claim budget restraints as a reason for not investing in the potential genius of each and every American. It is not the constraints on our budget but the constraints on our minds, and constraints on our hearts, that limit America now.

## The Abuse and Misuse of Government

In the 1830s, President Andrew Jackson sought to break the financial chokehold that he thought the Bank of the U.S. had over American life. His words make sense today:

> It is to be regretted that the rich and the powerful too often bend the acts of government to their selfish purposes. Distinctions in society will always exist... but when the law undertakes to add to these natural and just advantages artificial distinctions... exclusive privileges to make the rich richer and the more potent more powerful, the humble members of society... have a right to complain of the injustice of their Government. There are no necessary evils in government. Its evils exist only in its abuses.
>
> It is time to pause in our career to review our principles, and if possible revive that devoted patriotism and spirit of compromise which distinguished the sages of the Revolution and the fathers

of our Union.... [W]e can at least take a stand against all new grants of monopolies and exclusive privileges, against any prostitution of our Government to the advancement of the few at the expense of the many....

The 1997 proposed Republican budget cuts taxes on estates for the richest 1 percent of families, re-opens loopholes in the corporate income tax, would direct about 65 percent of their tax cuts to the richest 20 percent of American families, and only 13 percent of the tax cuts would reach the bottom 60 percent of families.

The problem in America is not that the majority of Americans like things the way they are. The problem in America is that the majority of Americans do not take part in democracy, do not even vote, do not own what power they have. The people most hurt by the system have understandably given up trying to change it. But we must reverse that trend. The only way to get power back to the people is for the people to remember that they have it.

We never lost our political power so much as we decided not to use it, and that has been our undoing. The reempowerment of the American people will stem from a collective shift in intention. A critical mass will say to ourselves, "Oh, I forgot. I'm a citizen; *I'm* the power here. I will think these things through, and reeducate myself where necessary. I will vote. I will write letters. I will communicate. I will organize. I will participate in the process. I will take back America, for the sake of my children and the sake of the world."

No amount of money will be able to prevail against a reawakened citizenry. The walls of Jericho came down, but only when the people shouted.

## Enlightened Economics

Change does not come from the top down, but from the bottom up. Each of us can help transform the financial ethos of the United States.

As individuals, and as a nation, we need to carefully watch our economic choices. They are powerful expressions of our values. Every time a screenwriter says, "No, I won't write a script in which the woman gets cut up into little pieces and the restaurant full of people gets blown away by a sixteen-year-old blonde bombshell carrying an Uzi, even if you do pay me $300,000," conscience takes an economic stand. Any time a lawyer says, "I won't let you buy my services so you can find a way to legally exploit old and feeble people out of their life savings," conscience takes an economic stand. Any time a business executive says, "I don't want to spend this meeting only asking ourselves how much money we're going to make this quarter, but first, how much good we're going to do for the country and the world this quarter," conscience takes an economic stand. Any time a Congressman says, "No, I won't vote to take money away from summer job programs for inner city youths, and then vote *for* further subsidies for wealthy businesses that don't need it," conscience takes an economic stand. Martin Luther King, Jr., once pointed out that money given to a corporation is called a subsidy, while money given to a mere human being is called a handout. The truth is, we should subsidize our youth and stop all the handouts we make to the very, very rich.

A true marriage of conscience and economics will not depress the U.S. economy; it will rebuild it from within, revitalizing it in a way no external economic machinations could ever do. The greatest unmined source of wealth in America is the potential peace and happiness of millions of now stressed-out Americans.

When we collectively return to our natural goodness, money will flow more easily for all of us. I heard a story once about a man who had some fishes and loaves. He always took care of the children. And He gave the moneychangers a piece of His mind.

## Economics, Shmeconomics

One of the twentieth-century Wizards of Oz (he was a fraud, you remember; he *cannot* take you home) is the so-called science of economics. Economist Hazel Henderson has written, "Economics is now revealed as a 300-year-old grab bag of unverifiable propositions too vague to be refuted." Economists are like a group of people who came out of nowhere and all of a sudden run the world. Who made them boss? In the words of Mahatma Gandhi, "Nothing in history has been so disgraceful to the human intellect as the acceptance among us of the common doctrines of economics as a science." Economists do not normally include in their calculations such spiritual precepts as the Golden Rule. But everything that goes around comes around—the universe is based on the Law of Cause and Effect—and that is as true for a nation as for an individual.

There are those who would say that to run a country with love in mind is not practical. But the argument that love is not *practical* is but a smokescreen. Of course, it is not practical. But what is practical? No one is saying love is practical, but only that it is *good*. Nowhere in the Bible, or in any other major spiritual source material that I have read, are we told to do what is practical. Would it take a lot of hours and debate and work and analysis to figure out how best to apply our resources toward the eradication of human suffering, here and throughout the world? Yes. Just about as many hours as it now takes figuring out how to wage espionage, create weapons of destruction, and produce the endless stream of things that we obsessively buy but do not need.

Love is as serious a subject, as difficult a subject, and as sophisticated a subject as money. Why should we treat economics more seriously than love? This makes no sense, and anyone with the slightest understanding of the metaphysics of money knows that ultimately, it actually stops the flow of wealth creation. God is love, and love is the only abundance. Everything else is just the toys we've been playing with at an immature level of our spiritual development.

*From a spiritual perspective, no nation as wealthy as ours, with as many underprivileged children as we have, has any basis for long-term economic optimism whatsoever.*

## I'll Tighten My Belt When You Tighten Yours

The leaders of Congress are very big these days on telling us that we're going to have to make very difficult decisions in order to balance the federal budget. What they seem unwilling to cut, however, is the unbelievable system of "corporate welfare" by which the taxpayers of the United States subsidize the country's wealthiest companies.

According to Common Cause, the progressive public-interest advocacy group, corporate welfare will cost us $265 billion over the next five years. We subsidize private California wineries, oil companies, timber and forest companies, the broadcasting industry, and others. We even gave McDonald's $1.6 million to help them advertise fast-food products overseas, and $78 million since 1986 to Sunkist so they could promote their oranges in Asia! With the latest tax bill, we've agreed to pay $4 billion over the next ten years to subsidize ethanol, a gasoline substitute produced by

Archer Daniels Midland. Last year, that company gave more than $1 million in political contributions to Democrats and Republicans. All of our subsidized industries, of course, are major election campaign contributors. That's the way the system works.

In the summer of 1997, the Senate began major hearings regarding foreign contributions to American election campaigns. This is a  perfect way to deflect attention from the purely legal contributions to political campaigns made by companies right here in the U.S.A., according to a system that has deeply corrupted our political process, but that neither major party has yet made a meaningful effort to change.

And yet we are told that we just "don't have the money" to provide more educational and job opportunities, or health-care benefits, to average citizens.

IN President Clinton's 1997 budget, he proposed $5 billion be provided as seed money to help repair and upgrade decrepit public schools. The Republicans cut the amount to zero. Neither side, however, was actually standing up tall to get the job done. According to government studies, it would actually take $112 billion to bring America's schools up to minimum building standards.

Notice that we're not discussing new educational programs that would help America's children reach anywhere near their full human potential. That seems to remain *way* beyond our current level of political consciousness. What we are talking about here is whether the richest nation in the world is committed to its children going to schools whose buildings satisfy minimum safety requirements, meet basic construction standards, and have adequate heating, not to mention even working toilets. And all those computers for the schools we're commited to hooking up to the Internet? Well, that won't be happening in

America's poorest schools, because they don't have adequate wiring for computers even if computers were provided.

Why? Because we just don't have the money . . . *they* do.

WHENEVER someone suggests a program to aid our children, support education, or rebuild our most devastated communities, they are liable to be criticized as supporting big government programs as solutions to society's ills.

This argument is an example of what happens when public-relations slogans begin to replace *thinking*. The biggest lies, repeated enough times, start to sound true. There are huge government programs we should be worried about, don't get me wrong. *The Pentagon is a big government program that receives $259 billion annually.* Education, job training, employment, community development, health and social services, however—*all combined*—receive $59 billion a year less than what we give to the military.

What's the answer? *Better* questions.

In the 1997 budget agreement, the President and the Republican-led Congress agreed to allocate $16 billion to cover medical-insurance costs for half of the 20 million low-income, uninsured children in America. The big question in Congress is over whether the money will be directed through federal or through state programming.

The more important question—the one we should be shouting from the rafters—is this: why are we only insuring *half* our needy children? It is now reported, in fact, that regardless of how the $16 billion is allocated, only 500,000 of the uninsured children will actually be covered by that money.

If America is to move in the direction of strength and healing and leadership in the years ahead, we must evolve to a state of awareness in which leaving our children underattended—physically, intellectually, or emotionally—is considered barbaric. For it is.

And to make children's welfare merely a "family" issue, while our economic policies continue to bear down more and more heavily on those very families—in the form of pressures such as substandard schooling—is a mental trick being foisted on the American people. The same Constitution that calls on the government to secure our defense also calls on government to secure the general welfare. It should be an embarrassment to a country priding itself as a leader of the free world that 22 percent of its budget is directed toward the military while a mere 5 percent is devoted to education.

Details often bore me. When I read books like this, I'm very tempted to skip such sections as this one. But I try to remind myself how much certain elements in American society are counting on my doing just that so they can go about their merry way.

## Tra La La La La, to Prison We All Go

Nowhere is our current government thinking more obsolete, or more corrupt, than in the area of crime and punishment. This issue is crucially related to other areas of public policy and poses a huge threat to the health and safety of American society. At present, our crime policies are more than anything else like a game in the hands of immature schoolboys: let's see which ones can look tougher—whether they actually are, or not.

Emotional, psychological, and spiritual wisdom play little or no real part, as yet, in the forging of our public policy. That is because they do not necessarily lend themselves well to soundbites. They don't immediately impact an electorate deluded into thinking that "getting tough on crime" actually solves the problem.

Violence is to love as darkness is to light. It is what happens in the *absence* of something else. Hitting it, fighting it, and suppressing it are merely temporary palliatives. If we want peaceful teens, we must ourselves, as a society, show peace and love toward our younger children. There will be no dealing effectively with crime until we decide as a society to massively invest in the care of our very young children. A child's major behavioral tendencies are set by the time he or she is ten years old. No amount of boot camp, midnight basketball, or tough prison sentencing can do a whole lot to change that. If a gang has created more sense of social belonging in a child's life than we have, guess what? We lost that one. We need to shift our emphasis away from punishment—or even prevention—as an answer to crime. We should turn our attention to actual *cause*.

Ninety-five percent of all prison inmates in this country are high school dropouts—many, if not most of them, are functionally illiterate.

It's easy to blame our juvenile crime problem on absentee parents, and drugs, but outrageously inadequate schooling and child social services don't help. They exacerbate the problem, making all of us accomplices in the criminal neglect of our nation's children. America gets what it pays for. We invest our money in our military and we have a fine military. We invest our money in businesses, and they thrive. But our children—why should we not invest massively in them? Money for childcare, for children's health care, for quality of life, for education? For the price of one B-2 bomber ($1.5 billion)—which we're building although the Pentagon doesn't even want it—we could pay for the annual salaries of over 56,000 new elementary school teachers or 125,000 child-care workers.

There are people in the U.S. today who, while acutely aware that it takes cash to achieve almost anything else, rhapsodize that "Money isn't what will fix these things!" whenever you're talking about education or social services.

While it is true that spirituality, not money, is the ultimate answer to our problems, who can be gentle and peaceful for long around hundreds of angry, frustrated children? It takes money to create the environments conducive to the flowering of human capacity. It takes money to hire creative educators. It takes money to provide adequate public schools. Of course, most of our federal lawmakers surely send their children to private schools, *so perhaps they do not realize how bad the situation is.*

The American citizen might ask him- or herself at this point: if we would have to spend $112 billion just to bring our school buildings up to minimum building standards (and if we can't get ourselves to fix the toilets, how much do you think we're spending on teachers?)—then which *neighborhoods* are most of those schools in, and are these not the neighborhoods where most of our prisoners grew up? If we would spend a fraction of the money we now spend dealing with criminals on the children of the United States, we would have a much more peaceful society at a lot less cost to the American taxpayer.

STATE and local federal prisoners more than doubled between 1985 and 1996, with the prison population increasing by 56,000 in 1996 alone. While some say these statistics are a good thing because they prove that America's getting tougher on crime, there is a reality behind those statistics which bodes very badly for all of us.

While there are brilliant, dedicated individuals working within our criminal justice system, attitudes which are beginning to dominate that system are barbaric. American society breeds hundreds of thousands of criminals and then says to law enforcement, "Here, you handle it." We treat our prisons like garbage dumps to receive society's refuse. The problem of crime has become so huge in the United States that our government has opted for a crackdown mentality in its search for an illusory "safety." Then we get all these great new wonderful crime statistics: crime is down! We got little Johnny on his first offense, see—which is great except that we'll have to deal with little Johnny again when he's *big* Johnny, who's just been let out of the prison where he was sodomized, beaten, and terrorized for ten years! Yippee!

What is going on behind bars in the United States today should be of serious concern to all of us. Even the significant minority who *want* criminals to suffer in prison would be horrified by reports of what is *really* going on there. Most Americans think of our prisons as at least humane, but there are increasingly terrible exceptions. Brutality throughout the system is epidemic. And now there is a drive, particularly on the federal level, to put more juveniles in jail with the adult prison population. The potential for human tragedy here is tremendous.

A sixteen-year-old schoolboy in Texas named Rodney Hulin, Jr., was charged with arson in 1995, in a fire *that did $500 damage to a fence*. He admitted his guilt and was sentenced to *eight years in prison*. After having been repeatedly beaten and sexually assaulted during his first thirteen months in jail, during which he asked his father to pray for him that he would get out of prison alive, he hanged himself in his cell. From Georgia, there are reports of totally sadistic treatment of prisoners: men who had not violated any rules, or even resisted their guards, handcuffed and having their faces and skulls crushed in against walls by prison officials.

Do we plan to keep these people in jail forever? Or will we be dumping hundreds of thousands of men, women, and children onto our streets at the end of their prison sentences, and then reap whatever havoc one might reasonably expect on the part of those who have been, themselves, so brutalized?

If we do not change our direction drastically, then within five to fifteen years our cities will be like war zones. We will all be living in gated communities. We will travel in security police–protected caravans. We will shop only at private, guarded entertainment and shopping complexes. In other words, *we* will be in prison.

But we will have plenty of military equipment to protect our precious way of life and plenty of toys to keep us happy. Don't worry about it: none of *that* will be endangered.

Even worse, we will have done this to ourselves.

## Honey, Six of Our Kids Are Sick; Let's Ask the Neighbors if They'll Read to Two of Them

In April of 1997, the President held a Summit on Volunteerism in Philadelphia. President Clinton was joined by ex-Presidents Ford, Carter, and Bush in setting an example of service for all Americans. Fifteen million children are at risk in America, and the goal of the summit is to help 2 million of those vulnerable children by the year 2000.

I understand the need for volunteers, I believe in the work of volunteers, and I support that work with my efforts. I had dirt under my fingernails in the nonprofit sector long before it was fashionable in my community. But for a government that has systematically dismantled programs that keep human desperation at bay for millions of people, to then produce a pep rally to get us all to volunteer each week to try to pick up the slack, makes me tilt my head.

*If 15 million American children are at risk, then it is 15 million American children we should commit ourselves to saving. Not 2 million in four years, but 15 million,* immediately. *Incremental change is a classic tool of a status quo that is committed to no real change at all.*

There is no resource—governmental, economic, or private— that should *not* be involved in the effort to lift up America's desperate children and their parents who want to work. Private charity cannot compensate for governmental neglect and injustice. And corporations throwing a few million dollars into the pot here and there is like you or me throwing a quarter to a homeless person on the street.

If you bought this book, I will receive money. Capitalism has been good to me. But there is no amount of money I can make that will protect my child from the explosion of horror which will occur in this country if we do not commit to a serious effort at universal access to the opportunities that capitalism affords.

I made my own way. But as a child I was fed, stimulated culturally, safe in my environment, and cared for medically. I was told I was valuable by the world around me—psychologically as well as materially, I had a reasonable *chance* of success. And it was not just my parents, or our religious community, that gave me those things. There was a larger culture of which I was part, believing in me and supporting me in myriad ways both large and small; in short, I was set up to succeed. But millions of American children today are absolutely set up to fail. It's one thing to say that everyone has to climb the ladder of success by him or herself; it's another thing entirely to make the bottom rung too high for a child to reach.

Children cannot provide their own health care; children cannot be responsible for their own education; children cannot create their own cultural stimulation before someone teaches them how. To provide those things to all of America's children is our responsibility as a society dedicated to self-governance. What are we thinking—surely we are not in our right minds—to abdicate our moral responsibility to the development of millions of American lives, and then act horrified when they turn to dysfunctional behavior.

We must awaken and act. Not because we are fond of this group or that, but because we love America. Because we love the idea of democracy and social justice. Because we love our own children. President Kennedy, in his Inaugural Address, said "The free society that does not take care of its many who are poor will not be able to save its few who are rich."

## To Dissent Is Noble

In the words of Albert Camus, "I should like to be able to love my country and still love justice...."

Economic injustice doesn't always violate the letter of the law, but it violates the *spirit* of the law. It might not subvert the Constitution, but it subverts the principles on which the Constitution rests. We must be as vigilant in our repudiation of economic injustice as we are toward any other form of oppression.

Economic injustice is an inevitable consequence of a market-based rather than a conscience-based way of thinking. Money as the bottom line is the shadow side of the American psyche. Putting money before heart, we offend the spirit of God and repudiate a core value of American democracy. When we place our freedom to do as we wish before our responsibility to do right by others, we desecrate one of our basic first principles: freedom for the individual balanced with responsibility toward the collective good.

There is no reason why the right to make more money should be seen as a more precious right than the right to be educated, receive health care, or to live in a clean and safe environment.

Money should be seen as a means and not an end; it should not be exalted for its own sake. Making money more important than people is tantamount to making money more important than God. Our biggest financial investment, as Americans, should be mining the genius within every American child, and the creativity within every American citizen.

It is immoral for big business—including the defense establishment—to receive more government support than children's health or education, or job training for people who cannot find a place for themselves in the new economy, or the disabled or the sick. It is wrong to organize the entire country in a way that leaves millions in near-desperate conditions with little hope of escape. That is the direction that America has been going in for years, but we can change it if we assert ourselves. We must vigorously dissent.

To dissent is noble. It does not mean to attack, to judge, or to whine. It is the role of a true patriot to dissent if the direction of one's country goes against his or her conscience. If the choice is between dissent or acquiescence, dissent is the moral option.

America has become like the story of the Emperor's New Clothes. Too many of us feel, in too many ways, that this country is merely pretending to be what it no longer is. We need that little boy to come along and say, "This whole thing is a charade."

## *Money Isn't Everything, But It Helps*

I was sitting having brunch with a friend at a trendy location in Los Angeles. Cindy Crawford's boyfriend had just walked by.

"It's not enough to just give money to the poor, Marianne," said my friend, sipping his mimosa. "The poor are going to have to change their *attitudes*."

I asked him who he thought had a better chance at a positive

attitude today: the people having brunch in this beautiful restaurant, or people about ten miles away on the other side of town.

Bobby Kennedy used to say that until you have spent one full
day in the neighborhood of the inner-city poor in our society,
you have no right to condemn them or judge them.

A classic tool of demagoguery is to identify a type of person
and then use that example to condemn the entire group they
belong to. Every group has its shadow face. Yes, there are Jewish
slumlords, but that is not who Jews *are*. Yes, there are Islamic
terrorists, but that is not who Muslims *are*. Yes, there are judg-
mental, hateful people who call themselves Christians, but that
is not who Christians *are*. Yes, there are screaming gay hysterics,
but that is not who gay people *are*. Yes, there are violent black
men, but that is not who black men *are*. And yes, there are lazy,
unreliable, up-to-no-good, just-wanting-a-handout poor people
in America, but *that is not who the poor in America are.*

The poor is who my grandfather was; was yours? The immi-
grant is who my grandparents were; were yours? The desperate
are who I once was; were you?

## *Money Money Money Money Money*

I once decided to set up a nonprofit group, the purpose of which
would be to promulgate principles of conscience within the
political arena. I called my lawyer and was told that, yes, it
could be done. It would cost me several hundred dollars. Fine, I
thought; it doesn't sit well with me that it should cost so much,
given that most people wouldn't have that kind of money to
spend on such a purpose, but fortunately I do have the money,
so I'll do it. Every day I spoke to the lawyer thereafter, the price
of the project grew exorbitantly higher. Like an auction bidder, I
had to quit at about the time I learned I'd have to spend thou-

sands of dollars every year, auditing the books of every state in which the group was operative. In other words, the situation is completely rigged to discourage "just anybody" from participating dynamically in the political process. "So basically, what you're telling me is that the law prohibits this kind of political involvement for almost anyone except for the very richest among us. Is that right?"

"Yes," she said. "That's right."

NEW paradigm thinking, relevant to all human endeavor, posits the interconnectedness of all people. The poet John Donne wrote, "No man is an island, entire of himself; every man is a piece of the continent, a part of the main." This is not just an economic, social, or emotional truth; it is a *spiritual*, or *ultimate* truth, and thus will always be reflected across the board in human affairs.

No one can win at the expense of another and long retain his or her advantage. If we severely oppress people economically, they will act out their desperation in ways that ultimately endanger all of us. Harsher prison sentences and other tightened screws will hardly set us free.

A critical mass of the American public has not fully awakened to the level of serious economic injustice in our midst. The average American, for obvious reasons, has not recently driven through the streets of our most devastated communities. With jobless rates three to four times the national average, the millions of residents of America's urban wastelands are caught in a culture of vicious poverty as deep as that of a Third World country.

So many millions of dollars have been spent on public relations to convince America that things are basically okay except for the suffering of a few lazy drug fiends and their liberal friends, that millions of Americans have been duped into believing that the victims are the bad guys and that those who disdain America's first principles are the saviors of our disintegrating culture.

When someone in America now says "the economy is good," we should ask ourselves, "Good for whom?" The inner-city poor in America have lived for nearly thirty years with social and economic conditions as bad as those endured during the worst days of the Depression. The Depression lasted for ten years maximum, and was considered a national catastrophe. It would have been inconceivable for Americans, or the American government at that time, not to try to alleviate the suffering of those whose lives were wrecked by the Great Depression. President Roosevelt created jobs through the Public Works Administration and the Works Progress Administration. President Eisenhower would later help rebuild the economy of the rural South through the Economic Development Administration, creating jobs by constructing the highway system that still runs through that region. To aggressively seek to rebuild the economy of a devastated segment of America is hardly counter to our traditions; what runs counter to our traditions is the way that, today, we do *not* help.

While the Labor Department released figures in June 1997 placing unemployment at a new low of 4.8 percent—prompting President Clinton to say that "America's economy is stronger than it's been in a generation"—the jobless rate remained at 10.3 percent for blacks and 7.4 percent for Hispanics. For teenagers, the rate was 15.6 percent, while 32.6 percent of black male teenagers in the labor force were without jobs. One is reminded of Dr. King's comment that, "When you have mass unemployment in the Negro community, it's called a social problem. When you have mass unemployment in the white community, it's called a Depression."

It has been fifty years since America had a massive repair of its infrastructure. Our schools, parks, libraries, and highways all need a major overhaul. The whole country would benefit from a massive job-training and job-creation program for America's poor. What we lack is the political will to do it.

The pain of millions of Americans now stuck in a cycle of poverty and hopelessness can only result in greater social dysfunction, such as family rupture, drugs, and crime. More prisons and tougher welfare laws will of themselves do nothing but add gasoline to the already raging fire. Hatred does not end hatred, and fear does not end fear.

Some say that America cannot "afford" a massive effort to rebuild its inner cities. Quite the contrary. The price we pay for *not* doing such a thing is much, much higher than we can afford; what we are paying in both inner and outer rage is more than the system will be able to bear indefinitely. A teenager whose life is "at risk" is a risk to you and me. Money should not be the first question when we are wondering how to put back together a terribly broken part of ourselves.

A return to economic and social justice requires exertion of our national will. A massive focus on education, job training, and job creation for the inner-city poor is, while not yet politically popular, morally correct. Some would say, "Well, they can get a job at McDonald's, if they want it," and that is a significant fact; but it does not substitute for providing a fair means to move beyond that job, for those who are willing to exert the effort. People need more than jobs; they need the opportunity to get a *good* job. That is what training and education provide, and child care makes more possible. Underemployment is a crisis in America for millions of people. Child care is a crisis in America for millions of people. It is very important not to let low unemployment figures obscure the reality.

A conscience-based politics cares less for political expediency than for spiritual truth. We should extend our hands to the struggling portions of our nation for no other reason than that it is the right thing to do. Why would we bail out another country, but not our fellow Americans? And why would we not want to help those in trouble, if we ourselves are in our right minds?

## The Kids Who Do Not Matter

In February 1997, President Clinton unveiled a plan to help combat youth violence. Saying that reversing a decade-long climb in juvenile crime and gang activity should be "the nation's top law enforcement priority," the President warned that if new policies were not enacted soon, "our country is going to be living in chaos."

While crime in most categories has been decreasing in America, youth violence continues to surge, juvenile homicides having increased more than two and one-half times since 1984. With a steady increase in gangs, 95 percent of large cities and 88 percent of small cities are afflicted with gang-related crime.

"We've got about six years to turn this thing around," said Clinton, or "my successors will not be giving speeches about the wonderful opportunities of the global economy—they'll be trying to keep body and soul together for people in the streets of these cities." His plan included a $200,000 subsidy to state and local governments to hire prosecutors focusing particularly on gang crime and juvenile violence, and $50 million for youth courts and probation officers. Instead of spending our money on lifting people up, we're spending it on the police we need to keep them in line.

The majority of these young people live in communities where, even if they follow all the rules and do their very best to win within a system so terribly stacked against them, the economic opportunity for even modest prosperity is nil.

Most Americans, while we know all this, do not *really* know.

—

We do not viscerally realize, on a mass level, the extent of the human misery and hopelessness in our midst because we are afraid to drive into the neighborhoods where it lives. When we have to go there, we lock our car doors, and in far too many cases, prompted by fear, we are tempted to lock our hearts.

## Our Money, Our Minds

According to Thomas Jefferson, all Americans were to have universal access to the opportunity to produce modest material abundance. America was not to rest until that was achieved. We cannot keep faith with this American first principle if we are willing to abide by the systematic unraveling of this basic democratic freedom. Millions of Americans can no longer be validly described as free to pursue the American dream.

Not every rich person is greedy—by a long shot—any more than every poor person is kind and noble. Indeed, many of the richest Americans are becoming alarmed at the increasing economic disparities in America, for they do not bode well for any of us. If this boat sinks, we're all going down. It will do us little good to be wealthy if we have to live in gated communities and in fear for our very lives. That is what will happen in America if the emotional violence already spawned by economic injustice spills over into more widespread and collective expressions of outrage.

After World War I, the European Allies made a terrible mistake. Punishment of the vanquished Germans was cruel and unrelenting. U.S. President Woodrow Wilson passionately argued against the punishing attitude of our European Allies, predicting exactly what occurred: that an economically and socially crushed Germany would be prey to something even more dangerous in the years ahead.

It is generally agreed by historians that if Germany had not been in such a desperate state in the years following World War I, Hitler would not have had such an easy rise to power. That is why we treated Germany and Japan so differently after World War II: we helped rebuild their economies, realizing finally that there is no greater threat to peace and security in the world than a large group of crushed and desperate people.

Should we not think on these things? Americans already employ more private than public police. Is this the direction in which we wish to keep moving?

## Creating the Alternative

Imagine three groups of Americans: those who drive fancy cars, those who drive basic serviceable cars, and those who drive clunkers.

While there are many activists in America who are concerned about the people driving clunkers, and do everything they can to help them, what we need is a concerted voice that says, "In the richest nation on earth, everyone should have a reasonable chance of driving a basic, serviceable car."

Some of the spokespeople for the financial status quo would argue that our tax structure and other economic policies should not be used for purposes of "social engineering." But that is in fact exactly what they are used for now. Our current disparity between rich and poor is the result.

We have to rethink money and its place in our lives if we are to transform American society. But the solution to economic injustice does not lie in making money bad. Spiritually, there is only one of us here; in the final analysis, there are no separate needs. Ultimately, what is good for Jesse Jackson is good for Rupert Murdoch. We do not have to choose between the rich and the poor, but only between a consciousness of abundance and a consciousness of lack.

The primary political issue should not be the distribution of wealth but the creation of wealth. That is why job training, job creation, and education matter so much. The creation of wealth should be validated, not undermined; but it must be validated for *all* American citizens. It is not a limited amount of wealth, but a limited amount of creative, compassionate thinking that is our problem as a nation. There is not a limited amount of potential prosperity in America because there is not a limit to human creativity. In the presence of love, integrity, discipline, and the commitment to excellence, limits fade away.

One day, our leaders say, "But there is only so much money to go around." The very next day, there are runaway tax revenues as a result of a booming economy. We wait until the money comes, and then fight over how to allocate it. Instead, we should set morally outstanding national goals—the best educated children, the eradication of economic injustice, the best system of job training in the world, the tools of democracy in the hands of all Americans, and proper medical care for all. Then, out of a mass intention to meet those goals and the spiritual authority behind it, we will manifest the money to make it happen.

We must turn from scarcity thinking to possibility thinking, in meeting not only our personal goals but our societal goals as well. The economic order in America is essentially unjust, but as solid as it appears to be, it is part of a system now passing away. As spiritual beings, we are outgrowing its tenets. As new structures of thought emerge, new institutional structures will follow. But it will take our material as well as spiritual efforts to transform a system so firmly entrenched.

We need a new paradigm of understanding, a moral commitment to express it, and a new kind of activism to bring it forth.

# 5

# YIN
# ACTIVISM

*"I must study politics and war that my sons may have liberty to study mathematics and philosophy. My sons ought to study mathematics and philosophy, geography, natural history, naval architecture, navigation, commerce and agriculture, in order to give their children a right to study painting, poetry, music, statuary, tapestry and porcelain."*

—JOHN ADAMS,
LETTER TO ABIGAIL ADAMS,
MAY 12, 1780

I N the May 19, 1997, issue of *Time* magazine, there is a major news story headlined "Too Good to be True—By almost any measure, life is swell in the U.S. What went right?" The article outlines the amazing string of wins that the United States has been enjoying for the last few years: we're breathing cleaner air and drinking cleaner water, crime is in a free fall and near a twenty-two-year low, and the U.S. economy keeps humming along beautifully. Skeptics like me are psychoanalyzed for our inability to take yes for an answer. All you have to do, according to the magazine, is spend enough time at the same restaurant I mentioned I was having brunch at with my friend in the last chapter to know that everything in America is really really really, really good.

When I was a child, we were warned of the evils of communist propaganda. But capitalist propaganda doesn't seem to bother many people today; it's just called "spin."

The article quotes former Labor Secretary Robert Reich, who served in President Clinton's first term, as saying, "There are still millions of people desperately trying to stay afloat.... But Americans are segregated by income as never before, so it is far easier to pretend the worse off don't exist. They're out of sight."

Then the article quotes a Clinton administration official as

———

saying this is no time to talk about anything downbeat. "There will be no return to Reichism," he said. "That would shatter the public mood."

Whoa, guys, thanks. I feel much better! What a *mood* I'm in!

I always felt that the Democrats whine a bit too much, and that the Republicans are right to point out the benefits of optimism. But optimism is very different from denial. We are a country in denial. Like Germany in the early thirties, Rome before it fell, and France before the Revolution. What we're experiencing is merely a sunset effect, where the sun looks so glorious just before it goes down to inevitably darkening skies.

Far be it from me to argue with all the economists, much less *Time* magazine, when they tell us that everything is fine, but I think I'll hold to the idea that "God shall not be mocked." That line means that He *isn't*. He is watching over every little thing, and there is nothing He does not see. An economic forecast is not the same as a moral forecast. What we do to the least of these, we do to Him.

What makes us think that we are so special that the lessons of history—much less the laws of God—do not apply to us? Economic forecasts can lie, and the media can lie. But history does not lie. And neither does the heart.

IN a land very very far away, so far that it exists only in our minds, there is a battle raging. It is more devastating than a nuclear war. The forces of fear have taken on the forces of love, and it is not yet clear which side will win the spoils of the modern world.

It is in our minds where the battle is raging, and it is in our minds where we must address it. The denial of darkness is just more darkness. The spiritual challenge of the times in which we live is to look at the darkness but not dwell on it. We must proclaim the light. We are in fact preparing for a climactic moment of life on earth, and while economists and journalists and political consultants can't necessarily see it coming, people all over the world can feel it. While our collective capacity for denial can be very great indeed, we are not dumb and we are not blind. From the Left and the Right, from all religions and no religions, from the hardest hearts to the most open hearts, there is a tremulous sense of a darkened sky and a star within it, appearing and reappearing, for all the world to see.

PEOPLE often ask what I think of all the prophecies that say the world is going to burn. I think it means that in one way or the other, the world as we now know it is going to pass into extinction. Only love is good enough to dwell on this earth. What is not love must go now. It is time for it to pass.

We have two choices, and we are free to make them for ourselves. We can willingly, through the sublime alchemy of God's grace within us, burn up and transform all selfish, fear-based thought forms that keep the dominant structures of this world in place,

OR

We can burn.

It is a metaphysical truth that it is not up to us what we learn, but merely whether we learn through joy or through pain. What America chooses to learn, what voices we choose to listen to, and which stars we choose to follow make all the difference for the entire world. The choices we make are determined by our thinking. We will shut down our thinking and hear the clankering of fools, or we will open our minds and hear the music of the heart.

—

## The Intention to Heal

America has no dearth of genius. A routine trip to any shopping mall in America shows this. If we spent a fraction of the energy we now use to manufacture things we do not need to instead create a society that truly works, we would be a completely different country. What we lack is an evolved sense of collective purpose for our talent and intelligence. Our awesome creativity is applied to mainly unimportant ends.

Each of us has within us depths of intelligence and creativity that come forth only in response to meaningful purpose. Changing the world is a meaningful quest. Millions of Americans want to see this country change in fundamental ways, and would be more than willing to help make it happen. But it feels as though there is no unified social forcefield for the effort, no number to call, no place to sign up. People are naturally attracted to a sense of higher, common need; watch any of us when there is a storm coming through town or a fire down the street.

But there shouldn't have to be a disaster to bring us together or to inspire us to serve a higher good. The ancient Greeks used the word *politics* to mean the involvement of the citizen beyond his or her own self, or even family identity, to the larger community of the nation. That is what politics should be. Politics should not be a place where we merely compete or even negotiate for who gets what, but rather a place where we creatively work together toward a greater good for all.

Service shouldn't be something we do separate from our daily lives; it should become a *way of life*. That, at bottom, is what citizenship is. "Ask not what your country can do for you; ask what you can do for your country" is something that Americans carry in our hearts, much more than we do the promise of a balanced budget. What we most need, as Americans, is to remember—and then act on the memory—that we were born for something far more important than the attainment of mere self-centered goals. We were born to glorify the love of God.

## Renaissance Politics

We need a new vortex of social energy in America, one that arises from the shared intention to heal our society. Minds in agreement form the most powerful force in the universe, and to harness that force would constitute not so much a bridge as a supersonic transport to the twenty-first century. What this vortex will look like, and how it will evolve in the material world, is almost unimportant. The most powerful manifestations occur where yin precedes yang.

To create a Renaissance politics in America, our first job is to create the thoughts and visions out of which new material structures will emerge. One of Taoism's highest principles is *wu wei* —"nonresistance" or "nonaction." But this is not at all a negative passivity. Quite to the contrary, what it means is that consciousness unburdened by material baggage has the greatest capacity to manifest a goal because it moves through life in a clear, clean line. As we transit from the Material Age into the Consciousness Age, the key to creative materialization is to work as much on the preparation of consciousness as on action. The issue is not only to "do the footwork" to achieve a goal, but to prepare a ground of consciousness from which the footwork can be most easily and effectively carried out.

Some might ask, if we are moving into an Ideational Era, why we need worldly institutions at all. They are necessary, in the words of Professor Huston Smith, to "give an idea traction." Heaven is already perfect; it's earth we must improve. The key to doing this is to keep our minds on the thoughts of heaven,

—

while grounding our bodies to earth. The reunification of these two realms is the goal of human evolution.

To achieve our potential and heal our society, we must address the realm of consciousness as seriously as we do action. Like a great athlete, we must have a very clear vision of what we want to accomplish before we make a move. Vision in preparation for an action is as important as the action itself.

The old political thought system looks at life through rearview mirrors. It is imprisoned within materially based mechanistic thought forms, and has little idea how—or even desire—to deal creatively with the personal side of political transformation. Thus the need for a new paradigm for social change infused with the yin of greater spiritual wisdom and the yang of an awakened citizenry ready and willing to act. From that combination will come our healing.

## The Power Within Us

A friend of mine is a doctor at a large hospital in southern California. During the spring of 1997, she attended Harvard's Symposium on the role of Spirituality and Healing in Medicine.

A week after attending the conference, one of my friend's favorite patients, a robust sixty-seven-year-old man, came down with what appeared to be routine symptoms of a cough and cold. He was treated early in the course of his illness with a very strong antibiotic, but developed pneumonia nevertheless. Admitted to the hospital, he was found to have a very virulent form of the disease and continued to rapidly deteriorate in spite of aggressive medical management. Multiple intravenous antibiotics were given to him, but within twenty-four hours his condition was critical. Within another twenty-four hours he was on a ventilator, comatose. Obviously, it was questionable whether the patient would survive. Several specialists working on the case felt that he would not.

My friend remembered that she had heard the doctors at Harvard speak about the role of positive intentionality and prayer, not only on the part of the patient but also on the part of those around him. My friend told the patient's family, "Your father is doing very poorly. The doctors are doing everything we can. Go into his room, surround him, send him loving thoughts and pray." She too prayed for him with her minister.

Within the first twenty-four hours, his physical deterioration stopped and his condition stabilized. Within the next twenty-four hours, he was weaned from the ventilator and awoke from his coma. Within another few days, the patient was well enough to go home.

His family would later say to my friend that it had meant so much to them to feel they could participate in their loved one's healing, rather than just passively waiting for doctors' reports. "That's what people want now," my friend told me. "They want to feel like they're contributing to a larger process, something bigger than themselves."

Later, the patient would say that he remembered, while in the coma, having a sense that a loving presence was sustaining him.

In medicine today, the "psychoimmunological factor" is seen as a serious element in the treatment of disease. Medicine has come to acknowledge that stimulation of our own healing powers is as valid an issue in healing as is an attack on our diseases.

The power of positive intentionality is the crux of alternative medical power, and alternative political power as well. What our founders referred to as "divine providence" doesn't register whether the condition to be healed is a human body, or a complex relationship of social factors affecting 266 million people.

The form of a problem is irrelevant before the power of God. Nothing on earth can make Him say, "I wish I could help you, but it's too big a job."

The physician studies disease, while the metaphysician studies health and healing. The Western allopathic doctor is taught to control symptoms, while the metaphysical healer seeks to address the nonmaterial factors that contribute to the cause and perpetuation of illness and the factors that stimulate our natural healing. Together, the two approaches form a holistic paradigm for the treatment of disease. The conscious patient doesn't just passively wait for the doctor to "fix" her: she participates in the healing process through mental, emotional, and spiritual work of her own.

Politicians can be likened to doctors. We have overestimated their role in healing society, as we once overestimated the doctor's role in healing our bodies. No doctor can guarantee physical health to a patient who refuses to take care of her body, and no leader can guarantee social health to a people who refuse to take care of their society. Every citizen can be likened to the immune cells of a body whose immune system is clearly compromised. Most of our problems in America are, at their core, opportunistic infections. They wouldn't be happening if individuals were more awake and vigilant to their responsibilities as citizens.

Metaphysicians are not doctors; their expertise is not in the area of disease, but in how people heal. A parallel phenomenon can occur in politics: there are many people who do not know that much about traditional politics, but they know tremendous amounts about people, about how groups operate, and how they change. As with any holistic vision, it is not just the material plane but the mental and spiritual planes as well that should now be addressed seriously as political factors.

Legislation can be likened to medicine: it can treat the symptom, but it does not necessarily treat the cause. The cause of all societal dis-ease is a tearing asunder of our experience of underlying unity. You can't just pass a law and say, "There! Be unified."

P O L I T I C S itself is now dominated by negativity and discord, and vessels of emotional and psychological violence have no capacity to bring forth peace. We ourselves must create an alternative political force that does. We must take responsibility for our own reunification as a nation, in relationships not manipulated by the press or elective politics. Without an emotional reconstitution of our social fabric, no amount of laws, police, or prisons will contain the violent eruptions inevitable in the presence of profound misunderstanding among people.

I call the inner work of creating this force "yin activism." It is made up of three main elements: the awakening of our minds, atonement for our errors, and the arousal of our spirits.

A W A K E N I N G
Whereby we find our own wisdom and
reassert our personal power,
reeducate ourselves concerning things we've ignored or
forgotten,
seek to be free thinkers,
rethink love,
reclaim the political process,
create a citizen-based politics,
move beyond war
and find the field of peace.

## *Personal Power:*
## *Repudiating Mind-Death*

The most critical political issue in America today is the numbing and suppression of personal power within the individual American citizen. Political power ultimately derives from the personal confidence and courage to express oneself. Where a social system has failed to adequately educate its citizens, bombarded our nervous systems with an overstimulation of mindless entertainment, promoted consumerism as the primary social activity, and accepted the numbing of the resultant pain with massive use of antidepressants as a substitute for questioning the pain itself, personal power becomes the purview of a lucky or courageous few. The game of the culture has been to respond to our feelings of disempowerment by exploiting those very feelings: trying to convince us that if we buy this or that product, or elect this or that official, our feelings of well-being will be miraculously restored.

Americans, as individuals, tend to be spunky and eminently decent. We are great to sit next to on airplanes. As a group, however, we have a capacity for denial and grandiosity that makes us increasingly easy targets for manipulation by the media, politicians, or false advertising campaigns. We have become completely taken in by the business of public relations.

Much of our education was training in passive acceptance of someone else's perspective rather than development of the ability to create our own; television has all but destroyed our capacity for critical thinking; our linear thought processes are jumbled like crackling cereal; and we are left with a dangerous propensity to be taken for a ride by anyone who can afford a specialist at scrambling our brains even more.

We have been lulled to sleep by an official culture that speaks nonsense to us as though it were reasonable and have been trained since childhood by a consumer culture to conspire in our own psychological bondage. The lullabies are compelling, but we must commit to our awakening.

As we meditate and pray, we begin to awaken. As we read good books, we begin to awaken. As we eschew bad television, we begin to awaken. As we serve our community, we begin to awaken. As we journey toward psychological health, we begin to awaken. As we think for ourselves, we begin to awaken. As we communicate more freely, we begin to awaken. As we take up the philosophical mantle of concern for the future of life on earth, and apply it as best we can to our social, professional, and political endeavors, we begin to awaken ourselves and others. And in that awakening lies hope for all of us. Mass awakening from our entrenched delusions is the only hope for America's healing.

It is up to each of us to make a stand for the things that will change society. Each of us has a potential for genius, for each of us is a child of God. Our genius lies sleeping in most of us because it is not yet compelled to come forth. Greatness unfolds in response to great challenge. Making money is not a great challenge, nor is fame or worldly power. But the challenge to transform the darkness of the world is a call from God Himself. This is not just some wonderful utopian thought; it is absolutely necessary if we are to survive and thrive in the century now upon us.

## Once We Wake

It's not an accident that Americans have become so passive in the face of systemic threats to our freedom. For decades, the American public education system tried to teach children what to think, avoiding its greater mission in a free society: to teach children *how* to think. Teaching children how to think means fostering minds that are questioning, assertive, open-minded, and creative. We should bring up our children to be creators, not imitators, for only that prepares them for the wonder of life.

That is an outlook that the perpetuation of democracy requires, but that an industrialized economic system came more and more to resist. While we were dominated economically by the rule of industrialization, the tacit pact that American education made with industry was to provide the system with masses of Americans who would show up on time, do as they were told, not ask a lot of questions, and not bother to assert themselves.

A child would enter kindergarten excited and passionate. By the sixth grade at the latest, his or her passion was squelched. Passion is messy for an authoritarian system and frightening to those who live under it. In the name of discipline and education, yet actually in the service of an economic system which had become our sacred cow, America taught its children to stuff their passions and forget their questions, and thus turn off their minds.

I'M not a conspiracy buff in the traditional sense. I'm not afraid of groups of evil people meeting in secret societies to plan world domination. Or if there are such societies, they're not the things I'm most afraid of. The conspiracy that concerns me is our very way of life, our conspiracy of silence about things that matter most. It's an invisible foe because it's the tenor of our collective being. There is no one to oppose because there is no monolithic power source that spews out all the poison of our forgetfulness. We want to forget, after all, because *we are afraid to know*. Direct confrontation, even if we knew all the ins and outs of America's deepest darkest secrets, is not an option. What we have got to do is rise above, begin thinking again and feeling again like the passionate, authentic, brilliant human beings we were created to be. From that place we will cast a web of insights and manifestation that will disperse malaise and malice, and bring us back to life.

The average European is much better educated, much more aware of the true political and social issues that affect his or her daily life, than is the average American. We have become so accustomed to allowing the media to do our thinking for us that we are dangerously ignorant of important issues.

What I've noticed, however, working on both continents, is that as intelligent as Europeans are concerning a particular subject, their enthusiasm for action is not the same as ours. Once we wake, we wake. You give a group of Americans a thumbnail sketch of an issue that demands their involvement, a 101 overview, and they are jumping up and down on chairs, organizing activity, creating solutions, preparing to act. We leave no doubt that we are indeed the psychological heirs of the men and women who, over two hundred years ago, had what it took to recreate the world.

We ourselves must take responsibility for our abdication of citizen authority. We abdicate our power every time we allow ourselves to surrender to the myriad forms of mind-death that pass for culture in America today. If we want a renaissance, we must take our minds back. If enough Americans would say, I will no longer watch too much TV; if enough Americans would say, I will read the books I know I should read; if enough Americans would say, I will seek my spiritual nature; if enough Americans would say, I will do the things that I know in my heart I should do, and make a stand for the changes that I feel are important— then America would have a renaissance. We've forgotten our identities as the source and protector of power in America, and as a consequence that power is seeping like blood from our wounds.

—

## Freeing Our Thoughts

Freethinkers protect our freedom, but often at great cost. Notice the projection of guilt onto Vietnam war protesters during the 1960s. Even now, when that war has been declared invalid from every military and political, as well as moral, point of view, we have not as a nation yet been able to fully retract our psychic disapproval from those who refused to shut up, sit down, and do as they were told. Then, and now, those who threaten our most basic democratic freedoms are often made to look like the patriots in America, while those who stand up for those freedoms are often made to appear as if they lack love for this country.

Without the strength of an enlivened mind we become passive observers to our own lives, easy to sell to and easy to control. Thus, the onset of citizen anemia. Universal education is important, not just so that we can get jobs, as the politicians keep saying, but because it is the greatest bulwark against tyranny. Freedom depends on people *thinking*. We know more about fashion at the Oscars than we know about issues that vitally affect our daily lives. If this continues, democracy will become a memory.

Democracy is like driving: you can't do it with your eyes shut. Democracy—a celebration of power of, by, and for the people —depends on our being intelligently informed, appropriately skeptical, and freethinking citizens.

American democracy carries with it extraordinary rights to express ourselves. It is not a political repression of our voices but a psychological and emotional invalidation of our opinions that poses the greatest threat to universal participation in our democracy today. Some of the people with the greatest gifts to give at this time would feel the most insecure about trying to do so. No American should ever feel, "Who am I to have an opinion?"

Democracy has been turned into a shallow well. It needs not to be extended around the world so much as to be extended more deeply into our own minds. When people have asked me what advice I might have regarding reading spiritual source material, I have had only one thing to say: Take it personally. I feel the same way about democracy in America. I think we should all take it personally.

## Expanding Our Concept of Love

America's destiny is to reflect the highest unfoldment of Western consciousness. When we are good, we are very very good, and when we are bad, we are awful. I have said to European audiences over the last few years, "I support your efforts to resist the influx of second-rate American television programs into your country; you shouldn't let Hollywood do to your kids what it's done to ours."

When America gets it right, however, we are a light unto the world. Part of getting it right in life is periodically taking the time to take stock of oneself. In many ways, that is what we as a nation most need now.

During a time of whole-systems transition, it is not enough to just fix this problem or that problem, for all our problems are interconnected. We must develop a broad-based, collective shift in consciousness. What each of us must learn—what America must learn—is that all problems ultimately stem from our lack of concern for one another.

When Americans are in a crisis, we come together and work together magnificently. What is happening now is that we are denying that there's a crisis and are pretending things are rosy. For those of us who believe there's at least as much danger in the denial as in the crisis itself, our challenge is to come together anyway. All strength is found in joining. But this time we must see the joining as more than an answer to a particular problem; we must see the joining as the necessary next step in our cultural evolution. We must consider what it means to join, and indeed what it means to love.

Romantic love is a wonderful thing—great for skin tone. But it is not the spiritual height of love, and the country must outgrow our false attachment to it if we are to heal. We are hooked through advertising on images that are so false even the models in the picture don't experience love in the ways that the pictures suggest. We are being beckoned by a higher love. We are being challenged by destiny to move beyond *eros,* beyond even *philia,* to the *agape* of love for all humankind.

Our lives are like a huge house, and we have relegated love to just one room of it: the bedroom. But God created us to fill the entire house with love. To embrace that more expanded sense of what love is, and how it applies to our collective existence, is the radical medicine that will heal us.

The love of which I speak is not made up of denial, enabling, or false posturing. It cries as often as it laughs; it admits of sadness and despair. There is nothing smarmy about it. It is not a less authentic, but rather a more authentic mode of human thought and behavior. Invalidating it on the grounds that it is touchy-feely is totally preposterous.

Our relationships are reflecting the chaotic shift from fear-based to love-based planetary experience. There is a larger romance waiting for us: our participation in a love affair with the higher possibilities for life on earth. And romantic, sexual love ultimately unfolds more easily when it is one fabulous room in the house but not the house itself.

As long as we stay resistant to a deeper, more penetrating discussion of the interior forces that rule the world, then our options for national recovery remain limited. Violence cannot be endlessly managed, but it can, through the grace of God, be undone. It is overwhelmed, as is all darkness, in the presence of love. God's love is not separate from human love, because God is one. To understand that mystery, and to learn to live it, is the salvation of the human race. God is one, therefore you and I are one. God is one, therefore all nations are one. That is not a thought humanity has outgrown; it is a thought we have not yet quite grown deep enough to understand.

We must free the subject of love from the mental prison where it has been relegated by our pseudo-sophisticated bias. We must eschew the tacit injunction against its discussion in any other context but the romantic or the mundane. We are quickly coming upon an age when the question of what it means to love will define our science, our educational systems, indeed our politics. As the philosopher Pierre Teilhard de Chardin said, "Someday, after we have mastered the winds, the waves, the tides and gravity, we shall harness for God the energies of love. Then for the second time in the history of the world, man will have discovered fire."

IT is very clear now that faith-based nonprofit organizations have greater success dealing with social problems than do traditional government programs. While some would argue that this means government should be less involved in such issues, I disagree. Why should government not help clean up the mess that in many cases its own policies helped create and now maintain? Even more important, the government has a proper role as community-builder because it is our only centralized voice. It's like the loudspeaker in homeroom.

Government should be involved in helping the disadvantaged among us, but in a very transformed way. Handouts and enabling behavior are low-level response patterns, spiritually and psychologically. Faith-based organizations are successful because spiritual tenets are more psychologically sophisticated than those that dominate most government programs. As a rule, the government looks to professionals in business rather than professionals in transforming people's lives, to do work that a traditional business mentality has no clue how to perform.

I read an article by a rabbi recently, in which he noted that while being a member of the clergy is considered the most prestigious career by most Americans, there is no way they could be regarded as the most influential. Faith professionals receive the message, "We have a lot of respect for you, but on the other hand, it's totally agreed here that you don't really understand how the world works." What is true is the opposite: people who know the world of faith know *more* about how the world works because they know how consciousness operates. Consciousness is *cause.* It is the place where we are stuck, and the place where we will be collectively released.

Faith should not be America's stepchild. In fact, its right use is the most intelligent response to the problems of our time. While it is important that nothing connected to the government ever be involved in proselytizing for a particular religion, the actual laws of spirit apply to every aspect of our lives. Stating the Golden Rule doesn't violate the separation of church and state. There are enough universal spiritual themes we can use, and all agree on. The twelve steps of Alcoholics Anonymous, with their reference to "God *as we understand Him,*" have clearly demonstrated how people of all religions, and no religion, can come together and feel included in a spiritual, though not religious, context. It is very possible to honor God without showing honor or dishonor to any particular religion.

What we need to concern ourselves with is not just the fact that faith-based social organizations work, but also *why* they work. Faith works because it opens the mind to more expanded dimensions of itself. It accesses the soul and the power of the soul to heal and be healed. It delivers us to our inner peace and power.

Faith is the miracle of love. It is effective because it doesn't stop at fighting a problem; it provides a solution. It doesn't just try to manage the effects of evil; it exalts the good that casts it out. It doesn't just say no to something; it says yes to something better. Without a spiritual experience, true change does not occur. The head without the heart has no idea how to heal anything.

It is part of God's law that love will ultimately prevail in this world. But it is also part of His law that we have total freedom whether to love now or later, whether to embrace it willingly or to put up a fight. History bears witness to the resistance of the human species to the love in our hearts. Love's pull, our resistance to it, and our final surrender back to love are the story at the center of all human existence.

Historic change doesn't just occur by itself, but necessitates a persistent and intense flow of energy as counterforce to the world's inertia. We can be that counterforce. We can be that love.

## The Inner Citizen

New paradigm thinking shifts our focus to the personal dimensions of worldly power. We must create a new political *culture* in America if we're interested in fundamental repair. We need to move from a government-centric political system to a citizen-centric political culture.

Most average Americans have, in critical ways, dropped out of the political process. Over the last few decades, the American citizenry has allowed itself to become infantilized, trying to find the perfect parent figures to fix us, unknowingly inching closer and closer to an authoritarian system every year as we search for an illusionary security. The security we wish to feel will come not from the power of government but from a power within us.

Too many Americans fall into a category that a friend of mine calls "the politically resigned." When she told me that she isn't even registered to vote anymore because she is so disgusted by politics, I questioned whether this is responsible behavior. "You're right," she said. "But it's all so complicated, and I don't want to vote unless I know exactly what I'm voting for." That's certainly reasonable. I suggested that perhaps she would want to watch C-Span, read some of the news each day, do whatever it takes to become aware.

My friend takes very seriously the issues of higher consciousness. People with a knowledge of philosophy and metaphysics have important understanding for this moment in history; they should be the biggest adults in American society. They are the last people who should be sitting out the political process.

I see Americans in three distinct groups. Let's imagine there's a door, and on the other side of it is an American paradise. One group says that paradise is not real and that therefore there is no door. Another group wants very much to unlock the door, but doesn't have the keys. The last group has the keys, sees the door, and knows there's a paradise—but is so busy staring at how beautiful the keys are (and endlessly talking about them) that it hasn't yet thought to use them.

We need those keys to unlock the door. Spiritual principles were not just created by God to save an individual; they were created to save the world. Nothing else will heal us. No external remedies alone can lift us up. As a prominent citizen of New Jersey said, "We had our tax break, and it didn't transform our lives."

## *Citizen-Based Politics*

A citizen-based political culture would have a different collective nervous system than the culture we have now. It might seem to lack sex appeal at first, compared to our current election-driven politics. We wouldn't place all our focus on a passionate courtship, culminating in one hot night when all the votes get counted and we finally release the mounting tension of the race to the top. As a generation we're addicted to the spectacle and the heat of big elections, not yet having found our passion for a sustained and steady love of country.

Our leadership plays into our immaturity, often acting as immature as we, promising us everything during campaigns, then delivering very little after the election. Mature leadership will not emerge from an immature body politic. Our leadership lacks because we lack, and at present the greatest gift our leaders give us is that they reflect back to us our own limitations.

It's very difficult to look in the mirror sometimes, for an individual or for a nation. But American individuals seem to be far more able to look deep within, and adjust accordingly, than our institutions seem capable of doing. It's one thing to admit to your spouse or children or therapist that your life is a fraudulent, big fat lie, and you're going to change it. It's another thing to announce that about a corporation if you're the CEO talking to stockholders, or about the nation if you're running for reelection. We, the people, must have the courage to face things as they are and speak the truth as best we see it.

## *Shedding War*

This country was born from a pioneer mentality, and it will be reborn from one as well. Americans at their best are a people psychologically suited to forging new ground.

But the early frontier mentality was, in some ways, almost the opposite energy from that which is needed now. Our new frontier is first and foremost within our minds; our greatest challenge at this time is not to dominate outer territory but to create internal healing. It is our own minds we need most to explore.

Throughout the twentieth century, our leaders have used the imagery of war to rally the American people. Our collective psyche is still stuck on the model of war as power; thus our War on Drugs, War on Crime, or war on anything else we don't like. The White House Plumbers were reflecting Nixon's perceived need to make a "war" on his enemies, and President Clinton waged his first Presidential campaign from a "War Room." We will never move beyond war so long as we ourselves are still so convinced of, and even attracted to, its power.

Janet Reno was perceived by many as a hero for her Rambo action at the Waco compound, even though that action resulted in the deaths of innocent children. Jimmy Carter was perceived by many as a weakling for his refusal to play Rambo in the Iran hostage crisis, though his patience and creative nonresistance brought all the hostages home alive.

People were more comfortable with the false security of Rambo-type action than they were uncomfortable with the deaths of those children; and more uncomfortable when confronted by a true demonstration of the power of a spiritual principle than they were made comfortable by seeing Americans come home alive. That is where our collective consciousness needs further evolution: we still see brute force as more powerful than soul force.

Peace is more than the absence of war. According to an ancient Indian sutra, peace is defined as "beingness grounded in nonviolence." We will not have peace in the world if we merely wish to eradicate war; we will have peace only when we have reached a level of humanity at which our shared intention is the creation of peace.

We have a drug problem in America because we have not yet, as a society, embraced sobriety; we have hatred in America because we have not yet, as a society, embraced love; we have violence in America because we have not yet, as a society, embraced peace. As long as we are unwilling to make the next evolutionary leap into greater light, there is no point in cursing the inevitable darkness that will be with us until we do.

## *There Is a Field*

I was watching television late one night, surfing through channels that all appeared uninteresting. I landed on a cable program featuring two radio talk-show hosts—one very conservative, one apparently liberal—going at each other in extremely adversarial, gladiator fashion. After a few minutes they began to read the news, trading stories.

Both men were obviously seasoned professionals with deep, resonant radio voices. Delivering the news, they were like professional soundboxes. They could tell you their hometown was burning with a seemingly calm objectivity and absence of emotion. But this was television rather than radio, and I saw chinks in their emotional armor.

The first newscaster reported that two teens, eighteen and seventeen, had shot and killed two pizza delivery men in a remote area of New Jersey "for the thrill of watching them die." The two murderers were described as "aimless thrill-seekers" by police.

Then the other newscaster reported that police had just buried a newborn infant found dead in a duffel bag.

Both men reported the stories with stoic detachment. But I saw in both of them split seconds of horror. A look that seemed to say, "What is happening to this country? This is too sickening to take," flashed across both of their faces. And it was in their horror that I saw hope for America.

It was in those moments of horror that they were spiritually awake, for they were emotionally honest. There is nothing spiritually awake about their supposedly objective reportage of the facts, nor certainly not in their attacks on each other. But in their both expressing revulsion—however brief, however squelched—at the sight of evil was, and is, their common humanity. It does not matter, in that place, who is Left and who is Right, how obnoxious their "act," or how differing their opinions. What escaped from behind their masks, much more clearly than is revealed through their worldly personae, was the fact that both are basically decent, civilized men with a sense of conscience and shame.

Carly Simon sings a song about how two people who have decided to separate slip, while in a state between sleep and waking, and say to each other, "I love you." That is where the planet is: we walk around pretending—first to ourselves and then to each other—that we do not love each other, that love is not our primary concern. But it is primary in our hearts because God placed it there. Can we evolve to a place where we are willing to bear witness in the world to what we know to be true in our hearts? This is a question that millions of people now ask themselves; imagine what the world will be like when entire nations ask it.

We do not admit our love because we do not admit the pain that stands in front of it. That is why America's internal work is so important; our society cannot heal until we move into a much more psychologically and emotionally mature way of structuring our lives. Emotional dishonesty is an American disease.

Looking at the two radio hosts, I wanted to reach my hand through the television and touch them. For in the place beyond their differences, beyond their opinions and beyond their neuroses, lies the truth of who we all are. If we can join there—and pray there together for the healing of our world—then there is no violence, cruelty, darkness, or perversion that will be able to stand before the majesty of that joining.

Persian poet Rumi, writing over seven hundred years ago, revealed a greater possibility for humanity:

> Out beyond ideas of wrongdoing and rightdoing,
> There is a field. I'll meet you there.

We need to all go to that field, where it doesn't matter what our politics are, before something happens to force us there. We must move as a society beyond the point where we come together only during times of crisis; we must evolve to the point where we come together because to do so is the reason we're alive.

"Our separation from each other," said Albert Einstein, "is an optical illusion of consciousness." Our long-term good—indeed, our survival as a species—depends on our finding our way past thought forms of conflict and separation to thought forms of peace and love. It is in that field beyond our differences where we find God. Let us go there and pray together: "Dear God, please heal America."

If the conservative talk-show host can say, "Dear God, I don't have all the answers, I know that," and the liberal talk show host can say, "Dear God, I don't have all the answers, either—but we are joined as brothers and sisters in asking that You restore to our world the spirit of peace," then America and the world will have a miracle.

> **Atonement**
> Whereby we make amends as a nation
> for our grievous errors,
> see where they're still hurting us,
> and seek to make things right.

## Forgiveness and Amends

This is not a time in America to minimize our antagonisms or pretend they don't exist. This is a time for serious people to try, with depth of intelligence and heart, to build new bridges.

The most important reconciliation needed in America today is in the area of race. With a nation, as with an individual, amends are necessary to free the psyche and allow it to move on.

When I have worked with physically challenged people, I have said, "If you can try to forgive whomever you haven't forgiven, it will help you."

I have usually then been asked how forgiving, or not forgiving, affects physcial healing.

The answer is because there is in each of us a reservoir of divine power, and unforgiveness blocks it. Liken this power to a Divine Physician within you. Call it God, Christ, the Holy Spirit, the Jewish *shekina*, the Atman, the Oversoul, nonviolence, universal love, whatever words you wish. It is the all-powerful action of God. But it cannot work against our free will. Every thought we have of judgment or attack is an obstruction to the flow of God's power within us. He doesn't ever withhold His power, but with nonloving thoughts we block it.

Anger is not the source of our healing; love is. As we make amends to those to whom we owe amends and try to forgive those who have hurt us, healing forces are released within our minds. There are times when unexpressed anger is itself a diseased condition. We must express it appropriately, but even then the point is to get to the love that is behind and beyond it.

In order to heal, America must atone for our violations against others, without which no true reconciliation among ourselves, or with other nations, is possible. We cannot move forward until we have made a serious effort to clean up the past.

ATONEMENT is part of spiritual law, built into human consciousness as part of the divine response to error. It is our opportunity, always present, to interrupt the Law of Cause and Effect, which otherwise holds absolute sway. Grace supersedes the law of karma. To atone is to admit our errors and ask God to free us from their consequences. In order to achieve this freedom, we must willingly and consciously unburden ourselves of the weight of our mistakes, asking God for the chance to begin again, to go forward in life from a healed perspective.

America's denial of our own violations of the principles at the core of the American ideal limits our capacity for renaissance. God will grant us new life, but only when we are willing to renounce our errors. He will not take from us what we do not consciously and willingly give back to Him. As long as dark, loveless thinking remains in our minds, it will have negative effects on our lives.

"It is the duty of nations as well as of men," said President Abraham Lincoln in 1863, as he declared a national day of prayer, "...to confess their sins and transgressions, in humble sorrow, yet with assured hope that genuine repentance will lead to mercy and pardon; and to recognize the sublime truth announced in the Holy Scriptures, and proven by all history, that those nations only are blessed whose God is the Lord."

America was blessed from the beginning—not because we were special to God, Who loves all His children equally—but because we were founded on a blessed notion: that here was a nation where men and women and children would find sanctuary from the tyrannies of the world. Our blessings now seem in many ways to have faltered, not because God has abandoned us but because we have abandoned God. We have reneged on our commitment to bless humankind.

We can still turn back. We can always turn back. That is the power of atonement.

There are three main areas where America's need to atone weighs greatly on our collective psyche: our cruel treatment, indeed genocide, toward Native American peoples; our racism toward African Americans throughout our history; and the terrible mistake that was the war in Vietnam.

## Dances with Death

Native Americans had lived on this continent for 1,000 generations before our European ancestors "discovered" it. The wisdom of the indigenous peoples of North America graced this soil for centuries before the white intruders arrived. In 1492, it is estimated that anywhere from 10 to 25 million indigenous people lived north of Mexico. Within 150 years, as a result of war and disease, there were fewer than a million Indians left here alive.

Part of the irony of the devastation of the Native American population by white expansion is that the Western world is now near the brink of global disaster because we lack contact with the very quality of consciousness that so many of the Indian peoples personified. We killed them, and now we need them. How much better off America would be today had our ancestors been wise enough to take advantage, on a mass level, of the extraordinary opportunity presented to them to marry European and Native American cultures. They opted, to use anthropologist Riane Eisler's term, for the dominator rather than partnership model of human development, a characteristic of the historical era now closing, yet hopefully not of the one now being born.

Blood stays on our hands unto endless generations, and only atonement washes them clean. There are things we could do in America to materially express our desire for healing the relationship with Native Americans. First, we should repeal Columbus Day. Christopher Columbus, for all the fiction created around him, was a murderer of indigenous peoples. Given the fact that his life was a model for the standard of enslavement and killing that came to characterize much of European settlement in the New World, to honor him is deeply insulting to our Native American brothers and sisters. Moreover, it stunts the collective psyche of the nation that we are so dishonest about our history.

In 1992, at the time of the quincentennial celebration of his "discovery" of America, there was a national rethinking of Columbus's appropriate place in history. The National Council of Churches, the largest ecumenical body in the United States, called on Christians to refrain from celebrating the quincentennial, saying, "What represented newness of freedom, hope and opportunity for some was the occasion for oppression, degradation and genocide for others." When it comes to celebrating Columbus or Columbus Day, we should *just say no*.

I have watched with interest New York City's efforts to clean up Columbus Circle; it seems like it just can't be done. Although

—

the intersection of Central Park South and Central Park West should be one of Manhattan's most exciting points, that circle has a seedy energy that, like blood on Lady Macbeth's hands, doesn't ever seem to wash away. No matter how many times they sandblast that statue, you never really want to look at it. And no matter how many ways they try to dress up that entrance to Central Park, it continues to be a questionable location. There's only one way to clean up Columbus Circle: take the statue down and rename the place. It's a moral black hole.

I have heard people acknowledge that Columbus himself poses a problem, yet they wouldn't want to give up Columbus Day as a holiday because it celebrates the contribution of Italians to American civilization. If what we are excited about, and indeed we should be, is how many people from other lands have enriched America, then perhaps we could change Columbus Day to Immigrants' Day. I realize how many people would not want *that*, of course—but that is all the more reason why we should propose it.

## Color-Blind, Like Hell

The United States is like a torch that has, at various times, both enlightened the world and burned the world. We should be the generation that commits to making right what still needs to be made right, in order that our children might have a fresh page on which to write their story.

A story very much alive in America is the tortured relationship between blacks and whites. For this, atonement is only the beginning of what is morally demanded of us. "I tremble for my country," wrote Thomas Jefferson regarding slavery, "when I consider God is just, and that His justice shall not sleep forever." By the time of the Civil War, clearly God's justice had been aroused. Yet political justice is just one form of justice; we must strive for psychological, social, and economic justice as well. We have *begun* the path to true justice for the African American, but we have not yet completed it. If we do not do that now, this country will face a terrible consequence. It is unreasonable to think otherwise.

While the Civil War could end an evil institution, it could not end evil thinking. And there, in our thinking, is where the cancer remains. In abolishing slavery, we did not abolish racism. Indeed, such societies as the Ku Klux Klan were founded after the end of the Civil War, in direct response to the abolition of slavery. While external, legislative remedies are an aid to racial healing, spiritual forces are necessary to heal the terrible wounds to the heart and soul. Cellular memory of hatred and abuse has accumulated among black Americans to such an extent that it has become a generational resentment leaving only two choices on the road ahead: the relationship between our races will turn to violence unless it turns to love.

White America must acknowledge its culpability in institutionalizing racism, including a formalized amends to the African-American people, and black America must have deep and serious permission to voice its frustrations in a dignified way, one that honors the depth of injury and insult to African-American people throughout our history. America must make a serious effort to atone for a racist past and present.

Many white people have expressed dismay that now, when in some ways we have indeed made real strides in the civil rights arena, more blacks who have fared well seem to be expressing increased anger. But psychologically this makes sense: once your stomach is full, you have more time to stop and think. "Black rage" is an accumulated response to generation after generation of insult. It's not just what people have experienced, but what their parents and parents' parents experienced that often moves through their veins and erupts like hot oil. At the end of the millennium, an unconscious message is breaking through from all marginalized people. "Enough is enough." That message isn't going to be getting any quieter.

I do not believe the average American is racist, but I believe the average American does not truly realize how racist our public policies are. If the residents of America's inner cities were primarily white, I cannot imagine that the notion of a Marshall Plan to redeem their economies would be considered such a long shot. Although the Emancipation of the slaves gave African Americans their political freedom, their bondage was replaced by a more subtle but equally oppressive form of slavery: an economic slavery that continues to this day. Dr. King saw economic injustice as the inseparable twin of racial injustice, and it still is.

One in three black Americans lives in poverty, three times the rate of whites. Half of all black children in America live in poverty. Unemployment for African Americans is twice as high as it is for whites, and has been for the last thirty years. For the same educational background, blacks can expect to make 82 to 86 percent of the income of whites.

Economic injustice toward blacks in America is a systemically racist phenomenon, and to minimize it is further racism. When blacks understandably object to their own oppression, they're liable to be told in one way or another: "There you go—complaining again!"

We must listen deeply to what black America feels now, even if it is uncomfortable to do so. People who haven't been listened to for over two hundred years have a lot to process.

PRESIDENT Clinton has proposed a major race initiative in which he plans to hold town-hall meetings around the country, and have a high-powered advisory panel write a report summarizing his findings. "It is really potentially a great thing for America that we are becoming so multiethnic at the time the world is becoming so closely tied together," he has said. "But it's also potentially a powder keg of problems and heartbreak and division and loss."

A large staff will work with the President, soliciting and gathering research on race relations over the last fifty years, and making projections on how they will change over the next fifty. When it comes to race, President Clinton's heart is clearly in the right place. When it comes to what he has actually done politically—signing the Welfare Bill, making the 1997 budget deal, and failing to act on his promises for serious investment in job training and education for America's poor—his heart and his head have clearly gone in different directions. The President has not yet put serious political capital behind grappling with fundamental issues—particularly economic issues—that cause and maintain division among races in America. It is unclear whether his current plans will be strong enough to overcome what is now institutionalized government inertia on this issue. In order to truly change things, his initiative must make the kind of raw, authentic statement that carries with it genuine moral authority. It will not have that authority, if it is merely words.

On May 16, 1997, President Clinton offered a public apology on behalf of the nation to the victims of the federal government's Tuskegee Study of Untreated Syphilis in the Negro Male, an infamous chapter in the history of American medical research. In that study, starting in 1932, 399 indigent black men from Tuskegee, Alabama, were told that they would receive free medical treatment for syphilis, but instead were left untreated and carefully monitored. Even after penicillin was found to be a successful cure in the mid-1940s, the men were left untreated.

"To our African-American citizens, I am sorry that your Federal Government orchestrated a study so clearly racist," said the President. The Government, said President Clinton, "did something that was wrong—deeply, profoundly, morally wrong. It was an outrage to our commitment to integrity and equality for all our citizens."

It is very heartening to hear the President make that statement, but it is also very important that we not use our apologies for specific instances of racism, to help us ignore the all-pervasiveness of racism in our society. It is not enough to treat the symptoms of racism; we must treat the disease itself. Tuskegee was part of a larger pattern of abuse that stemmed from a general feeling that the lives of black people do not deserve the same respect and consideration as the lives of white people. President Clinton's action was a good beginning, nothing more and nothing less. I hope it will help us open our eyes to the plight of millions of black children today, whose diseases of poverty, ignorance, and substandard medical care are going every bit as dangerously untreated as was syphilis in Tuskegee sixty-five years ago. The bigger problem is far from behind us.

We need rituals of atonement and apology for American racism, past *and* present. I have led atonement prayers throughout the country, with whites collectively apologizing to blacks; the experience for both groups can be extremely powerful.

## Racial Atonement

The nation now debates whether or not Congress should officially apologize for slavery. For those Americans who think that blacks need to just forgive slavery and move on with their lives, I would like to point out that it is much easier to forgive someone when they have had the courtesy to apologize.

A sincere apology is not just "emotional symbolism," to quote Newt Gingrich's comments on the idea of a Congressional apology. An apology is an act of atonement. Only in a society that trivializes faith is atonement viewed as mere symbol.

Faith, for those of us who embrace it, is as *real* as a car, a house, or a piece of legislation. The power of God in our lives is no less *real* than technology, business, or sports. The fact that the action of faith is invisible to the physical eye does not make it a mere function of our imaginations or a metaphor or psychological child's play. A mass act of faith, performed sincerely in the hearts of white Americans, would carry tremendous power because it would affect our collective consciousness.

The trivialization of faith by the political status quo—from the left, with its rolled eyes, to the right, with its hypocritical words of support—has created a huge void in the center of American political consciousness. Faith in God is not faith in a particular religious dogma. Faith in God is faith in love, faith in a higher power, and ultimately faith in each other. Atonement means the turning back of darkness through a prayerful embrace of the light.

The reason a national apology for slavery is a good idea is that it would help awaken our national conscience. Maybe, just maybe, if our national heart was touched for a moment by our collective shame over that one enormous violation of God's law, then we could move more easily to a mass awareness of what matters now: the racial and economic injustice that still permeates American public policy today.

The apology is the yin we need; serious restitution is the yang. When African Americans say the word "reparations," you'd think they had suggested something completely outrageous. But the concept is legitimate. Germany paid somewhere around $50 billion in restitution to Jews after World War II. The United States paid $20,000 to every Japanese American who had been sent to concentration camps here in America during World War II. Nothing short of a massive investment in America's poor black population—the true legacy of slavery—is a responsible sign of America's willingness to heal itself racially. The most depressed communities in America, which are primarily African-American, cry out for help and we act like it's some major liberal coup every time we even throw them a crumb.

Human beings, on the level of spirit, are not separate but joined as one. In the words of Dr. King, "We are all caught in an inescapable network of mutuality. . . ." The reason the Golden Rule is essential to all religous thought is that what we do to others *will* be done to us, and if not to us then to our children or our children's children. We *will* reap what we sow, and what we withhold from others *will* be withheld from us. Time itself is a trick of the mind. This realization is at the core of new-paradigm thinking, and it is critical that it become part of our political calculations. We must give justly, not merely because we're "good," but because we understand cosmic law. It is no longer possible to be realistically satisfied with our own circumstances if the opportunities for the same abundance are unfairly denied to others. The day of reckoning—a kind of instant karma—is at hand.

The black poor in America can be likened to a patient bleeding to death in an emergency room. One side of the political spectrum says, "Let's do nothing for him. It's a free country and he could walk out of the emergency room if he wanted to. He's probably faking this illness, anyway." Another side says, "Let's give him a manicure while he's lying here. Perhaps it will make him feel better. If he's still weak after that, let's be modern about this and give him some vitamin C."

Add to that the fact that he is bleeding to death because of a congenital disease he inherited from his father, who got it from his father, who got it from his father, whose father got the disease through injection from *us*.

This is not about money, but atonement. Money will not solve America's problems; only spiritual power will do that. But spiritual power is not released in the absence of serious intent and sincerity. It is neither serious, nor sincere, to apologize but not to back up the apology with action where action is appropriate.

There are those who would point to blacks who have behaved criminally or dysfunctionally, and try to use that as a justification for not performing our ethical duty toward the African-American community. Or, conversely, one can point to black stars who have triumphed, and try to claim that because they made it big in America, that proves there's no real problem. But neither argument is valid. Every group of people has its shadow element, and every group of people has its geniuses. Neither is an excuse for failing to do what needs to be done. America has a *huge*—not a nonexistent, not a small, nor even a medium-sized —problem on its hands. We must see it for what it is and act accordingly. It is the only way to clean up what needs to be cleaned up and to heal what needs to be healed.

If America will take this time to seriously right itself on this issue, God will royally compensate us for our righteousness. White America will not lose money or power if it pays off its moral debts: the whole country will become richer and more powerful beyond our wildest imaginations. We will take a quantum leap forward as a nation if we embrace the opportunity before us and genuinely atone.

"The holiest of all the spots on earth," according to *A Course in Miracles,* "is where an ancient hatred has become a present love." Let us imagine the glory that could be, and pray to bring it forth.

A PRAYER OF ATONEMENT

Dear God,
Please forgive us our grievous errors.
We atone and ask forgiveness for
our early treatment of the indigenous people,
the natives of the North American continent
who suffered devastation at the hands of our forefathers.
We atone and ask forgiveness for
the racist streak in American history,
the slavery in both body and spirit
of African-American men, women, and children,
who have lived among us and suffered among us
the sting of our unfair dominion.
We atone and ask forgiveness for
the mistaken places in us,
wherein we have sought to suppress and harm
the children of the Lord.
We atone and ask forgiveness for
the places where we do this still,
where we hate, dear Lord,
and do harm, dear Lord,
and lay unfair judgment on our brothers and sisters.
Help us, Lord,
so mend our thoughts that we no longer
rebel against Your Spirit, which is Love.
Forgive us now.
Turn our darkness into light, dear God,
through Your power which does these things,
that we might awaken to a new America.
May hatred be replaced by love here,
and true justice prevail.
May we meet each other in reborn brotherhood
now and forever.
Take from us the burdens of our history,
our transgressions toward others.

To people of color whom we have offended,
please forgive us.
We acknowledge the evils of past behavior
and the suffering which it caused.
We ask that God in His glory
compensate for the evil done unto your people.
We apologize for the past,
and ask that you open your hearts to us now.
We bless your children, and acknowledge their brilliance.
Please bless ours.
Wash us clean, dear God,
and heal us.
Amen

## And He Was Good Enough to Mention It on His Book Tour

One of the reasons we need to atone for our treatment of both Native Americans and black Americans is that it will help us break the chain with that part of our national character that still wants to grab for what it wants in the world, without regard to the life or livelihood of others.

Robert McNamara, who was President Johnson's Secretary of Defense during the Vietnam War, has written in his memoirs that the war was "a terrible mistake." After hearing that, if we were an enlightened society, we would all have gone to bed for three days. We would cry, moan, get sick, scream it out, punch punching bags, do whatever it takes to get the pain up and out of our cells. There is an inestimable human tragedy stuck to this nation as a result of that war, a significant aspect of which is the ever-more-frayed bond of trust between the American people and their government.

The Vietnam War Memorial is a uniquely powerful place because it is emotionally true. It doesn't lie. It pictures the war as a huge black gash across our landscape, which it is. It appropriately memorializes the lives of those who died such purposeless, tragic deaths in Vietnam. And it helps us grieve not only for them but also for who we were as a nation before that war so wounded us.

At a traveling exhibit of the Vietnam Wall, I saw the following letter posted by an ex-Marine:

> On the Second of July, 1967, Alpha and Bravo companies of the First Battalion, Ninth Marines were on patrol just a few hundred meters south of the DMZ.
>
> Bravo blundered into a well set ambush at the marketplace; soon, Alpha, too, was in the thick of it.
>
> The enemy consisted of a regiment of the North Vietnamese Army supported by artillery, heavy mortars, rockets, anti-aircraft guns, and surface-to-air missiles.
>
> Charlie and Delta companies were rushed to the field in support, but the outcome had been decided. The Marines were overwhelmingly outnumbered.
>
> But, worse than that, they were equipped with Colt M-16 rifles. Their M-14 rifles, which had proven so effective and reliable, were stored in warehouses, somewhere in the rear.
>
> The M-16s would fire once or twice—maybe more—then jam. The extractor would rip the rim off the casing. Then the only way to clear the chamber and resume firing was to lock open the bolt, run a cleaning rod down the barrel, and knock the casing loose. Soon it would jam again.
>
> This was the rifle supplied to her troops by the richest nation on earth.
>
> The enemy was not so encumbered. They carried rifles which were designed in the Soviet Union and manufactured in one of the poorest nations on earth—the so-called People's Republic of China. *Their* rifles fired. Fired every time. They ran amongst the Marines, firing at will.
>
> Sixty-four men in Bravo were killed that afternoon. Altogether, the Battalion lost around a hundred of the Nation's finest

men. The next morning, we bagged them like groceries. We consigned their bodies to their families and commended their souls to God. May He be as merciful as they were courageous.

Today, people are still debating the issue: Was it the fault of the ammo? The fault of the rifle? Neither. It was the fault of the politicians and contractors and generals. People in high places knew the rifles and ammo wouldn't work together. The military didn't want to buy the rifle when Armalite was manufacturing it. But when Colt was licensed as the manufacturer, they suddenly discovered it was a marvelous example of Yankee ingenuity.

Sgt. Brown told them it was garbage. Col. Hackworth told them it was garbage. And every real Grunt knew it was garbage. It was unsuited for combat.

There was no congressional investigation. No contractor was ever fined for supplying defective material. No one uncovered the bribes paid to government officials. No one went to jail. And the mothers of dead Marines were never told that their sons went into combat unarmed.

To all outward appearances, those Marines died of gunshot and fragmentation wounds. But a closer examination reveals that they were first stabbed in the back by their countrymen.

The politicians, contractors, and generals have retired to comfortable estates now. Their ranks have been filled by their clones —greedy invertebrates every one. They should hope that God is more forgiving than I.

Brave men should never be commanded by cowards.

First Lieutenant Harvey G. Wysong
0100308
United States Marine Corps Reserve
First Battalion, Ninth Marines

It was not just Johnson and McNamara who made a terrible mistake in Vietnam; the entire nation made a terrible mistake in letting them do it. One would think that, after such a debacle,

America would no longer allow those in power, in uniform, in "command," to so easily make absurd decisions on our behalf. And yet we do. What a tragedy, all that false respect we had—and still have—for the trappings and illusions of worldly power over our original ideals. We still have not opened ourselves collectively to the shame and horror of that huge mistake. We have not atoned, to our vets, to their families, to God, to other nations involved, or to ourselves. Until we do, we shall remain in some way under the effect of that mistake. Even worse, we will continue to repeat it.

America is still weighted down by the mass of our unprocessed guilt and the sickness of our secrets. Ever since the sixties, America has been besieged by lurking shadows. You cannot dedicate a nation to the high ideals to which this one was dedicated and not expect the soul to rebel in some way when you start acting like you didn't really mean it.

From the genocide of Native Americans to our systemic racism to the Vietnam War, the United States needs, as they say in the twelve-step recovery program, to take a "fearless moral inventory." We are not to spend the rest of our lives in an endless string of *mea culpas,* but as soon as we say at least a few sincere ones, the miracle of atonement will begin to release our collective soul.

## America's Finest

While it stands to reason that the tragedy in Vietnam would serve to bust our illusions regarding the military, almost the opposite seems to have occurred. In the last few decades, America has if anything turned militarization into glamor. Rarely does a politician speak anymore that he or she does not at some point mention "our fine young men and women in uniform."

Meanwhile, almost every other day we read about one of our

"fine young men" who sexually harassed or even raped someone, commited a hate crime, or even murdered a U.S. citizen. What's with all this false respect? Timothy McVeigh, remember, was one of those "fine young men" who fought in the Gulf War. Let's at the very least admit that military and police personnel are as fallible as anyone else.

In Redford, Texas, in the spring of 1997, four Marines patrolling an area known to be heavily infested with drug dealers shot and killed an eighteen-year-old high-school student named Esequiel Hernandez, Jr. The young man had the nerve to be herding his family's goats at the time, as he did every day after school. Esequiel was known in his town for his politeness and respect, and according to one of his neighbors, "the only way [the soldiers] could have botched this up more was if they shot Mother Teresa." While the Marines have claimed they shot in self-defense, their stories bear profound inconsistencies and are currently under official investigation.

The U.S. Constitution enshrines the principle of civilian supremacy over the military. One reason for this principle is that during the years leading up to the American Revolution British authorities tried to use British troops to maintain order in Boston—with often tragic results, such as the Boston Massacre. Our Founders remembered that history, and wanted to prevent its ever happening again.

A critical issue here is this: soldiers are trained to fight wars, not to do police work. They are understandably focused on the idea of an enemy. That is why their presence in domestic situations is so potentially dangerous, and the death of young Esequiel Hernandez is only the latest example of that danger.

While the Constitution seeks to protect American citizens from the imposition of military personnel in our midst, we have in the last few decades exercised very dull vigilance on this subject. In the 1980s, the Reagan administration secured the right of the government to use military personnel in domestic law-enforcement operations, and there are those in Congress today who support such use enthusiastically. Let's think this one through: Marines roaming through our border towns looking for drug dealers...then, once we're desensitized enough, Marines roaming through our city streets, looking for suspected "violent criminals"...and then, once it's way too late, Marines roaming through a shopping mall looking for you.

## Getting It Right

After I had spoken at a seminar in Seattle about the power of atonement in society, a gentleman came up to me. As I shook his hand I heard him say, "Ms. Williamson, my name is Egil Krogh. I used to work for President Nixon."

I stopped in my tracks, for I remembered that name well. Egil "Bud" Krogh was head of Nixon's "special investigations unit" that became known as the "White House Plumbers." Assigned the responsibility of finding out why the Pentagon Papers had been released to the *New York Times,* the Plumbers had broken into the Beverly Hills office of Daniel Ellsberg's psychiatrist, Dr. Lewis Fielding. I was very interested to hear Krogh's personal story, and marveled at his transformation from the head of an illegal intelligence operation to spiritual seeker.

When the seminar continued the next day, Bud rose and spoke to the entire room. He said who he was, described what he had done, and spoke of the time he had spent in prison for his deeds. "I spent time in prison, so I paid my debt to society," he said. "But I need to apologize to all Americans whose trust and confidence in the President and government were violated by the actions I approved. Please accept my apology now." He proceeded to say that the violation of Dr. Fielding's civil rights had cast a spectre over the entire nation—a spectre in some ways still with us—that he very deeply regrets.

There was a stunned silence in the room. During an intermission in the program, people gathered around Bud to speak to him and thank him. One woman said, with tears in her eyes, "I didn't know how much rage I still had within me regarding those events, and hearing you today has helped me process some of those feelings."

I hope Bud Krogh felt freed by his apology that day; he had freed many others, and such actions go deep into the psyche of a nation. There is a level on which we are all connected and we all know everything. On that level, we are waiting for release.

### The Arousal

Whereby spirituality comes out of the closet,
we begin to realize the power of intention,
we start to question the materialistic basis of money and
    business,
we take a good look around us,
we question patriarchy
we see the Mother,
we remember the witches,
we get hip to the press,
and we reembrace the magic.

## Private and Public Spirituality

American society has developed in such a way as to keep spiritual seeking in the private domain. There is a level at which this bias is appropriate, and a level at which it is not.

While the separation of church and state is an important and enlightened concept, it has been at times strangely interpreted.

It is damaging to America—not liberating—that soulful, spiritual dialogue has been relegated to the margins of our cultural conversation.

For centuries, the Church held indomitable sway over the thinking of the Western world, often abusing its influence in such a way as to suppress legitimate rational investigation of the universe in which we live. In the modern era, a fashionable cynicism that opposes any kind of faith has become the new intellectual tyranny in American society. Often even the most legitimate religious and mystical paths are invalidated in a way no less oppressive than how science was suppressed in earlier days.

The status quo seeks to trivialize and diminish the efforts of almost anyone seeking to bring spiritual principles and depth psychology into the cultural mainstream. The press has led the charge. But I sense that we are on the verge of a sea change, for a critical mass has gathered around the new frontiers of knowledge. As German philosopher Arthur Schopenhauer said, "Whenever a new truth enters the world, the first stage of reaction to it is ridicule, the second stage is violent opposition, and in the third stage, that truth comes to be regarded as self-evident."

The creative challenge of spiritual life is to know enough about the world to be informed and enough about God to be hopeful. From Jesus to Buddha to Moses to Mohammed, way-showers have risen out of the timeline of history to draw maps and pave roads to a more perfect world. From Jefferson to Lincoln to Gandhi to King, world leaders have injected into history the political principles of higher awareness. If we ourselves follow as best we can—applying eternal truths to our own historical circumstances and bringing forth even a fraction of their power—then we will be a generation that does much to repair the world.

## New Economic Engines

There are economists who believe that as technology continues to replace human labor, unemployment around the world will rise to the point where the majority of people will not have jobs. They will not be needed to produce goods and services. According to a Swiss study, within about twenty years, as little as 2 percent of the world's current labor force will be needed to produce all the goods necessary for total demand.

So where will people get jobs? What will be the nature of work? And how can America lead the way? If we trust in the economic theories that have dominated the era now closing, many experts agree there will be widespread global destitution within the next fifty years. New-paradigm economic theory places doing good before doing well—indeed, sees doing good as the *key* to doing well—and views the realm of consciousness, rather than the material world, as the source of job creation.

The highest level of job creation is the ability to dig deep into ourselves, not narcissistically but authentically, to discern how we might best serve a larger world through our talents and abilities. The desire to serve is the most inspired motivator, and where we are most inspired, we have the greatest potential for creating material abundance. Education and inspiration—not material substance of any kind—are the real engines of economic power.

OUR new business model, then, should not be how to make money, but rather how to further the human good. Free-market capitalism cannot legitimately claim that, where more money is produced for a corporate entity, life is by definition made better for everyone. If the cost of doing business is ecological distress that threatens the health of people and the planet, if American workers continue to lose social and economic ground in the unraveling of the social contract between management and labor, if executive compensation packages continue to eat the lion's share of this country's profits, if money continues to rule Washington and turn the American government into little more than a slave to the market, then we will lose all that is most precious to us. This is the central sickness in America today: our almost tragic deference to the needs of the free-market capitalist economy. At the rate we are going, our system will be torn apart by internal contradictions, just as communism was. That which does not honor life will find itself no longer honored *by* life.

One of the things I find most odd about what one might call a "money-grubbing" mentality is that it doesn't create an environment where people work hard. As America's greed factor has increased, our work ethic has decreased. Work is good not primarily because it creates money but because it contributes to the higher unfoldment of humanity.

## Blood Money

Money is, at heart, the great moral issue of our time. America must have a very serious discussion with itself about the wisdom of allowing the market to drive us. From the Left and from the Right, voices are beginning to rise up to protest the market's unbridled power.

We can no longer afford to look the other way, as American economic interests systematically compromise our societal values. From American companies doing business with totalitarian regimes, to our government putting the sale of Boeing jets before support of pro-democracy forces in Communist China, to record companies selling rock 'n' roll lyrics about devil worship to our children (protesting, of course, that what they're *really* concerned about is the First Amendment!), we must reconsider the phrase "blood money."

American companies doing business abroad are beginning to feel pressure from a public increasingly aroused by stories of government brutality toward citizens of those countries. ARCO Oil and Gas Co., which does business in Myanmar—formerly known as Burma—is an example. ARCO refuses to abandon its investments in Myanmar, even though brutal rape, forced labor, and summary executions are clearly carried out by the military government on a regular basis. ARCO and other such companies seek to hide behind a clever public relations ruse: they claim that the presence of American companies in these countries is actually a service to the people living there, as contact with good American ethics will help influence the governments to become more open and free. But what good ethics? Good ethics would demand that we not be there to begin with, that we not put the financial demand for more stockholder share value over the demands of conscience. Such governments as that of Myanmar separate economic freedom from political freedom; therefore, the "our being there will actually do more good than not" excuse is bogus. The presence of American business does nothing more than prop up those brutal governments.

Thankfully, the President has placed sanctions on new investments by American businesses in Myanmar. The Myanmar government responded by arresting pro-democracy leaders. This is hardball; it is more necessary than ever that ARCO make a stand for freedom over money. The Chairman of the Board and Chief Executive Officer of ARCO is Mr. Mike Bowlin. His office is located at 515 South Flower Street in Los Angeles, California 90071, and I am sure he would love to hear from you.

• • •

—

WHILE many Americans in government and business circles argue that doing business with totalitarian regimes is the best way to promote democracy, this argument bears a closer look. There is in the world today a new marriage between the forces of economic freedom and political repression. There are places where the value of economic freedom has been clearly recognized while political freedom is still undervalued. This is very different than in the old Communist order, where political repression and economic repression went hand in hand.

Our doing business in such places doesn't pose an opportunity for the businesspeople there to see the light regarding political freedom, any more than it offers an opportunity for American businesspeople to see the light regarding political repression.

Let us admit to this one basic realization: political freedom is not easy. It is not orderly. It takes effort and is often inconvenient, particularly if your primary goal is to make money. The primary value of democracy is not just that it helps us get rich; in fact, our neighbors who have forged the economic freedom–political repression connection present a logically valid argument that economic growth is actually slowed down by certain democratic freedoms.

Therefore, if fast economic growth is what we value most as a society, then our pact with the devil is already signed. Once people have bought into the idea that economic growth is the highest good—and that is how America acts now, though of course it is not the way we talk—then the slow but steady march toward totalitarianism is established. Its cornerstone has been bought into. Such a prospect does not loom in America; the cornerstone of that house has already been laid.

The U.S. Trade Representative is now a Cabinet-level position, but we have no Secretary of Citizenship.

Why don't we just cut to the chase and go the route they've decided to take in Hong Kong? Let the business tycoons be the bosses; let's stop pretending and just let the power elite have the power. We could appoint our most successful moguls to a committee and just ask *them* to run the country! It would be faster, more efficient, and—just like Mussolini—*they* could make the trains run on time.

## None of Us Know, All of Us Know

A healthy skepticism regarding the government's official posture on an issue is essential to our freedom.

In the late sixties, millions of Americans who protested against the Vietnam war wouldn't have dreamed of believing something just because the Pentagon said it. Now, however, we live at a time when TWA Flight 800 en route from New York's JFK airport to Paris explodes inexplicably in the air, and all rumors of "accidental release" or friendly fire from the U.S. military trying out a new defense system in the area are struck down fairly easily. According to "serious" journalists, we're not supposed to believe such preposterous stories as the "friendly fire" theory because (1) the Internet cannot be trusted for reliable information (like *they* can) and (2) the military already *told* us they had no planes in the area at the time (like, right, they would *tell* us).

So we're supposed to scoff at anyone silly enough to buy into the notion that TWA 800 came down because of friendly fire, yet on February 6, 1997, a chartered jet landing at JFK in New York City had to take sudden evasive action so as not to collide with two New Jersey Air National Guard F-16s that had erroneously been cleared by the Navy to fly in that airspace.

Referring to the four-hundred-foot distance registered between itself and the F-16 by the civilian craft radar, the Air National Commander claimed, "I won't rule out it was close enough to set off the collision-avoidance system. I would rule out that it was any threat at all." When the television program *Sixty Minutes* got hold of a swatch of material from a seat in Flight 800's cabin, purportedly covered with missile fuel, the swatch was confiscated by the National Transportation Safety Boad (NTSB).

And Americans should be waking up any minute now. We have been trained over the last thirty years to believe our military and intelligence agencies slavishly and unquestioningly, though that is decidedly *not* how our Founders thought things should work. That is why we have the right to bear arms and why we have, in the President, a civilian commander-in-chief. In fact, it was President Eisenhower who, upon his departure from the Presidency, warned America of the "military-industrial complex." Noting the already growing pressure to thoughtlessly expand military budgets for no other reason than to create and maintain an economically gargantuan defense industry, Eisenhower, who himself had been Commander of all Allied Forces in World War II, said, "I know how these guys think."

On the other hand, the NTSB says the real issue with Flight 800 had to do with a problem in the center fuel tank of the 747. This theory is reasonable, as well. The NTSB claims the Flight 800 disaster was an accident that could have been prevented had the Federal Aviation Administration followed the board's recommendation regarding the installation of a corrective feature to the tank mechanism. That recommendation has not been followed, according to FAA officials, because the cost analysis doesn't measure up. They put a price of somewhere around $2.8 million on the head of every human being and, since making the correction would cost more than the figure tallied up if you calculated how many people would be flying in 747s, the airline industry decided not to make the correction.

People don't even pretend anymore. You'd think FAA officials would say something like, "Of course, no human life could ever be measured in terms of dollars and cents, but ..." But the dominant ethos in America today allows people to just say what they're *really* thinking: an FAA official put it this way: "Every human life has its price."

So we have two choices: either Flight 800 came down because a Navy missile accidentally hit it and there is a huge government cover-up, or Flight 800 came down because money is put before our safety: the recommendations of a federal safety board aren't followed because the Federal Aviation Administration is more of a protector of the airline industry than of our lives.

Either way, are you happy?

A country is like a huge family system. One of the most potent psychological factors in that system is "family secrets." Mommy and Daddy say everything is fine, but little Johnny is cutting his wrists and little Gloria hasn't eaten in months. What are Mommy and Daddy not facing?

Privacy and discretion among individuals are positive things, but undue official secrecy is negative. Truth heals; secrets destroy. With the establishment of the Truth and Reconciliation Commission in South Africa, those who perpetrated crimes under the rule of apartheid are now given amnesty in exchange for admitting the truth; it is officially acknowledged that getting the facts out is necessary to that country's healing process. This is not some New Age slobber. In fact, if anything, the tendency of so many Americans to self-indulgently reveal *too much* of their personal stories today—and of the press to dig so rudely and inappropriately into people's personal affairs—is an unconscious effort to get to a level of truth that we all feel is missing. We itch in one place and scratch in another.

The rules of psychology and group dynamics apply to our entire nation, and increasingly they affect our political behavior.

If a missile brought down Flight 800, does that mean the U.S.

military purposely did such a thing? Absolutely not. Does it mean an accident occurred? Yes, probably. But *why?* Does the military play war games with civilian aircraft? Would that not explain the cover-up, if indeed there is one?

I have no idea what brought down that plane, any more than anyone else does. But I know this: People have gut feelings, and the American gut is still very tense about that crash, as it is still tense about the Kennedy and King assassinations—indeed, about almost everything related to "official" explanations over the last thirty years. That tension is at the root of our group malaise. We are cynical, but we did not start out that way. We began with what is basically a healthy skepticism on the part of free and sovereign people, but the system that was devised to be a two-way street between citizen questions and government answers became monopolized by official PR blasts. The average citizen doesn't know where to direct questions anymore, much less outrage.

So we pretend we don't care, or that someone else is going to fix things. Which fits perfectly into their plans, whoever "they" are.

Every once in a while we get our hopes up again, but what we long for is one of the hardest things for most of today's politicians to give us: an honest conversation. Just put the facts on the table, guys. Democracy cannot survive in an environment where the electorate is treated like children who are not quite mature enough to be told the truth. Especially when the ones *withholding* the truth are the ones going around acting like children.

George Stephanopoulos, writing in the *Los Angeles Times Book Review* in June 1997, said the following:

> One of the first rules you learn in American politics is never blame the voter for anything at any time. The voters are right even when their demands are contradictory or just plain wrong.

During my time at the White House, we plundered the thesaurus each year to find synonyms for the word "strong"—the only politically appropriate way for a President to describe the State of our Union.

Gee. That's really wonderful. If their first rule is never to tell us what's wrong with *us*, then they're sure as hell not going to tell us what's wrong with *them*.

THE best education there is regarding what Americans are really thinking may be found on airplanes. You sit talking to someone you wouldn't necessarily be talking to under any other circumstances, in a situation that makes most people more honest than usual because our mortality at those times is so obvious. If conversations take hold, you can really get the scoop.

One gentleman I met on a plane during the early summer of 1997 told me he was the chief financial officer of a large public company. Early in our conversation, I asked him, "So, what do you think of the economy?"

"Oh, well," he smiled. "It's good."

Then after a couple of minutes of silence, he said, "Well, actually, I think there's a false sense of security."

I laughed, "Boy, that's America today. Ask someone what they think and they give you the official line. Then within five minutes they tell you what they *really* feel."

"You've heard that before?" he said.

"Oh, yeah," I told him. "We all have instinctive information about everything. America's head and America's gut are very divergent these days. Especially about the economy."

"That's so true!" he exclaimed. "A friend of mine personally manages twenty-four to twenty-five million dollars of other people's money. He invests it for them. But for himself, he won't touch the market. 'I only put my money in conservative things like CD's,' he says."

"Um-hmm."

We started comparing oyster crackers to heated nuts.

"I'm on my way to New York for a big meeting," he continued. "My company is being sold. One prospective buyer would keep the management team that's there now. The other would fire all of them. They have no heart, that's for sure."

"Can you voice any opinion about that?" I asked.

"Of course not," he said. "Have you ever been to a business meeting at that level? All those guys care about is the bottom line. And I have to answer to our shareholders. I have to sell to whomever gives us the best price."

"Well, all I know," I said, "is that something's got to change. It's nothing we can legislate, but we're going to have to introduce more compassion into business, or the whole system is going to go down out of sheer moral corruption on the inside."

He gave me a knowing look. I've seen it hundreds of times. I've seen it on conservatives, I've seen it on liberals, I've seen it on libertarians, and I've seen it on the most apolitical people. It's America's most common expression of political opinion now: *the knowing look*. Everybody knows what's really happening in this country. Most people just don't say it.

Or at least, not at first. . . .

## The Myth of the Powerful White Male

White men constitute 33 percent of the U.S. population, but 80 percent of the members of the House of Representatives and 90 percent of the U.S. Senate. At 33 percent of the population, why aren't *they* considered a "special interest group"? They are just a *piece* of the fabric that makes up this country, no better or worse than the rest of us. They don't always *think* the way women do or blacks do, or any of the other groups *who live with them in this country, which supposedly belongs to all of us.* It is not just that all of our needs need to be represented in a democracy; how we all *think* needs to be represented in a democracy. The way it is now, one group gets away with calling any other kind of thinking less serious than its own.

The military is a perfect example of why white men shouldn't run everything. The military is a phallic fantasy. It's an archetypal role for men to see a phallic image and say, "Wow, this thing is wonderful," and an archetypal role for women to say, "Maybe yes, maybe no—It depends on what you *do* with it." American women shouldn't spend time fighting for the right to fight in the military, so much as fighting for a say in what we *do* with the military. And what we *do* with our Congressional budget. And what we *do* with our children's lives. The same denial-based mentality that looks the other way rather than deeply question the presence of military aircraft in civilian airspace also looks the other way rather than question our national priorities.

Certain people in the government use the need to balance the budget as justification for slashing social programs: "We're doing this for our children's future." But when they discuss bankruptcy, perhaps we should lift our voices and say, *"We are already spiritually and morally bankrupt* if we continue to spend approximately $33.7 million an hour on national defense, while only $2.1 million an hour on education and $1.8 million an hour on children's health care."

We should put feeding our hungry children before feeding our fat defense establishment, and we should keep an eye on them, and discipline them, at just about the same rate.

Women, and men as well, must find a way to break the chain of co-dependent acquiescence to patriarchal ideas, when they are dangerous for our children and the future of the world. I realize that some men are more feminist than some women, and that some women are more patriarchal in their thinking than some men. I do not think women are necessarily less violent than men. But I do think women are generally more relationship-based than men are, and obviously tend to live closer to the children. We can see with our eyes, and avoid less easily, the sight of children's bodies and souls as they fall apart from lack of care.

As women, we need to do more than just enter the halls of financial or governmental power. We must do something much more difficult than that: we must change things once we get there. How co-opted we have been in the last thirty years, breaking through glass ceilings, only to go to lunch and then out shopping. Feminism is a failure if ultimately all it means is that women have the same right to worldly power as men have. The higher significance of power is not the struggle to attain it but, rather, what we do with it. The feminist perspective in society should stand to remind us that the *point* of power is to make the world a better place. And that means something much, much more than just making some people richer.

The Western world is having an identity crisis, striving to balance itself after centuries of patriarchal leanings. Many men are joining women in leading the way to a more balanced consciousness and a fairer society. They are finding, among other things, their silence; women must find, among other things, our voices. The children need us.

EVERY once in a while, I see an article about unpaid "women's work": if babysitting, cooking, driving the kids here and there, and so on were counted for their financial equivalency, how much of the nation's productivity would come from women? Viewed this way, our earnings would add up to more than men's.

—

But even this doesn't begin to tell the story. During that drive to the roller-skating rink, the two five-year-olds in the back seat ask questions that demand an extraordinary amount of sophisticated understanding and emotional mettle in order to answer well. Some of those hours shouldn't be considered worth $6.50 an hour for a babysitter, but more like $100 an hour for a child psychologist. Guiding one young person through adolescence in America today is not just equivalent to a $10- or $15-an-hour job. It is a job that demands a wisdom and fortitude that make being a lawyer look like small potatoes.

Notice how economics works: it is based not on some inherent value in a product, but rather on the value we place *on* the product. The ultimate economic issue, then, is not value but *values*. We place far too little value on things having to do with childhood and the care of children. As a consequence, we underinvest enormously in our children, costing us tremendously on the other end, in everything from health care to drugs to crime.

Raising a child is not just the most important job in society; it takes much greater skill than most. American culture patronizes its parents, teachers, and other child-care professionals—throwing on the verbal support ad nauseam, but withholding financial and material support such as child care, health insurance, tax breaks, and educational funds. In addition to that, the government tends to cave in rather than stand up to the television industry on the subject of TV violence, making a parent's job even harder.

Americans have been treated by both political parties to endless varieties of the "$500-a-year tax break for the American family" theme in the last few years. What Americans should wake up to is the insult of the entire picture: it's like saying, "I love you so much, and I support you 100 percent—to demonstrate this, here's a peanut."

Make no mistake: the affluent can avoid America's major problems, and increasingly, we do. Our children can go to private schools, therefore we don't have to face the woes and undue strain on the public educational system every day; we can and do hire private police and security forces to protect us from the violence in our society; and our elected officials have effectively removed the most harrowing signs of mass despair from our line of vision. Political awareness will not knock on your door in America today; you have to consciously and willingly invite it in.

## Feminine Force

For the traditionally minded, feminism in politics means more women voting and more public policy supporting us. Certainly those things are important. But feminism should have a much more expanded meaning. It is not just the role of women in society but also the role of genuinely feminine, yin facets of consciousness that must emerge reborn. In the century now dawning, spirituality, visionary consciousness, and the ability to build and mend human relationships will be more important for the fate and safety of this nation than our capacity to forcefully subdue an enemy.

For the last five thousand years, human civilization has developed in a way that suppresses the natural power of women—and thus the emotional, spiritual, and relational talents of both sexes. True feminism should be a champion of spirituality, and concern for the natural harmony of life. This would be a triumph for men as well as for women, restoring to our collective psyche the beauty of the internal world. We must strive for whole personhood. "The opposite of patriarchy," wrote Germaine Greer, "is not matriarchy but fraternity." Feminism should restore balance to the world—between women and men, of course, and also between the inner and the outer realms of our being.

The feminine archetype is making a dramatic new appearance in modern consciousness. She opens a psychic curtain to reveal a radically different worldview than our own, where the female is freed from age-old prejudice and expresses her total nature without fear. No human law can free a Western woman from the heaviest chains that hold us back, for those chains are not material. For most Western women, it is our hearts and not our bodies that are bound. It is in understanding the true nature of our bondage, including the ways we tend to conspire with it, that we learn to leave behind us the ravages of an over-externalized society. From the various ways we allow ourselves to be co-opted by the patriarchal system, to the appalling lack of sisterhood engendered by the new level of economic competition among us, we allow ourselves time and time again to confuse female liberation with the freedom to be as masculine as men are. The last thing the world needs now is twice as many unbalanced thinkers as there were before.

Yang, or externalized activism, has defined politics in the age now passing; yin, internalized activism, will be a political force in the age now dawning. Yin activism is *force*—as Gandhi and King would say—not brute force, but soul force. Soul force emanates subtle energies that invisibly move and heal the world. Soul force is part of the feminine domain in human consciousness, an aspect of the inner life. Suppress that in religion and religion becomes mere external authority, more concerned with doctrine and dogma than actual religious *experience*. Suppress it in society and civilization devolves, for we lose the bond with our natural selves. That disconnection is the root of all evil.

The feminine force of consciousness is the invisible womb out of which all manifest creation springs. It is the force of the mother and the force of the earth.

—

In *The Education of Henry Adams: An Autobiography,* published in 1918, Adams ruminated on how the power of American industrialization came to replace feminine spirituality as the Western world's vision of ultimate force:

On the one side, at the Louvre and at Chartres, as he knew by the record of work actually done and still before his eyes, was the highest energy ever known to man, the creator of four-fifths of his noblest art, exercising vastly more attraction over the human mind than all the steam-engines and dynamos ever dreamed of, and yet this energy was unknown to the American mind. An American Virgin would never dare command; an American Venus would never dare exist.

The Statue of Liberty, note, is a woman. She represents the Roman Goddess Libertas, who "lights the way." She is the vision that gave birth to this country, without whose guidance we cannot *see.* Liberty's crown symbolizes the power of consciousness; her torch, the illumination of higher truth, which we are to share with all the world; and the book she holds, a commemoration of the Declaration of Independence.

Emma Lazarus's poem, "The New Colossus," engraved on the base of the Statue of Liberty, reads in part:

> "Keep, ancient lands, your storied pomp!" cries she
> With silent lips. "Give me your tired, your poor,
> Your huddled masses yearning to breathe free,
> The wretched refuse of your teeming shore.
> Send these, the homeless, tempest-tost to me
> I lift my lamp beside the golden door!"

We look at that statue all the time. We see her, but we don't seem to hear her.

## *Witchpower*

The European Renaissance was, according to most historians, part of a huge historical counterforce to the oppressive elements of the Middle Ages. The Inquisition, in all its fierce and fiery assault on the human spirit, had finally ended. People throughout the Western world were opening mental windows and letting in the light.

The Civil War stopped slavery but it could not of itself end racism. Similarly, ending the Inquisition meant that so-called witches would no longer burn, but it did not mean that passionate women would no longer have every shadow element of the human psyche dangerously projected onto us.

Supreme Court Justice Louis D. Brandeis wrote, as part of an argument for freedom of thought, "Men feared witches and burnt women."

During the Middle Ages, every feudal village in Europe had a group of women called the "witches"—literally meaning "wise women." They were the herbalists, midwives, and healers of their world. They facilitated community rituals, which held the inhabitants of a village in sacred connection to nature, each other, and themselves. They held a space, as it were, for the individual's sense of personal connection to the divine. Some of them were called "hags." The word *hag* originally meant "mature woman who carries sacred knowledge."

The witch burnings of the Middle Ages, which historians now believe claimed anywhere from several hundred thousand to 9 million lives—85 percent of whom were women—was a systematic effort by the early Church to eradicate the passionate, free-thinking woman. Why? Because such women tended to raise passionate, free-thinking children. And such children tended to become passionate, free-thinking adults. Passionate, free-

---

*231*

thinking adults are very difficult to manipulate and almost impossible to control. Any time a group or institution seeks to gain control over human minds, one of its first attacks is on passionate women.

What do the witch trials have to do with modern America? A tremendous amount. There is in modern Western women a cellular memory of burning at the stake, just as there is in modern American blacks a cellular memory of slavery. Many women today are still afraid to speak their piece, and there are those who feel it the most natural thing in the world to burn us when we do.

Several male clergy have been respectfully referred to as President Clinton's spiritual advisors, but author and scholar Jean Houston's career, after consulting with Mrs. Clinton, was undermined by lies and innuendo. Her prodigious intellect was trivialized, and a standard gestalt technique she used in her work was irresponsibly called a "seance." As Houston said regarding her accuser, "Mr. Woodward confuses the fringe with the frontier." We have so dumbed down the entire culture that anything that doesn't fit into the white bread section of the supermarket is deemed way too controversial for America to handle.

That is very sad for all of us, because the nourishment we most need will not come from white bread. We need expanded frontiers of knowledge, new sets of questions, and a more sacred, piercing sensibility. We are comfortable with male ministers being at the White House because we know what they're saying there; *they stay within the boxes.* But the man who announced in the light of day his need for male ministers was tended to in his darker moments by mature women of spirit, and that is fact.

# The Press

Instead of endeavoring to genuinely increase our understanding of the events and forces that shape our society, much of the media presents stories ensured to be as superficial as possible. They have mastered rather than obliterated obfuscation. An artificial appetite for titillation and sensationalism has replaced our demand for truth.

The press seems to lead the push to keep the mainstream stuck at mid-century. Many of them seem willing to use any means of falsehood or innuendo to invalidate new-paradigm thinking. Instead of watchdogs, they have become guard dogs for the old order.

Far too many journalists are drunk on their rights and blind to any ethical responsibilities. "What's the story? What's the *hook?*" carries more weight as a question than "What is the actual truth?" Often, when there is no "story" or "hook" to feed their insatiable hunger for a sensational headline, then a story, myth, or caricature is manufactured instead. When a lie is printed enough times, it carries a veneer of truth; people's lives and careers are casually smeared. I know.

President Kennedy once said, "For the great enemy of truth is very often not the lie—deliberate, contrived and dishonest—but the myth—persistent, persuasive, and unrealistic."

In a court of law, there are laws of due process: circumstantial evidence is thoroughly scrutinized, the defense is able to question the witnesses, unfair commentary and leading of a witness are ruled out. But now Americans are put on trial by the media themselves, where there are no laws of due process. If they're unfair, they're unfair. What will happen if this continues—indeed, what is already happening—is that Americans with the greatest gifts to give society will only give them privately. Our most brilliant minds are already congregated too heavily in the private sector, while in former times government—at least the public sphere—was considered the grandest place to put one's talents. A sensitive heart would have a hard time enduring the meanness of the media today. Who wants to risk the pain? I heard someone say, "The abuse of leaders is the last unchallenged oppression in America."

A man I know told me recently that there are too few "significant" people in the world today. I do not agree. There are exceptional people doing amazing things. But American culture —particularly the press—has become so intent on selling personal destruction as a form of popular entertainment that we do not allow people to publicly *show up* in their significance anymore. Would Thomas Jefferson, with his affection for Sally Hemings, have been allowed to be significant in our lives today? Would Franklin Roosevelt's adultery have remained hidden? John Fitzgerald Kennedy, forget it.

And I hear Mother Teresa is tough.


DURING the seventies, investigative reporting was heroic. Woodward and Bernstein revealed the dark underpinnings of the Nixon White House, leading ultimately to the resignation of a president. It was an example of the press being society's watchdog, which in fact they were intended to be. But now something very odd has occurred. Investigative reporting seems to have been mainly reduced to embarrassing people, to personal destructiveness, and to casual demolition of lives and careers. A category now reigns called, "Who can I destroy today, possibly winning myself a Pulitzer, without leaving town or doing any real work?"

Much worse, truly dark things are going on in America that *should* be investigated fully, yet don't seem to be. Intelligence secrecy, of course, is one. But how about this? Two former cadets from the Citadel military academy, Craig Belsole and Dan Eggars, charged the following in court papers filed in May 1997: "There appears to be a tradition of Nazi symbols among some Citadel cadets, concentrated among cadets who the Citadel has chosen as officers and leaders." The account goes on, "The Nazi symbols are treated as badges of honor and passed on from year to year."

According to the Southern Poverty Law Center, a public advocacy group in Alabama, hate groups—from neo-Nazis to skinheads—have developed a vast following over the last few years in as many as forty-three states, and have infiltrated the military. The Center's Militia Task Force and KlanWatch Project report that the "patriot movement," with its extreme and violent anti-government doctrines, has permeated all fifty states. Surprisingly, this powderkeg situation has generated very limited reaction from our leaders in Washington. More than two years after the bombing of the Murrah Building in Oklahoma City, the federal government seems to be hoping that it will all just go away.

The government doesn't respond because they're not hearing much from us about it; we're not responding because we're not hearing much in the press about it; and the press isn't responding because such stories don't sell papers.

But we *all* know *this:* Gwyneth Paltrow and Brad Pitt *broke up!!!!!!!*

We're sleeping through a very critical part of the movie.


## Drugs, Sobriety, and Magic

A system that makes a lot of noise about fighting drugs is itself invested in our being stoned. A critical mass of clear thinkers is the one thing that would change this country. We sometimes spend a lot of money trying to fight a problem, merely masking the fact that we have no intention of solving it.

While our politicians are big on discussing America's drug problem, they hardly ever discuss sobriety. There is a reason for this: sobriety doesn't yet play a serious part in mainstream conversation because America hasn't yet decided to become sober. The most significant drug stash in America is in our collective medicine chests. America has become a legally ordained drug culture.

Americans act these days as though taking a prescription drug is not really taking drugs, which is much like saying that using a credit card isn't really spending money. Our mass consumption of legalized chemicals should show us how oddly selective we are in our condemnation of drugs.

Legal, though not necessarily morally legitimate pharmaceutical company campaigns have set out to drug America, with far too many doctors as their willing accomplices. We drop antidepressants like candy, often giving them to our teenagers for no better reason, from what I can see, than that the kid is acting like a teenager. I can't imagine Beaver Cleaver's mother looking at the antics of one her sons and saying, "Oops, that's a case of obsessive-compulsive disorder if I ever saw one! Dope him up!"

America's overmedication of itself and its children is our biggest "dirty little secret." Notice how illegal drugs are called drugs, but legal drugs are called "medication." "So-and-so thinks I should go on medication" has replaced what we used to say in the old days: "Do you know where I can get a gram?" "My doctor prescribed it" has replaced "I'm not addicted—I just do it every once in a while."

The kid's a problem? Attention deficit disorder—put him on

Ritalin. Can't deal with the pressure of work and home? Prozac might be the answer. I'm not saying that there are never legitimate reasons for psychiatric drugs, because there clearly are. But the bigger issue is America's hypocrisy in not facing up to our addictive patterns, preferring to suppress the symptoms rather than legitimately deal with our pain. We have allowed billion-dollar industries to grow up around ways to manage and suppress our misery.

Psychologist Carl Jung said, "All neurosis is a substitute for legitimate suffering." As a culture, America lacks a deep understanding of the value of suffering. Contrary to popular opinion, there are times when allowing ourselves to suffer is the only way to get through the pain.

American popular culture is a cult of pleasure, which is an inappropriate response to deep unhappiness. The happiest life is an authentic life, which is not necessarily one of constant delight. Our obsessive pursuit of entertainment and cheap pleasure is both a response to and a masking of deep unhappiness. When, after fifteen minutes, the pain comes back—no matter how much fun we had and how many games we bought—we should do more than just seek to numb it.

It's important that our bones hurt when we break them. Otherwise, how would we know that they're broken? But if you have a broken bone, you don't just take painkillers; you have to reset the bone. So it is with our society: the fact that so many of us endure deep psychic pain on a daily basis—one in four women in America will be diagnosed as clinically depressed—should be something more significant than a gold mine for drug manufacturers. It should be the source of deep questioning regarding what has gone so wrong, and the embrace of real solutions—*like maybe a serious spiritual life.* Why is a pharmaceutical company that makes billions of dollars manufacturing antidepressants called a legitimate capitalist concern, but someone who suggests that we pray and meditate regularly to help treat depression liable to be called a snake-oil salesman?

Americans don't need to *treat* our unhappiness so much as we need to *respond* to it. Unhappiness is here for a reason; it is trying to tell us something. It is a sign that who we have been in our lives, and what we have been doing with our lives, is an inadequate structure for the energies trying to emerge within us. Usually it is a sign that on some level we have been playing way too powerless; responding to that powerlessness with drugs is like saying that we'll respond to a cut by cutting ourselves again.

Our war against drugs is odd, at best. It's basically a prohibition that hasn't worked, undertaken by a society that is itself addicted to drugs. I think we keep fighting the drug war for that reason: like any addict, we try to deflect attention away from our own use. The criminal underclass created by the "drug war" costs America more in lives and money and outright human tragedy than any straight-out use of the outlawed drugs ever would if they were legal. Even more important, our children, in taking drugs, are far too often merely imitating us.

If we were intent on fighting drugs in this country, we would seriously foster recovery. We would have twelve-step recovery meetings in the high schools during the afternoons. I've heard that a Recovery Channel is going to start broadcasting on television soon; for a fraction of the money we spend fighting drugs, we could have federally funded such a network years ago.

And most important, we should begin asking ourselves, what is the hole inside our children, and inside us, that we are all seeking to fill so dysfunctionally? What is it about the world we have created for ourselves that we so don't want to *be* here?

Saying that we are going to win the war on drugs is like saying that we'll get rid of the Viet Cong. Damned if there wasn't always another one right behind that next tree. So there will be drugs on our streets, no matter how much money we spend trying to stop them, as long as there is a spiritual wound in the gut of America's children. And there will be that pain in them until we have adequately addressed the pain in us.

The issue is a paradigmatic one: we are on the verge of out-growing a mind-set that says "I will deal with this problem by saying *no* to something" and embracing one that says "I will deal with this problem by saying *yes* to something else." Notice we have a Drug Czar, but not a Sobriety Czar. It's as though our government is run by a group of old-fashioned father figures who rarely spend any time at home, but then love to come into the house and start giving orders. The kids look at him like he's crazy. Who's done more to get America off drugs—Gerald Ford or Betty Ford?

Our drug war should be replaced by a national sobriety campaign. And that means a whole lot more than just saying no; it means saying yes to some things that America, deep in its heart, has not yet decided it wants to say yes to.

The only way America is going to solve its drug problem is if we retrieve our spiritual awareness. That is what sobriety is. There is a magic within each of us that we consistently deny, because it lies in the realm of the imagination. We have been trained since childhood to view the imagination as a less im-portant function than the intellect. This has left us emotionally and spiritually bereft. Taking drugs is a desperate effort to com-pensate for the loss.

The most dangerous thing in the world for a free society is for a critical mass of people to lose conscious contact with the place within us that says, "Hey, something's fishy here. I feel something rotten in my gut." Not everything that is happening in America today would make a person who is in their right mind happy: that's why we have to *be* in our right minds. Our right minds are our salvation.

## *Magic People*

What do so many of us wish to bring back to civilized awareness in a more potent, alive way? Mystery, intuition, ritual, relationship, healing, emotion, soul, community, imagination. Important parts of who we all are. The stuff of magic and magical people.

The peoples who never dropped those things from the forefront of their consciousness are the peoples who have lived at the margins of power in Western civilization during the era now drawing to a close. They have been suppressed, at the deepest level, not because the prevailing patriarchal consciousness thought that they were *less* than. They were repressed because, unconsciously, it was suspected that they were *more* than. All people, through the grace of God, have mystical power greatly underutilized in this now-passing millennium, but it is people who have been historically held down, whose inner strengths have been simmering within the pressure cooker of their profound long suffering, who now stand at the forefront of humanity's rebirth.

The following stanza from G. K. Chesterton's poem "The Secret People" is one of my favorite expressions of how the magic of the soul has been shoved aside in the consciousness of the modern world:

They have given us into the hand of the new unhappy lords,
  Lords without anger and honour, who dare not carry their swords.
They fight by shuffling paper; they have bright dead alien eyes;
They look at our labour and laughter as a tired man looks at flies.

And the load of their loveless pity is worse than the ancient wrongs,
Their doors are shut in the evening; and they know no songs.

The magic people haven't been invited to attend the party in America, for fear that they might dance. They haven't been invited to speak at the party, for fear that they might sing. They haven't been invited to run the party, for fear that they might change it.

They would have, and now they're going to.

# 6

# HOLISTIC
# POLITICS

*"Never doubt that a small group of concerned citizens can change the world. Indeed, it is the only thing that ever has."*

— MARGARET MEAD

*"Politics should be the part-time profession of every American."*

— PRESIDENT
DWIGHT D. EISENHOWER

BEYOND the appearances of history, there is a great and glorious, unfolding plan for the destiny of nations. God carries the plan within His mind and seeks always, in all ways, channels for its furtherance. His plan for humanity, and the preparation of teachers to guide it, is called within the esoteric traditions the Great Work.

Contribution to this work is not unique to any one nation or people. Worldly structures are instruments for the advancement of God's plan, to the extent to which the ideals of that structure reflect the highest philosophical truths. Where immoderate ambition or selfishness take hold, the bond is broken between the spirit of the work and the structure that held it. The Work continues; it always continues. But it leaves behind what becomes unworthy of it and gravitates toward truer hearts.

In modern sociological terms, there is a phenomenon called the "local discontinuity of progress." The next step forward in a system rarely comes from a predictable place. Grace is not logical, nor can brilliant insight be rationally formulated. Where human beings pride themselves, the spirit of God departs. Human arrogance is not a container for God's greater work, nor will it ever be.

When a particular group or structure fails to keep faith with

God—not measured by its words but by its actions—that structure then loses the privilege of guardianship of the great Work.
The plan passes on to other groups or structures. Human beings
cannot stop or pervert the works of destiny, but we can dissociate
ourselves from its higher unfoldment. When we do, we cease to
share in its blessings.

America has been a vessel for the great Work from its incep-
tion. Now, however, we have lost our conscious contact with the
greatness of our destiny. We ignore invisible principles, yet ob-
sess about all manner of visible pursuits. We allow our time and
attention to be frittered away in a scramble for things too shallow
to satisfy us, even if we can attain them. Having overcome so
many forms of external bondage, we are now so internally bound
that we are yet to be set free.

Still, powers greater than we continue to minister to humanity. Today, as it has been and shall forever be, any heart that
surrenders itself becomes a channel for the vibrations of love
still emanating from the mind of God. It is not too late to change
our minds.

America keeps trying to find the right drivers, when instead
we should be questioning what road we're on. Contrary to what
we are told, the road ahead is not full of just light; the road
ahead is full of consequences. But there is another road that
America can take, the road we have always known that we be-
longed on. It is the road of high and enlightened purpose, a
pursuit of the expansion of truth—in who it touches and how
deeply. Material expansion will take care of itself if we take care
of all things true and beautiful. For those whose hearts respond
to this thought, it is time to break through the superstitious
thinking that would have us believe it's too late to change. We
can change, we will change—in fact, we are changing. That is
our destiny. A question that faces us is this: can we recreate
politics to reflect these things, or must the pursuit of higher

truth remain separate from the public sphere? This moment is one of opportunity for the creation of a new political forcefield. It is up to each and every one of us to decide where America goes now.

## David and Goliath

One of the greatest religious tales is the biblical story of David and Goliath. Like all powerful allegories, "it is true even if it didn't happen," to use the words of Jack Kerouac. It reveals an eternal truth about the nature of man, the nature of God, and the nature of the world.

David was a young boy when God first looked into his heart and chose him to become the King of Israel. During the years of his circuitous route to the throne, he was, among other things, King Saul's personal musician and a shepherd.

As a youth, and with no professional military training, David seemed an odd choice to kill a giant. Yet Goliath threatened the nation, and none of Israel's warriors were brave enough to confront him. They all trembled at the sound of the giant's roar, and only young David volunteered to take him on.

Goliath was not only a giant; he was also equipped with 150 pounds of armor, carried a massive spear, and had "a javelin of bronze slung between his shoulders." He had all the ego and bravado of a warrior villain. He taunted and mocked David, who had no armor or ammunition except a sling with five smooth stones. Yet David solemnly proclaimed that he would win victory over the giant, "that all the earth may know that there is a God in Israel, and that all this assembly may know that the Lord saves not with sword and spear, for the battle is the Lord's and he will give you into our hand."

With that, David shot his sling, landing one smooth stone

right in the middle of Goliath's forehead. Goliath dead, David then used the giant's own sword to behead him.

FOR the spiritually motivated activist, that story is everything we need to know, revealing the Achilles' heel of a monstrous status quo. *Its meanness, but also its vulnerability, is its dissociation from its own soul.* When its conscience is struck, it is automatically transformed.

David had the power of God's love on his side. Contrary to appearances, the giant was the one who didn't stand a chance. There is one power that a mean, soulless, worldly juggernaut cannot defend against or effectively destroy. That is the power of love, and its weapon of faith.

Goliath is a giant, symbolizing worldly power bigger than any one person. He is heavily armored, symbolizing something impossible to touch, emotionally or physically. He has a piece of bronze slung between his shoulders, symbolizing something which is heavily armed.

David is a musician, which symbolizes the intuitive, mysterious power of the right side of the brain. He is a shepherd, symbolizing the caretaker, or those who "take care of the lambs of God." The great artists of the world make manifest the subconscious yearnings of the human race; Michelangelo, in shaping the *Pieta, Moses, David,* and other great works, created that which we were already longing to look at. Renaissance art hearkened back to the idea of human perfectibility as expressed by the ancient Greeks. That ideal, weaving through the Bible, Michelangelo's hands, and now our own souls, beckons us to dig ever more deeply into the miraculous possibilities of our being. David is one of the most powerful symbols of who we are, what we struggle with, and what God wants us to achieve.

David's youth and faithfulness gave him the courage and

power to confront the giant and to have victory over him. Today in America there is a new Davidic impulse: the young, the used-to-be-young, and the faithful joined together. If we have courage and we have faith, we too will slay the giant in our midst.

## The Will-to-Good

Great religious symbols represent the intersection of human and divine will. In the Jewish Star of David, the pyramid pointing to heaven intersects with the pyramid pointing toward earth; the Christian cross similarly reflects the power pointing to heaven as it "crosses" the power that covers the earth.

The point of living in this world is that we transform it back to the ways of love: to create a life "on earth as it is in heaven." From an esoteric philosophical perspective, the point of human evolution is that we hasten the day when heaven and earth no longer exist as two separate states.

Human power is the power of will, a power that can be either constructive or destructive. Divine power is the power of love. The spiritual and psychological evolution of the species is the march toward their union, or a consciousness of Will-to-Love.

*Energy* is a word that denotes the presence of a spiritual vibration, while *force* describes the human use, or application of that energy. The energy of love is a given, because it streams from the mind of God into all of us. Our choosing on a mass level to turn that energy into a social force for good is our next evolutionary step. That is why Gandhi and King were both shadows of our future.

We must *will* into the world the love in our hearts, not through self-will but through surrender to God's will. That is our spiritual as well as our psychological maturity. Love, to be God's love, is not a passive but a participatory emotion.

## Faith and Action

Two things make David important: who he is and what he does. We must address both those issues within ourselves in order to become serious vessels for transforming the world.

David's two significant aspects are his faith and his action. Faith is the belief in things unseen, a hearkening to principles that a materialistic world does not acknowledge. It is an experience that far transcends religious dogma. Faith gives a different set of eyes, that we might see a different world.

David had faith, and from it he drew his power. Faith brings not a weakening of the personality but a strengthening of it, for it provides more data to the brain as well as to the heart. It expands one's awareness by positing the reality of a world beyond the one we perceive with our physical senses. It is not an irrational, but a superrational take on life. It represents a shift from living one's life based on extrinsic calculations to one based on intrinsic understanding.

There are universal themes and articles of faith. At the center of them all is love. Faith in God is faith in love and its power to ultimately sustain us, renew us, and make straight our paths. It is the ultimate power because love casts out fear.

MANY Americans have the unfortunate habit of waking up every morning and surrendering their lives to fear. Newspapers, radio or TV news, caffeine or nicotine get hold of our nervous systems and hook us into the anxiety-ridden miasma we call contemporary culture before we're even out the door.

A path of love takes conscious effort. The cultivation of hallowed silence, meditation, or prayer; a small amount of inspirational literature; a minimum amount of yoga or centering exercise—these are things that counter the fear and help to lift us above the ream of our popular hysteria.

*After* we meditate, we're ready to read the paper; after we're inspired, we're better prepared to be informed.

Every time we pray or meditate, we go home to God. There we are given the spiritual food we need to continue on our journey here. We are shown the light that it is then our job to help bring to all the world. Devotional practice gives us conscious contact with our higher selves, our higher purpose, and our power to express them both.

"The first responsibility of love," said philosopher Paul Tillich, "is to listen." We cannot learn to deeply communicate until we learn to listen, to each other but also to ourselves and to God. Devotional silence is a powerful tool, for the healing of a heart or the healing of a nation. We must break the addictive chain that binds us to the chatter and noise of our cultural nonsense. Avoiding too much television, for instance, is a revolutionary act today. It is part of the effort to retrieve our right minds.

From there we move up to the next rung on the ladder of healing: our capacity to so communicate our authentic truth as to heal and be healed by its power. While there is nothing about this that can be organized or imposed in any top-down, authoritarian way, a revitalized democracy suggests a grassroots movement of people gathering for the purposes of personal and planetary healing.

## A *Wealth* of *Genius*

Our Founders were children of the Age of Enlightenment, believing in the ultimate goodness of man and endeavoring to bring forth on earth a system that attested to and gave power to that faith. For us to find our inherent goodness, and express it, is our highest calling. A transcendent politics recognizes the inherent goodness of the average citizen as the crown jewel of American democracy. It is the lure of the spirit—not the lure of money —that shall uplift us and place us on the path to an American renaissance.

The external world is a world of dwindling resources, while the world within is one of infinite store. We have created a culture that denies its own gold mine. Our wealth is not our money but our genius, and a society that cannot promote genius has no access to the well of its own creativity.

That creativity feeds democracy. That is why education is so important in America, and why we must teach our children not just facts, but wisdom. The citizen should be a deep thinker because the citizen is supposedly making the decisions that determine the fate of this country. Democracy is a great potential vehicle for the creation of a worldly paradise—greater than any other system of government—because it is a container for whatever we decide to do.

America did not give birth to democracy; there had been democracies in Greece, Rome, and the city-states of Renaissance Italy. But our Founders synthesized all that had gone before. Every other free government had come about through evolution, as in the case of England, or through one great lawmaker, as in the case of Solon of Athens. Ours, however, was the first nation *founded* on democratic principle, dedicated to the notion that group involvement, consensus building, deliberation, and reference to our Constitution could produce the context necessary to organize the social functioning of countless millions of people. Alexander Hamilton began the Federalist Papers by declaring, "it seems to have been reserved to the people of this country ... to decide the important question, whether societies of men are really capable or not, of establishing good government from reflection and choice...."

As I drove past a Planned Parenthood clinic in the town where I live recently, I noticed that on one side of the driveway were protesters with picket signs, while on the other side of the driveway was a woman wearing a bulletproof vest, on the top of which was written "Clinic." I almost cried when I saw that sight: how far we have descended from our Founders' vision of a creatively deliberative group of people.

People who are free to debate their views but define that debate as screaming at each other, people who are free to express their opinions but dishonor the opinions of others, are not practicing democracy; they're in the process of destroying it. Our forefathers foresaw for us a deliberative, consensus-building, reasonable form of political debate. A generation for whom after-dinner conversation has been replaced on a mass level by after-dinner television has difficulty developing the social maturity necessary for the authentic practice of democracy. Such practice demands our capacity to speak from our depths, and listen from our depths. Cultural cacophony is an enemy of democracy.

Once I was giving a lecture to a large audience, and the subject of abortion came up in the discussion period of the program. Tensions began to surface, and a slight rip appeared in the psychic fabric of the room. One choice was to go for a false positivism, pretending we're all so "spiritual" here that we don't have to delve into issues like that. Such a choice is not transcendence but denial, healing nothing and no one. Another choice was to open the discussion—go for it and see what happens. A third choice offered a different way. I asked the people in the room to close their eyes and silently remain that way for two minutes. I asked the audience to look within themselves and call on the spirit of goodness that resides there. I asked them to ask the soul for its wisdom regarding this issue, to deliver their perceptions of this subject into the hands of God.

After our two minutes of silence, we resumed conversation. Everyone in the room was quieter, more accepting and compassionate toward the views of others, and more eloquent in stating their own. What came forward, then, was not so much anyone's particular opinions but everyone's capacity to communicate more deeply. The "right answer" is not a particular view on policy, so much as an experience of each other in which the process of meaningful democracy is restored.

We don't need to extend democracy outward on a lateral access so much, as we need to extend it vertically into our own minds and hearts. Democracy has become a shallow well in America, and remedying that *is* our "answer." The day after that lecture, someone who was there remarked to me, "I felt like last night I had an intimate living room conversation regarding abortion with two thousand people."

## Habits of the Heart

In Harper Lee's *To Kill a Mockingbird*, Atticus Finch tells his daughter, "You never really understand a person until you consider things from his point of view—until you climb into his skin and walk around in it." Where that kind of understanding occurs, hearts merge. Where hearts merge, miracles happen. More dimensions of the mind become operative, and more possibilities for healing develop naturally.

Where hearts remain separate, however, the mind miscreates. It moves instinctively in the direction of fear. That is why we must seek to remain in open-hearted relationships even with those with whom we disagree. Some of my most interesting

conversations—and definitely the most illuminating ones—
have been with people who view politics very differently than I
do. That is a problem only if the opportunity for stimulating
debate turns into personal insult. The highest exercise of democracy demands personal and spiritual maturity. Courtesy plays a
significant part in the process. Who among us has nothing left to
learn from someone else?

Too many Americans today define a political meeting as a
place where we go to be with others who are smart enough to
look at the world exactly the way we do, all of us joining together
in a self-congratulatory spirit to figure out how to impose our
opinions on those not yet intelligent enough to agree with us.
We must grow to the next level of our political maturity. Our
most critical need is for a mode of genuine reconciliation and
synergistic dialogue among opposing viewpoints. That is the
new politics because it retrieves the process of real democracy.
The adversarial games that define politics today are psychologically and socially destructive.

BOTH conservative and liberal principles are heightened when
seen in the context of a broad appreciation of the moral concerns
of the other. Part of our problem is that American popular dis-
course regarding morality and ethics and even government tends
to exist at such a sophomoric level. Our best minds often disdain
the subject of what makes something ethical and good, while in
other nations such subjects are hot topics at sidewalk cafés. Far
too often, Americans stop discussing anything philosophically
meaningful once we leave school.

Between a public education system that can hardly be cred-
ited with stimulating critical thought and television program-
ming that absolutely destroys it, we are left a dumbed-down
culture, ever ready to fight each other but almost incapable of

higher debate. Higher questions go right by us, and that is an inestimable loss for any culture. For only when we put the bigger questions on the table can we hope to arrive at bigger answers. Questioning is messy, but that is how it should be. American politics should have the feeling of one big college classroom, rather than gladiators fighting the lions.

IN his classic *Democracy in America*, the French philosopher and statesman Alexis de Tocqueville wrote of Americans' "habits of the heart." The practice of democracy is indeed a habit of the heart—the habit of voting, to be sure, but also much more than that: of reading, of becoming and staying aware, of communicating, plugging into the system, and owning one's voice.

An agreement among two or more people is a mighty power in the universe, and words in support of the agreement gives it added weight. There is an exercise where a group sits quietly, much as in a Quaker-style meeting, and when the spirit moves an individual, he or she says loud enough for all to hear, "I see an America in which..." One night we had done this exercise at one of my lectures in New York City. Hundreds of people were in the room, and probably seventy or so made their declaration of what they'd like America to be like. (Always very interesting and sometimes very funny: I've heard people in New York City say they see an America without lawyers, and people in Los Angeles say they see an America without agents.) After the completion of the exercise, the group took a twenty-minute intermission.

When I came back on stage, it was time for a different part of my presentation: responding to questions handed in from members of the audience. I have been doing this format—lecture, intermission, then questions and answers—for years.

But this night was different. Almost every time I read a question, before I could even say anything in response, someone in the audience would speak up! Not raise a hand, but just blurt out an answer—and always a good one. I realized that something significant had occurred here: from merely participating in that exercise, people had subtly shifted from passive to active, from nonparticipatory to participatory, from a mode where "someone else has the answers" to one where "I have the answers." People hadn't *become* wise that night, of course, but many had come closer to *owning* their wisdom that night.

Within minutes, people were talking—completely un-prompted by me—of which companies produce their products in countries where child labor is used; the tenets of responsible investing; how to include infant and child care in a corporate environment; economic injustice and the U.S. tax code; and what really happened to Flight 800. That, to me, is democracy in action: average citizens joining in a dignified environment to deliberate issues among themselves. And when that starts to happen, how intelligent we are. Group intelligence and group conscience both exist: the true political issue is to invoke them.

Too many times in America today the social maxim among us is, "Let's not talk about religion or politics." Boy, does that leave *me* out at dinner. We don't need to talk less in America; we need to talk *more* about the things that matter most.

## Coulda Been Like David, But We Caved

One day I took my daughter and one of her friends to an arts and crafts shop to play. While the girls were deciding whose ceramic cat should be black with white spots, and whose should be white with black spots, I sat editing the manuscript of this book.

The owner of the store stopped at our table. After playing with the girls for a while, he looked over at me and said, "What are you doing?"

"I'm writing a book," I said.

"What's it about?"

"The healing of America," I replied.

He smiled knowingly. "Oh, yeah? You think America needs to be healed? What do you think is wrong with it?"

"Well, first of all, I think a lot is right with it," I said. "But I think a lot of things are wrong, too. What do *you* think? Do *you* think we need a healing, and what do *you* think is wrong with the country?"

"I think there's a lot of good too, but also a lot of bad," he said. "The gap between rich and poor is so big—did you know that a small percentage of Americans own most of the wealth? And this country is practically becoming a police state. Everybody else in the world is becoming freer, and we're just one 'You can't do this, you can't do that' after another." He was getting excited. "I can't even paint my condo the color I want, or let my kid play in the grassed-off sections of the building where we live. Nobody seems to notice how much we're all being lined up in a row all the time now, just trained like dogs to say, 'Okay, you make the decisions for my life.' Even in business. It's all these huge companies that come in everywhere; the mom and pop stores don't even have a *chance* anymore."

He started to put glaze over one of the ceramic cats, and spoke more softly. "There's a lot of desperation out there, and now you read about how good everything supposedly is. Give me a break. Not for the average American worker, let me tell you. Millions of people are having a very hard time, no matter what they do."

"It's interesting that you feel that way," I said. "You know, you would probably like Robert Reich's new book, *Locked in the Cabinet*. Have you read it?"

All of a sudden a look came into his eyes that seemed to say, "Hey now, don't take me *too* seriously." He laughed a little. "No, no no. I don't want to read anything like that. I'm a Tom Clancy man myself. I just want to read another detective story and escape all this."

It was an odd switch, but one I've seen before. Someone so passionate about his views one minute, in the next minute resists the suggestion that he actually go further into them.

So isn't the real problem here that so many of us feel strongly about what we think has gone wrong in America, but have become too cynical to do anything about it?

When I've said this before, I've been told by people like him that there's no one issue to rally around; that if there was, they would definitely do something; that they feel there's no one else who really cares.

But there seems to be no issue to rally around only because there is no one *single* issue. There are many to rally around, in fact; our worst problem is a mind-set, but that doesn't mean there's any less to be done about it. And a lot of people care about our collective problems—many millions of us do. It's no one's fault but our own if we choose not to participate in solving them. What we need in America now is less a visionary leader than a visionary constituency.

Life has been so relatively easy for many of us that we haven't developed a healthy capacity to burst through obstacles. We cannot allow ourselves to remain stuck at an adolescent level of whining and waiting for someone else to fix things. We must develop the patience, the fortitude, and the strength of personality to use the tools we have.

And we *do* have tools. We have many.

• • •

AT exactly the time I was having that discussion in the arts and crafts store, the U.S. Senate was debating—and then turned down—an amendment to the budget bill that would have added a 43-cent tobacco tax on every pack of cigarettes, creating $30 billion in revenue to pay for health insurance for millions of children of the working poor. The amendment, which lost by only ten votes, had been proposed by conservative Republican Senator Orrin Hatch of Utah and liberal Democratic Senator Edward Kennedy of Massachusetts.

President Clinton had helped defeat the amendment because Republican Majority Leader Trent Lott had called it a "deal breaker" in working out the budget agreement. Opponents of the amendment were saying amazing things like, "Voting for this bill will actually hurt the poor because they'll just keep on smoking but it will be more expensive."

Senator Hatch said, "It's Joey versus Joe Camel, and no procedural niceties can obscure this reality and everybody here knows it." Senator Kennedy said, "We shall offer it again and again until we prevail. It's more important to protect children than to protect the tobacco industry."

I saw in the newspaper that one of my Senators voted to defeat the rider. She's a good Senator and I respect her, but on this one issue I strongly disagreed with her vote.

I called the main switchboard at the Capitol in Washington, D.C. [(202) 224-3121], and asked for her office. The switchboard connects you immediately to whatever office you request.

"Senator Feinstein's office." A nice young staffer was on the other end of the line.

"Hello," I said. "This is a constituent call. My name is Marianne Williamson, and I'm calling to express profound disappointment that the Senator helped defeat the rider yesterday that would have provided money for children's health insurance. Could you explain to me why she did that, please?"

"Certainly," he said, and put me on hold. In a few seconds he was back. "The Senator felt she had to do it because the Majority Leader said it was a deal breaker for the budget deal."

"Yes, I know that he said that. I read that in the paper. But quite a few people argued that that was a bluff. Why must we so consistently cave in to those who would have us balance the budget on the backs of our children, rather than on the back of the tobacco industry? Could you explain that to me, please?"

"Yes, certainly," he said, and put me on hold again.

In a few moments, he returned. "I was told to tell you that the President himself called here yesterday, and asked that the Senator vote the way she did."

"Would you please tell the Senator that my response to that is, 'So?'"

"Yes, of course," he said.

"Please tell the Senator that at least one of her constituents wants to go on record saying that doing the right thing is never a wrong move."

"Thank you," he said, "I will tell her that."

Like hell he will, I thought, as I put down the phone. I had no illusions, of course, that the Senator would be told what I said. But I know this: if she received a hundred calls like that—or, better yet, two hundred—she sure *would* hear about it, and I even think she would care. These people still run for election.

There are millions of people in America who read about what happens in Washington, and are disgusted at how we keep selling out to various industries at the expense of American families, day after day. But too many of us don't call Washington and don't write any letters; we just feel the darkness in our guts, knowing what we know but doing nothing. It's like David saying about Goliath, "Geez, he really *is* big. Maybe I won't do this."

But Goliath isn't *that* big. Things aren't *that* bad in America. And each of us has a slingshot.

## Using All Five Stones

"Words are also actions," wrote poet Ralph Waldo Emerson, "and actions are a kind of words." Goliath has the power of money; we have the power of citizen action.

Conventional wisdom holds that, on the state level, twenty calls on a particular issue matter. On the federal level, if a Congressman or Senator receives 200 calls, it matters.

There is only one force strong enough to create a wave of effective resistance to the buying and selling of America's general welfare. That is for a critical mass of Americans to emerge from the political silence that has gripped us for the last thirty years. Too many of the same people who marched in the streets to protest an unjust war now limit their political expression to screaming at the television set. While Americans are aware that something very corrupt has gotten hold of America, the corruption is so systemic that we are tempted to think there is no effective opposition one person can wage.

That is the delusion we must abolish, through reinvigorating democracy and reinvigorating ourselves. I have watched how groups form. Hearts resonate to truth. What each of us must do is speak it.

## The Kvetch Patrol

It is important that we avoid the temptation to indulge ourselves in whining, without taking constructive action. There is no meaningful freedom in the absence of personal discipline. Taking part in the political process through writing letters, making calls, signing petitions, and so on, is a *habit* we must develop if we want the process to transform.

David didn't just pray or complain; he acted. And so must we.

Paradoxically, part of the problem with an overly yang culture is that it produces overly yin personalities. Without the yin of peace and serenity, there is no character formation; without that, there is no capacity for the yang of powerful personal action. We desperately need both. There is no machine, technology, or scientific project that can renew and restore democracy. If we want it done, it's a job that we have to do ourselves.

IMAGINE a politics infused with the following principles:

RENAISSANCE POLITICAL PRINCIPLES

1. The power within us is greater than any power outside us.
2. Government should concern itself less with how to allocate our external resources and more with how to harness our internal ones.
3. The source of wealth is our capacity for genius. Creation of wealth through the stimulation of creative thinking is thus the primary source of economic recovery and stimulation.
4. The highest political dialogue is not adversarial but rather a synergistic conversation between high-minded liberal visions for the country and high-minded conservative ones.
5. The politics of hate is a branch that does not bear fruit. That is why another branch is starting to grow. Love is a more powerful political and social tool than hatred.
6. We will not move forward as a nation without repenting for our lack of righteousness toward other Americans in the past and present, and all other nations of the world.
7. We must acknowledge the power of the inner life, the wisdom

found in silence, and the primacy of the voice of conscience. Otherwise, the American experiment will end. It shall have failed.

Renaissance politics would not necessarily win anybody election or reelection to office, but it would profoundly affect the country if enough of us embraced its principles.

Mass adherence to an idea that the heart feels to be true has been and will forever be the strongest force in the world.

## Citizen Power

The key to America's repair lies in the tools of democracy— their proliferation and widespread use. After he left the Presidency, Harry Truman was asked how it felt no longer being President. He responded that he had gotten promoted to a better job: "Mr. Citizen."

Most Americans do not even vote, feeling politics is like a fading reality having little to do with their actual lives. In many ways they are right. It is a spectator sport now, when it was intended to be a participatory drama. No American citizen should be watching the action from the sidelines; each of us has lines to say.

And to say that I vote and therefore participate fully as a citizen is like saying that I pay child support and therefore I'm a real parent.

"The people of every country are the only safe guardians of their own rights," wrote Thomas Jefferson, "and are the only instruments which can be used for their destruction. It is an axiom in my mind that our liberty can never be safe but in the hands of the people themselves. . . ."

Many Americans do not exercise their rights because they have come to take them for granted or underestimate their power. It is often when people have been denied their civil rights that they most appreciate how important such rights are.

Michele McDonald, an African-American single mother who lives in the inner city of Hartford, Connecticut, said regarding the Summit on Volunteerism, "That Conference is a nice concept, but it's missing the element of real democracy. What we want are the tools of power. We want to be the driving force of the richness of our own community.

"We want to be the ones to determine the needs of our own community; we appreciate people coming in to help, but we don't want to just be an object of someone's 'needs assessment' program. That makes us victims, and it disempowers us. What we want is to learn the tools of democracy, so we're not just drowning in the system—we want to learn *Civics!*

"The system shouldn't be deciding what I need; I want to tell them what I need. I want to learn how to be a better citizen in my community and my nation. I want to help my neighbors be more focused on their gifts than on their deficits. What I want to know is how to empower my own community, so we've got real input on where we're going. We want to be empowered to run and take care of our own neighborhood.

"Those people don't want us to have the tools because then we'd have real power. That's what's really going on.

"Sometimes they say they want parents from the community to sit on their boards and things, but once we get there, they don't want us to know how to really use the system. We're supposed to just sit there and be quiet, but they can point to us and say, 'See, they're included.'"

This woman understands the game that's being played here: a system that constitutionally owes her much is patting itself on the back for giving her just a little. Michele is part of a burgeoning impulse to take back the tools of democracy. We take them back by using them.

Even Michele's nine-year-old daughter, Giavanna, has gotten into the act. She took part in an essay-writing contest sponsored by the local police department. Giavanna won first prize—a new bicycle—with an essay entitled "How a Bill Becomes a Law." The bill that she and her classmates worked on was titled "Having Ice Cream Every Day for Lunch."

What neither the Democrats nor the Republicans have emphasized is how to empower Americans as citizens. John Perkins, leader of the Christian Community Development Association, has said, "It's not enough to give someone a fish, or even to teach them to how to fish. Now we have to ask who owns the pond."

## Holistic Politics

An idea grows stronger the more it is shared. If we are to revitalize our experience of citizenship, in certain ways we must do so together. It does not matter that we think alike about the issues —freedom is a state in which, by definition, we do not—but it matters very much that we think about them, period.

Imagine becoming involved in a citizenship gathering—say, on a weekly or monthly basis, held in your living room, or your neighbor's—a kind of Citizen Salon. The purpose of such gatherings is that you might become, as a citizen, more involved in the political process. It doesn't matter who at the meeting considers himself or herself liberal, conservative, neither, or even apolitical. If you're an American, you belong at such a gathering.

One would attend a Citizen Salon not just to voice his or her opinions but also to deeply listen to other people's views. Respectful exchange is an extremely important element in democracy; we must refuse to model our political conversations after "Crossfire."

Political debate should be a liberating force, not a culture war. Civility must be more than a goal; it must become the ground of our social being. For our characters are formed by the political discussion as much as the discussion is formed by our characters. It is hard to imagine the Constitutional Convention ever having produced a meaningful document in a political climate such as ours today.

That is very important because some of America's truly best and brightest today are so emotionally beyond wanting to take part in mean-spirited and emotionally violent interactions, that they have repudiated politics altogether. Public life should represent not our lowest but our highest sensibilities.

That does not mean we should avoid confrontation at all costs. Healthy debate is part of the democratic process. There is rarely a "right answer" in politics; the ultimate "truth" has elements of almost every intelligent person's opinion. If this were not so, we could have a computer make our decisions for us. Nuance, reconciliation, and compassion are things that must be brought to the political table, and the most awakened people bring them.

We need a holistic politics now, that our spirits might join the process of our citizen involvement in a meaningful way.

THE key to successful Citizen Salons is that we speak from the heart about subjects that matter. Possible items to include as part of such meetings are:

1. Silent meditation or nondenominational devotion.
2. Discussion or visualization of what we as individuals would wish America, or the world, to be like.
3. An educational element such as a group reading and discus-

sion. If the meeting is weekly, perhaps one member of the group brings in an article or chapter of a book for group discussion.

4. Citizen lobbying. With every article or discussion, the group should then plan a specific lobbying action, such as letters to an elected official. Remember, we do not all have to be lobbying for the same things or expressing the same opinions.

5. Part of the value of these meetings is that they provide a chance to hear the views of those whom we know are just as intelligent as we, but see things from a different political perspective. If splinter groups grow out of that, whereby we lobby for common things, that is fine and good. But listening to other people's viewpoints keeps our own from calcifying.

Reconciliation should be at the heart of holistic politics: blacks with whites, gays with straights, women with men, Jews with Christians, etc. Mutually respectful, dignified, authentic discussion among members of such groups is part of the value of a holistic political movement. If we don't like the mean-spiritedness of politics as we know it, it is up to us to reinvent it.

### THE POWER OF SILENCE

A minimum of two minutes of devotional common silence before, during, or after a Citizen Salon is highly recommended. Remember the power of prayer, meditation, and positive intentionality. An opening prayer might be as follows:

> Dear God,
> We come together,
> different perspectives,
> different politics,
> different cultures,
> to ask that you heal our country.

> We surrender to you
> the thoughts and attitudes we now hold,
> and empty our minds that they might
> be filled by You.
> Show us to each other,
> as You would have us see each other.
> Show us the world,
> as You would have us see the world.
> Guide our listening,
> as You would have us hear each other.
> Teach us, and inspire us.
> Use us on Your behalf.
> Amen

In an environment where prayer is either inappropriate or perceived as threatening to some members of the group, a generalized reference to "the spirit of goodness within all of us" or "the love [or light] within our minds" carries with it the power to bring groups of people into spiritual alignment with each other and a higher power.

Martin Luther King, Jr., said, "I am convinced that the universe is under the control of a loving purpose and that in the struggle for righteousness man has cosmic companionship. Behind the harsh appearances of the world there is a benign power. To say God is personal is not to make Him an object among other objects or attribute to Him the finiteness and limitations of human personality; it is to take what is finest and noblest in our consciousness and affirm its perfect existence in Him."

### GROUP PRAYERS

The following are some suggestions for the kinds of prayers that break up old political thought patterns:

—

1. Pray for every one of the fifty states.
2. Pray for help in giving up judgment toward whatever person in public life, or group of people, you tend to judge.
3. Pray for the children of America.
4. Pray for the leaders of America.
5. Pray for the poor in America.
6. Pray for America's criminal population.
7. Pray for all drug addicts and alcoholics.
8. Pray for America's sick.
9. Pray for America's relationship with all other nations.
10. Pray for atonement and amends toward those who have been wronged by us as a nation.
11. Pray for racial healing. Atone for the systemic racism that permeates our social policies today, even if you personally don't consider yourself a racist.
12. Pray for parents and children in America.
13. Pray for husbands and wives in America.
14. Pray for all lovers and friends.
15. Pray for America's environment.
16. Pray for the American economy.
17. Pray for American education.
18. Pray for American health care.
19. Pray for America's homeless.
20. Pray that you might become a better American citizen.

### PRAYER VIGILS

In 1995, a woman from Finland came up to me at one of my lectures in New York City. She said she worked at the United Nations and was wondering if I would help the then war-torn Bosnians. "What could *I* do?" I queried. "I don't know," she said. "But please say you'll try." I gave her my phone number in New York, but said that I was rarely there as I was living in California;

there was no phone machine, and I asked her to please understand that as sorry as I was about what was going on in Bosnia, I
knew nothing about how to deal with such things.

Months later, I was in New York again. Reading the newspaper one day, I read of the outrageous atrocities being committed
in Bosnia on a regular basis against men, women, and even
children. I thought to myself that what the world needed was to
be surrounded by a circle of prayer for the people of Bosnia. I
remembered the woman who had approached me months before, but I couldn't even remember her name.

Within an hour, at the apartment I rarely visited, on a phone
that had no answering machine, there was a ring. It was the woman
from the U.N. She asked me if I would come to the United Nations
with her that day, to hear the Bosnian Ambassador and Foreign
Minister present a press conference. I did, and what resulted were
plans for an international prayer vigil. The following is a letter
that then went out from the Permanent Mission to the United
Nations of the Republic of Bosnia and Herzegovina. Elvi Ruotti-
nen's efforts, scores of volunteers, faxes, letters, and Internet
postings were put to use, spreading the word to all like-minded
people of an international thirty-day prayer vigil for Bosnia.
Unity Churches throughout the United States and abroad were
particularly helpful. The vigil was officially sponsored by the
Cornerstone Foundation.

We began the vigil with an interfaith ceremony at the United
Nations chapel.

### Republic of Bosnia and Herzegovina
*Permanent Mission to the United Nations*
*New York*

July 24, 1995

Dear ———

On behalf of the people of Bosnia and Herzegovina, we formally request your participation in activating collective spiritual power in response to the forces of destruction now plaguing our nation.

The people of Bosnia and Herzegovina are a multi-cultural and multi-religious community. We ask for spiritual support from not one religion but all religions, not one spiritual path but all spiritual paths, in calling on the power of the divine to shield and protect our nation.

There will be an interfaith prayer vigil held on our behalf, from August 11 through September 11, inaugurated by interfaith prayer services on August 11 throughout the world. A fact sheet of the event is included with this letter. We do not ask you or your congregations to take any political position whatsoever, but merely to join with people of faith throughout the world in the creation of a powerful band of prayer.

Our prayer is that God's will be done; we trust He wills our people be saved. May peace be restored to all the world.

Please help us.

Sincerely,

Ivan Misic
Ambassador to the United Nations

Muhamed Sacirbey
Foreign Minister

*Prayers for Bosnia and Herzegovina*
*A Plan for Collective Activation of Spiritual Power in Response*
*to the Suffering of the Bosnian People*

On August 11, 1995, throughout the United States and abroad, interfaith prayer services will mark the beginning of a monthlong prayer vigil to activate collective spiritual power in response to the suffering of the Bosnian people.

Two minutes of silent meditation and prayer, at 3 P.M. in New York City, 12 noon in Los Angeles, 9 P.M. in Sarajevo and 8 P.M. in London, every day from August 11 through September 11, will bring millions of hearts and minds together in the application of spiritual force.

For people of faith, prayer is not a mere symbolic event. Rather, it is a harnessing of the power of consciousness to uplift the energy and spirit of the world. Through worldwide prayer, the power of darkness which now permeates the area called Bosnia-Herzegovina can be radically dispersed through the power of light. We pray for Bosnia-Herzegovina and we pray for all the world.

The highest form of power is not the allocation of external resources, but the harnessing of internal ones. Let us harness the love of all the people of the world. Love and love alone, can undo hatred.

The only spokesperson for this event is the voice inside each person's heart. Please work to organize whatever spiritual event will best inaugurate and hold firm the prayers of the people in your community. Above all, join the vigil yourself. Spread the word however you can, to best extend the love.

| Sarajevo | 9 P.M. | Mexico City | 1 P.M. | Athens | 10 P.M. |
|---|---|---|---|---|---|
| Paris | 9 P.M. | Jerusalem | 10 P.M. | Rome | 9 P.M. |
| Honolulu | 9 A.M. | Washington, D.C. | 3 P.M. | Kansas City | 2 P.M. |
| London | 8 P.M. | Cairo | 10 P.M. | Denver | 1 P.M. |
| New York | 3 P.M. | São Paolo | 6 P.M. | Moscow | 11 P.M. |

---

| Los Angeles 12 noon | Johannesburg | 9 P.M. | | |
|---|---|---|---|---|
| *One day ahead:* | Sydney | 5 A.M. | Beijing | 3 A.M. |
| New Delhi 1:30 A.M. | Tokyo | 4 A.M. | Taipei | 3 A.M. |

During the thirty days of the vigil, NATO forces acted, causing a profound shift in the course of the Bosnian war. Many thousands of people all around the world had given prayerful support to the effort to stop the violence.

At the end of the thirty days, Unity Church congregations who had participated in the vigil from around the world were joined in a transatlantic telephone call to declare praise and thanksgiving. I felt I had an awesome glimpse of a newer world.

YOU might wish to participate, by yourself or with others, in a prayer vigil for the United States.

The following are some prayers which might assist your efforts.

> Dear God,
> There was born on this land
> a possibility of freedom
> more expansive than the world had ever known.
> And the promise still exists.
> There is freedom here
> for some,
> dear Lord,
> but clearly not for all.
> And the promise still exists.
> Help us, Lord,
> to free our country from the chains
> of our hardened hearts.

---

And the promise still exists.
Amen

---

Dear God,
Please bless our children
and the children of the world.
    May their innocence remain.
Dear God,
Please bless their tender souls.
Lead them away from harsh stimulation
and the violent ways which hurt them.
Cast out of us the things which offend
the spirit of love
in all of us.
Make our children free of all the darkened things in life,
and make us free as well,
dear Lord.
Make us free as well.
In these United States
and in the world,
may only love remain.
Amen

---

Dear God,
We are
the richest nation,
the most blessed of places,
We praise you, Lord, and thank you.
Surely the bounty You have given us
is meant by You to bless the world,
Please show us how,
dear God.

---

Please recreate our culture,
renew our tired lives.
Let light and love
flow down on us,
our country
and our world.
Amen

---

Dear God,
We bless the souls of those who founded these United
States, of all who came before us,
and who struggle still today,
to bring forth all the greatness
and the glory
of America.
Thank you, God,
and them.
Amen

---

Dear God,
Please bless the people of America,
and all people throughout the world.
Use me, God,
in whatever way
You would have me serve.
Show me how to live my life
in such a way as to spread the love
which feeds and redeems us all.
Amen

---

Dear God,
May the angels
of America
burst forth across this land,
healing hearts and
blessing souls.
May they awaken yet
the cry of freedom
in one and all.
Release us from bondage,
release us from fear.
Amen

—

Dear God,
Turn back the fist
that sits upon the process of our furtherance,
limiting our good.
Remove it from our hearts,
remove it from our streets,
remove it from our government,
remove it from our land.
Thank you, God.
Amen

—

Dear God,
Please forgive this country
for the racism,
past and present,
which so hides Your light.
Take from us any thoughts we hold,
or feelings we have,
which make firm the darkness.

—

Please show us how to create anew
American society,
that truly we might be as brothers.
Thank you very much,
Amen

—

Dear God,
We don't even know
all the things which are wrong in this country,
but You do,
dear Lord,
You do.
Please reveal to us
what You would have revealed,
and take from us what You would take.
Thank you, God.
Amen

—

Dear God,
May we not be slaves to money.
May our hearts serve higher things.
May money flow into us
abundantly and freely,
according to Your will,
and may it serve Your purposes.
Show us how to hold it in the light.
Amen

—

Dear God,
May our essential nature
as a country

—

and a people,
awaken on this day.
May the glorious possibilities
of our miraculous beginnings
once more enchant our hearts and
set us free
of limitation.
Break the chain
of dominance
which false power holds upon us still.
Renew the spirit
of freedom and love
which are Your truth within us.
Amen

―

Dear God,
Please help us change America,
from a land of violence
to a land of love.
Where there is separation,
please bring union.
Where there is distrust and pain,
please bring reconciliation of our hearts
with each other,
and with You.
May all be blessed
and prosper,
here and throughout the world.
And so it is.
Amen

―

Dear God,
Lead us
where You would have us go,
Show us
what You would have us do,
Guide us
in what You would have us say,
and to whom,
that we might serve You best.
Give us hope
that there is yet
another way.
We are open,
we are willing,
we are waiting for Your hand
upon our shoulders and our hearts.
May Your will still yet be done on earth,
as it is in Heaven,
Amen

———

Dear God,
Please give every mother's child
enough to eat,
in America
and everywhere.
Give every mother's child
good work to do,
and the strength to do it,
in America and everywhere.
Give every mother's child
the wisdom to see,
and the courage to act,
and the heart to forebear,

———

in America and everywhere.
Use us to help You, Lord,
to make these things so.
Amen

—

Dear God,
Please forgive us
for how we offend Your spirit,
ignoring the poor,
yet feeding the rich,
not fostering peace,
yet making fortunes
on the instruments of war.
Please turn us around, dear God,
and heal our minds
and hearts.
Please open our eyes,
transform our minds,
that they might be of You,
and You only.
Amen

—

Dear God,
I know not where to go,
but You do.
I know not what to do,
but You do,
I know not how to be,
but You do,
to change this world,
to heal this country.
Please show me, Lord,

—

For I would do my part.
Amen

—

Dear God,
Please bless our Congress,
our President,
our judges,
and elected officials,
and the people of the United States,
with wisdom
and light
and love.
Please bless those who have no voice,
and lend them mine.
Amen

—

Dear God,
There are those
who have too little hope.
There are those who try,
yet feel their dreams
shot down.
There are those who love,
yet feel forgotten
in the madness and the crowds.
Please help them all.
Open wide our hearts
and eyes
and ears,
that we might know and hear each other,
in our joy
and in our pain.
Amen

—

## *Putting Feet to Our Prayers*

### GETTING INFORMATION ON BECOMING INVOLVED

There are many avenues through which one can find out what is happening on a daily, weekly, or monthly basis in our government, both on Capitol Hill and at the White House, and at the state and city levels.

Cable television seems to launch a new all-news channel as often as they break a story. C-Span and C-Span2 show live coverage of Congress when it's in session, important political speeches and panels, as well as programs with viewer call-in segments.

One of the easiest ways to become informed is to read the newspaper. It's true that you don't want to overdose on this, but a daily scan of one major paper, particularly the op-ed page, keeps you generally well informed. Most major newspapers are now available on the World Wide Web, as well. Most important, don't forget alternative press like the *Utne Reader*.

### WRITING TO ELECTED OFFICIALS

It is estimated that fewer than 10 percent of voters will ever write to elected officials. Yet *contacting your elected officials with a letter is an important part of making a difference.* They *work for you.* They theoretically want to hear our views, and they definitely can't afford to ignore them. It's our responsibility to express those views.

Like voting, communicating our views in the political arena metaphysically increases our own power. The universe registers our every serious intention, and vigorous action, on behalf of what we perceive to be a greater good.

You may think your elected officials are flooded with letters on issues you care about. The truth is that most members of Congress receive fewer than 100 letters on any one issue. On the state level, elected officials often receive fewer than ten letters on a particular issue. Your letter can carry a lot of weight.

Your opinions are particularly important when an issue is timely—for example, when a vote is expected or when there is a lot of news coverage of the subject.

Tips for your letter: Be brief, address only one issue at a time, keep the letter down to four or five sentences; say why the issue or legislation matters to you; state your reasons for opposing or supporting a particular bill. If you have particular expertise, then say what it is. Be positive and constructive; give compliments if they're sincere. Send a copy to your local newspaper to help build support for the issue. Use the appropriate title of the elected official. (Note: A country music star's mother recently met Al Gore and asked him, "And what do you do?" When told he was the Vice-President, she said, "Of the record company?" It couldn't have gone over well.) After you have written once, then keep up the contact and periodically communicate that you're following closely what happens; thank the official and state that you'll be following up with a phone call in a week to receive a response, and then do so.

As effective as one letter is, twenty-five on the same issue are even better. Getting others who are concerned about the same issue to send letters is not as hard as you might think. Use a Citizen Salon; write letters together.

## KNOW YOUR REPRESENTATIVES

On the Web, www.vote-smart.org/congress/congress.html is a government-run website that allows us to find our representatives in Congress by entering our zip code.

Send your letters to:

The Honorable _____
United States Senate
Washington, D.C. 20510

The Honorable _____
United States House of Representatives
Washington, D.C. 20515

Or you can go straight to the source via computer. Both the Legislative and Executive branches have Web pages: www.House.gov, www.Senate.gov, and www.White House.gov.

## DON'T HESITATE TO PICK UP THE PHONE

By phone, you can call the Capitol Switchboard at (202) 224-3121. The switchboard can connect you with your Representative's or Senator's office.

The White House Switchboard is (202) 456-1414, and the White House Comments Line is (202) 456-1111.

Say who you are, why you're calling, give facts and background about the issue, state your position and why, say what you want, and use a pleasant but firm closing that lets them know you'll be contacting them further. Make sure you follow up with a letter.

My experience calling Senator Feinstein's office made it clear to me that such calls are expected and are treated with respect.

## WRITING FOR THE OP-ED PAGE

This is easier than you might think. If you have a strong idea or opinion about a public issue that you'd like to express, write it out. Write it well, communicating your personal experiences. Make your position clear from the beginning, get right to the subject, make your sentences relatively short. Be sure all names are correct and all quotations accurate. End your article with a forceful conclusion, and write your name, address, and phone numbers on your submission. A good op-ed piece is about 750 words, or three double-spaced typewritten pages. Write in the active voice, get your facts right, and make sure you're adding some new insight to the argument.

## MEETING WITH ELECTED OFFICIALS

Visiting elected officials is an important part of promoting our points of view. A citizen visiting his or her elected officials is visibly identifying himself or herself as a constituent or a voter. Because the official is focusing on you as an individual and as a voter, a visit will have a great impact.

One of the important ways of effecting change with elected officials is by building a strong relationship. Developing strong relationships with them is an important part of exercising our power in a democracy. It is especially important to develop relationships with staffs of elected officials. Elected officials and their staffs are eager to get information that they can use in speeches and when working with constituents.

1. Make an appointment by calling the elected official.
2. Indicate the issues you want to discuss.
3. Study the issues to be covered in the visit. Keep the discussion to one or perhaps two issues.

4. Keep the atmosphere friendly and open. You are there to exchange ideas; under no circumstances should you become angry.

5. Limit the time of the meeting. Don't let the conversation drag.

6. If you don't know the answer to a question the official asks you, just say so and explain that you'll get the information. Make sure you follow through.

7. Leave some information with the elected official on the issue. This will help him or her remember your visit.

8. Follow your visit with a thank-you note. Remember—your main objective is to establish a continuing dialogue with your elected officials.

## WORLD WIDE WEB: WWW.VOTE-SMART.ORG:

There is a wonderful website that is a kind of all-purpose citizen activism guide. At the Project Vote Smart webpage, www.vote-smart.org, entering your zip code will tell you not only who your elected officials are and their addresses but also everything from their voting records to their biographies to their main funding sources.

If you're online, this is a wonderful opportunity to learn how to express yourself and participate powerfully in the process.

## DON'T FORGET THE COMPANIES THEMSELVES

When you think a toy is dangerous, or a television show irresponsible, or a corporate position immoral, write the company and let them know. They register complaints more than you might think they do.

Look to the Appendix at the back of this book for ways you can contribute to the waves that create an ocean of power. At

my website, www.Marianne.com, you can join with others in
sharing your thoughts and experiences.

## How It Could Work

Liberals are correct that we need to actively help the poor, while
conservatives are correct that just giving them handouts makes
things worse. The culture of dependency is not good, but the
answer is not to abandon a population in dire crisis. Some of the
people we're most fed up with are the way they are *because*
they're in crisis. Our myriad social dysfunctions are not going to
go away just because we throw people off welfare and claim that
move as some tough-love stroke of genius.

There are nonprofit models of success all over America, dealing with the deepest layers of the social cancers that plague us.
They are usually faith-based operations in which community
activism occurs at the most grass-roots level. While it is true
that such work as theirs is superior to most governmental action,
that does not mean that there is no creative role for the government in supporting and complementing their efforts.

There is a difference between a lot of enthusiasm to do something, and an army set up to do it. President Roosevelt didn't
just say, "If you're in Germany this summer, kill a Nazi or
two, will ya?" The government didn't fight World War II—the
American people did—but the government certainly called up
the troops and coordinated the effort.

It's an interesting thing: in business, if someone is a success,
his or her work is used as a model throughout the organization.
But when it comes to social problems in this country, our government doesn't usually tap into our best resources in the civil
sector. Someone doing good work with gang members in Philadelphia? Oh, let's have him up for the State of the Union so the

President can wave to him from the rostrum. The camera will pick that up. That's good. She has success teaching poor kids to read in Oakland? Great, we can have the Mayor sit with her on the podium during a rally. There's a photo op here, I can feel it, absolutely.

That's far from inviting a person to sit at the table of power. Civil sector efforts should not be patronized by an arrogant governmental system. We need to declare national recovery, not just as a tired campaign slogan, but as seriously and powerfully as we at other times have declared war. And that means we need every able-bodied American to feel drawn to the effort. The American citizenry must be inspired to wage a peace as seriously as we used to be drafted to wage war. The effort itself must have a field to hold it, to give it traction. There should be an 800-number that any American can call—a high-tech setup whereby anyone can find out via phone or Internet where to go and what to do to help with whatever problem we feel moved to help with. It's going to take a lot more than a pep rally to get people involved in a massive effort to heal America; it will take a seriously coordinated effort—yes, involving money—but also involving the most sophisticated organizational and motivational wisdom.

Mentoring, for instance, is the only known antidote to juvenile delinquency. One hour spent with a responsible adult each week can turn a young person's life completely around, even if that adult is not a family member and even if the young person is already in his or her late teens. Millions of Americans would respond to an intelligent call to join a citizen crusade to mentor our young and otherwise repair the broken places in American society. They would do it if they actually knew where to go, who to call, and how their work might make a difference.

This is ridiculous. Look at the Cabinet: Why do we have a Secretary of Agriculture but no Secretary of Childhood and

Teen Development? Why do we have a Secretary of Commerce, but no Secretary of Poverty Eradication? Why do we have a Secretary of Transportation, but no Secretary of Citizenship? And I love how Health and Human Services have to share one seat at the table. Of course, Housing and Urban Development are small things too, so they can go together.

We have Cabinet Secretaries for those segments of society that make money. There was a time when this made sense, but it doesn't make sense anymore.

We still do in government what we no longer do in business: we make management functions more important than creative functions. That reality not only reflects an economic ordering of society, but an *old-fashioned* economic order.

The truth is, the country's mood doesn't react to the market so much as the market reacts to the country's mood. We keep trying to make more money in order to make things right, when the more modern reality is this: make things right in a higher sense, and out of that abundance more money will flow for everyone. If we seek first the kingdom of Heaven, all else will be added unto us.

## Mission Statement

The biggest problem with the U.S. government today is that it has no mission statement. There is no overriding sense of purpose, other than a vague sense of "handling whatever comes up." There is much ado about various pieces of a puzzle, but no one in government seems to have much sense of what the finished product is supposed to look like. There is no overarching vision. As the Bible says, "Where there is no vision, the people perish."

A national vision is a national goal. For any organization to work, there must be a goal at its core. Whether the goal is higher productivity, good given to the community, or artistic production, the most powerful tool for group productivity is a shared intentionality among the people who work for that goal.

We have not healed America, but not because our policies are too liberal or too conservative. We have not healed America because we have not, as a nation, decided to. As a society, we have not *decided* that we want to make America the happiest, most creative nation in the world. There are too many short-term economic interests still placed before that goal.

## The Magical Bird

When I had very little money, my mother used to say that I was the only poor philanthropist she had ever met. Every month I would take the various requests for charitable donations that came in the mail, and put them across my bed. I would read each request very carefully, as if my donation was going to *really matter*. I would think very seriously about how I was going to spend my 10 percent tithe to those less fortunate that month. We're talking about five, ten dollars, *maybe* more to these various charities. Every time I saw Danny Thomas with those kids at St. Jude's Hospital on late-night television, I felt that I, having given my $16 each month, was personally responsible for serious research being done on finding a cure for childhood leukemia.

It is not an accident, as the years went on, that the money multiplied. That story is not about money, but energy. All contribution matters, regardless of size. I never thought that I would necessarily have any more to give than I was giving then. I did not think my giving might some day matter more; to me, my giving mattered then.

All energy—all power—multiplies according to the seriousness of intention with which it is expressed. You don't have to be speaking in front of a Congressional investigation tomorrow for your opinion to matter. Your opinion matters now, if you express it. It is being registered by the universe, by invisible traces of energy that connect your every thought to every thing. The universe takes you as seriously as you take it. You're a player in this world if you play. But if you don't play, you will have the awful feeling that the world goes on without you. It's just a trick of the mind to sit out the process and then tell yourself that there isn't any room for you. Write your Congressman like it's the most important letter he or she is going to receive all month. Because, in a way, it is. It is *your* letter.

ABUNDANCE comes not from without but from within. Consciousness precedes matter. Our economic policy should be this: to teach and remind every American of his or her inestimable value and potential, to create the contexts in which those gifts are most easily mined, and then strictly adhere to the ethical standards by which each person is held accountable for what he or she does and does not do. Banks should not be at the center of our economic policy. The stock market should not be at the center of our economic policy. *We* should be at the center of our economic policy: our ideas, our creativity, our potential for genius.

We have been schooled in the ways of exploitation and greed. We were taught that this is the way to win, to sell the product, to get the ultimate reward. But the days are nearing an end when that kind of thinking will produce even a simulated version of abundance. It is thinking that is spiritually impoverished and will ultimately produce only material impoverishment.

The operative word in the phrase "wealth creation" is not *wealth* but *creation*. Our greatest untapped gold mine is the place within us where we learn to create material wealth out of the wealth of the spirit. And that we cannot do by making money our goal, because the spirit will not be bought. While counterintuitive to current social wisdom, it is our purity and not our lack of it that is the key to manifesting wealth. It is a riddle, of course, because once you say, "Okay, so I'll be pure if that will make me more money," then you've lost your purity. Money comes from energy. That energy is like a magical bird that flies away from greed, overattachment, and lack of integrity. Working on our characters is the most powerful way now to work on our careers.

When I was in my twenties, I worked many jobs. At one point, I was scooping soup at Salmagundi's restaurant in San Francisco. In walked a young man one day, an old friend I had not seen since high school, dressed in a pinstripe suit, out for lunch with his legal associates. He had been one of the smart kids at school, but so had I. I was traumatized to see him: I didn't want him to register the fact that while he was now a hot shot, I was scooping soup.

He was friendly to me, but there was pity on his face. I have never forgotten that moment.

For what had happened in Charles's life that had not happened in mine was that he had figured out how to make it in America. I had fallen through the cracks, though that was not supposed to happen given my family and background. I couldn't get myself to think the way I was told to think or move ahead in the ways I was supposed to move ahead. Yet I knew that day at Salmagundi's that I was carrying a diamond in my pocket. I hadn't gone to law school, but I had been traveling far and wide. I had experienced, while most of my friends were climbing ladders, realms of adventure that they thought they had to leave behind. I didn't know if I would ever get anywhere in the world, but I knew that there was an inner dimension to the life I was living that was brighter and cleaner than the world my friends were hailing as true success.

—

I have seen incredible things in my life, and one of them is that the spiritual diamond in my pocket became a key to success as the world defines it. Unknowingly, I had visited the void out of which comes overflowing materialization. That void, or no-thing, is the creative source of all abundance.

## Loaves and Fishes

We live in a society organized according to economic principles that no longer suit who we are. We are tied to this obsolete structure only because we have not yet *imagined* it any other way. The argument of a higher-consciousness perspective is not that money is unimportant, but that it can flow as easily from love as from fear. It is time for fear to surrender its dominance over human affairs. The creation of wealth can flow from an open heart as easily as it can flow from greed. That is why the story of the loaves and fishes is so potent.

Several years ago I was producing a fund-raiser for an AIDS organization in Los Angeles. Some of the city's top interior designers were contributing their time and efforts to create a huge showcase to be used as a charity auction. Before my first meeting with the designers an assistant said, "You're going to have to be careful with these people. They're all very successful, so they have huge egos. They're all stars, you know, and they're very competitive. Try to make each one feel that *they're* the one we really needed here."

As the designers introduced themselves, most of them gave me some version of the following: "Look, I'm glad to be here, and what you're doing is great. But what you have to know is that I am very busy, and I have very limited time to give to this project."

They sat next to each other in their chairs, but for the most part you could feel the emotional distance between them.

About half-way through the meeting I said, "Ladies and gentlemen, this is not business as usual. You are not here *competing* for business; you are *joining* to help people with AIDS." I thought I could feel some ears perking up. "We have all been trained to think of other people doing what we do as the competition. I understand that. But that model of thinking has absolutely no place here, except in a good sense, a friendly sense. If you keep yourselves separate from each other, everyone will lose. The organization will lose, which means people with AIDS in this town will lose and, to be honest, you'll lose. You'll lose at the very least an opportunity to have an intensely satisfying experience. This event should receive our very finest efforts because we are here to create a vortex of love so powerful that it is stronger even than the disease of AIDS."

The energy in the meeting transformed. The designers became a group of the most committed, gracious people I ever worked with. The same people who came to the meeting saying, "Look, I can only give an hour or two" became people working twelve- to fifteen-hour days, still at the site at three or four in the morning, making a charity auction one of the most glamorous events in town. We raised, on a shoestring budget where no one was even receiving production salaries, over a million dollars. Money flowed into that event, quite simply because it was filled with so much love.

All it takes is a slight introduction of a higher perspective to remind people who they really are. People *want* to rise to the occasion. In my work as a nonprofit organizer, I got at least as many thanks from volunteers as from clients of the organizations. What they had received was a sense of themselves as participants in something important; they were making a difference in people's lives. And that is what many of us deeply want, because a life devoid of service to others is a life devoid of meaning.

## They're Not Fun Anymore— Should We Still Call Them Parties?

The failure of American politics to engage us fully is not an inherent weakness in the American system of government, only in the entrenched political establishment that would have us believe we have no alternative to them. There's nothing in the Constitution that says, "You will be divided into two main political parties, Democrats and Republicans, and together they will determine the direction of the country, even if that direction is into the ground." Their shared dominance of our political system is merely a product of our own malaise. They're so big for no other reason than we've all played so small.

In his Farewell Address, although he himself could not be called nonpartisan, George Washington had the following to say regarding political parties:

> They serve to organize faction, to give it an artificial and extraordinary force; to put in the place of the delegated will of the Nation, the will of a party; often a small but artful and enterprising minority of the Community; and, according to the alternate triumphs of different parties, to make the public administration the Mirror of the ill concerted and incongrous projects of faction, rather than the organ of consistent and wholesome plans digested by common counsels and modified by mutual interests. However combinations or Associations of the above description may now and then answer popular ends, they are likely, in the course of time and things, to become potent engines, by which cunning,

ambitious and unprincipled men will be enabled to subvert the Power of the People, and to usurp for themselves the reins of Government; destroying afterwards the very engines which have lifted them to unjust dominion.

He added, "Let me now...warn you in the most solemn manner against the baneful effects of the spirit of party."

Power is beginning to recycle back to the citizen now, not because of a change in government but because of a change in us. The era of *passive citizenship* is over.

## The Current System

While the American political system should be a context for the discovery of solutions, the system itself is beset by some of our most severe wounds. The selfishness, violence, absence of teamwork, shortage of creative thinking, lack of courage to take risks, propensity to put the protection of entrenched interests before the pursuit of truth, obsolete hierarchical management systems, glorification of external resources, underemphasis on internal resources, lack of integrity and diminished standards of excellence that are all hallmarks of a crumbling system are, if anything, more prevalent in politics than in any other institution in America. A weakened structure cannot give us strength. Far from being a fount of answers, politics in America is a big part of our problem. If democracy is a river that would provide the water to help us spring back to life, current politics is a dam that holds the water back. It is a conversation stuck at the level of a shouting match, an adversarial us-versus-them debate of total polarization and very little synergy.

Instead of endeavoring to present the political issues of our time in as historically and socially significant ways as possible to ensure the deepest exercise of democracy, the political establishment has turned itself into a clone of the advertising industry and the workhorse of a ruling class. It works less to serve than to exploit us, to manipulate the electorate for the sake of its own power.

Neither Democrats nor Republicans seem to see the writing on the wall; perhaps it is still written in invisible ink. But it is bold and in caps nonetheless: our political parties have abdicated the sacred trust we placed in them and we are married to them in our minds no longer. They have undermined the moral authority of the American political system; we do not trust them any more. Their eviction notice had already been signed, though they seem not yet to have received it. We have emotionally pulled away. It is a mistake to think our lack of expressed anger at the consistency of sordid government dealings and the obvious selling out of the average American's greater good means we're not interested or that we do not care. What we feel in fact is more potent than anger; we feel the kind of detached disgust that is significant because it *isn't* angry. We're not even interested in struggling with them anymore. That's when you know that a marriage is over.

Most of us used to think, "If *my* political party was in power, then things wouldn't be this way." But we don't think that any more. They have both contracted the same virus. We are living, for the first time in our generation, at a moment in which a critical mass of the electorate feels "a plague on both their houses."

Political parties at their best stand for something: ideas about what the country should be, ideas about how to achieve that, and ways for the average citizen to be involved in the effort. The average American citizen today can feel that we are mainly seen by the major parties as mere cannon fodder in their fights with each other over the prizes of office. When parties are what they should be, people are legitimately willing to commit their loyalty. Today, this is less and less true.

Our political energy is up for grabs, or for reinvention. We no longer feel positively connected to the system as it is. The largest voting bloc in America is independent, and it's growing. We are open to the possibility that there might be a better way.

## Serious About Democracy

If we were serious about democracy, voting eligibility would occur automatically on an American citizen's eighteenth birthday, voting would be held on a Saturday or a Sunday and possibly for more than one day, and the polls would be open twenty-four hours. It cannot be said that the current system *encourages* voter participation.

If we were serious about democracy, we would mandate free TV time for all candidates, where *they* are free to speak for themselves but their Madison Avenue handlers have to keep their paws off our brains. Our political candidates should not be sold like soda pop.

If we were serious about democracy, our legislators would not feel free to continuously avoid grappling with the challenge of limiting the influence of money on the electoral system. Americans have turned off to politics now because they know it's all just become a game. What we need to remember, however, is that while current politics *is* just a game, democracy is not. It's as though we own a house and we do not like the current tenants. You don't avoid the house or burn down the house; you remove the tenants. *N'est-ce pas?*

• • •

———

I remember when Lamar Alexander was running for President, and he wore a red plaid shirt *in order to stand out.* To show he was *different,* you understand. And in a way, he was right. American politics has become like Russia's grocery store shelves, while Russian politics has become like American grocery store shelves. We have variety at the store, but a scary level of sameness in our political pickings, while Russians still have very little variety for the consumer to choose from, but a wide spectrum of political viewpoints represented in their political process.

The Democratic-Republican machinery is practically a political mafia in America, and the media act like their puppets. God forbid Americans should get to seriously hear what various third-party candidates actually have to say. During the 1996 Presidential elections, the "Debate Commission" (who *are* these guys?—former Democratic and Republican operatives, of course) determined that only Clinton and Dole could participate in the debates because they were the only *serious* candidates. I love this; isn't this what they used to do in the Communist world—determine people's choices for them? Capitalism keeps us so busy with a variety of choices concerning the things we buy, that we don't stop to ask ourselves why it is that we get so little to choose from in politics. We wouldn't stand for it in our favorite store. We shouldn't stand for it in politics.

During the 1996 Presidential election, there was no serious debate regarding race, education, or the welfare of America's children. Why? The candidates didn't have to go there. The current system created a giant red herring called the balanced budget, and we, the people, swallowed it hook, line and sinker.

## And in the Middle of the Party They Bring Out the Cake

I heard quite a few people speaking on television before the last Presidential election, bemoaning the choice between Clinton and Dole, unhappy that neither candidate represented their highest hopes. And yet most Americans, even if there is a third-party candidate who more nearly expresses their views, are afraid to vote for that person lest the Democrat or Republican who most offends them might then win. This makes logical sense, but not quantum sense. Democracy should mean that we are cowed by nothing and no one. We need to retrieve our capacity to say "This is what *I* think." Remember when we were kids and we used to say all the time, "This is a free country!!"

## The No-Flow of Information

Secrecy and good PR are the armor behind which Goliath hides, and it is extremely important that we see this. It isn't fun to think about, but what will *really* not be fun is what will happen if we don't. It is not an issue but a condition that poses the greatest danger to America.

The following account is from *The New York Times*. In the May 1997 newsletter of the Organization of American Historians, Professor George Herring of the University of Kentucky, who served for six years on a CIA advisory panel set up to declassify records on the agency's most famous covert operations, called the agency's now years-long promises of openness "a carefully nurtured myth," a "brilliant public relations snow job" devised to make people think that our intelligence agencies are becoming more open, at a time when in fact they are becoming more closed.

Even the CIA's yearly espionage budget is secret. It's believed to be somewhere in the vicinity of $29 billion a year, and the Federation of American Scientists is suing the CIA to get it to reveal the specific number of the "black budget." President Clinton said in 1996 that he believes the number should be published, and his press secretary said this proved "the President's determination to promote openness in the intelligence community." Then the CIA agreed that publishing the number was not a problem. But it remains classified.

What does this have to do with your life and mine? Do the details of electronic eavesdropping and spy satellites really matter anyway? Yes, they do. First, let's remember that for all their gargantuan budgets and high-secret carryings on, these people didn't know that the Iron Curtain was about to fall. So the trust factor should be down, don't you think? What exactly do these people do with all that money that could be going to build and support our schools, create jobs, and help provide opportunities for Americans? And why for a minute should a reasonable human being assume that these people are going all over the world looking at absolutely anything they want to, spending whatever money they want to in complete secrecy—and then stop like good Boy Scouts when it comes to peeking at you and me? Secrecy is a bulwark of totalitarianism, and the free flow of information is a bulwark of democracy. U.S. government operations are becoming more and more secretive every day.

There are people in the government who realize all this, and who themselves try hard to change it. But they are for the most part overruled, even discredited for their efforts. Some of them have even been punished for trying to blow the whistle.

In 1913, the Lloyd-LaFollette Act was passed in Congress. It says that "the right of Federal employees to furnish information to either House of Congress, or to a committee or member thereof, may not be interfered with or denied." The basic message of that law has been repeated in several acts of Congress since 1987.

In plain English, what that means is that if someone is working for the CIA, the FBI, or any other department of government and he or she sees something that stinks—that is against the law, that violates what Americans like to *think* this country *stands* for —then the individual can call up his or her Congressman, or the appropriate Senator, or whomever, and tell what he or she knows. This is part of the free flow of information.

But in 1996, Richard Nuccio, a senior State Department official charged with leading our efforts to end the war in Guatemala, found that he had been mistaken when he had denied before Congress an American woman's claim that her husband had been killed by agents connected to the CIA in Guatemala. Upon reading a classified CIA document from 1993, he found that indeed the woman was correct; her husband had been tortured and killed by CIA-linked operatives. So he did the right thing, morally as well as legally: he contacted then-Representative Robert Torricelli of New Jersey and let him know.

So what happened to Richard Nuccio? Well, he had been a friend to his country, certainly, but not to the CIA. It was claimed by the Bush administration, and is now claimed by the Clinton administration, that *a U.S. Government official can only reveal information to Congress if he or she has been given "official approval" to do so.* Mr. Nuccio's high-security clearance was withdrawn (like, right—*he's* the risk); ultimately, he was so squeezed out of power that he resigned his job.

Given that the separation of powers among the three branches of the federal government is one of our Constitution's most important elements, certainly our Founders would be enraged.

What is significant in America today is that we're not. The media barely cover these things. We have allowed our narcissism and lethargy to diminish our capacity for political outrage. If this continues, our generation will be remembered as the one that brought the entire democratic experiment to a halt.

Were people that I know to read the Richard Nuccio story, they would shake their heads with a definite look of "Ain't it awful. It's disgusting that this happened." But we need another synapse after that. What is *really* awful is how muted our dissatisfaction is. For such a loud nation, we're unbelievably quiet about things that matter very deeply. Most of us feel so disconnected from the democratic process that we're just standing here watching, while our basic rights as a democratic society are being taken away right in front of our eyes.

The holistic political question is this: what's going on right now, at this moment, in the mind of the reader who read the last few paragraphs? Some might think, "Big deal, it doesn't matter if people can't freely talk to Congress." But many would think otherwise. The words *secrecy* and *government* are an extremely dangerous combination. To legally create, maintain, and perpetuate their connection puts your freedom, and mine, way too close to the line.

## What Should I Do?

Sitting around waiting for someone to tell us what to do is not the pulse of the moment or in keeping with the gift of democracy. The zeitgeist now is to do the thing that each of us knows is the one pure thing that stands before us on the road of life, the undone task of personal growth or community involvement that paves the way to our higher becoming. That is the critical issue in democracy today: that each of us rises to the nobler places within us, to the stuff of integrity, excellence, and love.

No one can lift the fog in your mind except you, yourself. Some of us need to read more; some of us need to pray more; some of us need to go to therapy; some of us need to get a job; some of us need to be more generous; some of us need to participate more fully in our family or our community; some of us need to forgive someone; some of us need to ask forgiveness; almost all of us need to become more politically involved. All of us need to do something that we know is the next step in the journey of our soul's unfoldment, and most of us know deep in our hearts what that is.

Leadership itself is changing, from a top-down, old-fashioned Newtonian model of someone acting on a system from the outside to try to change it, to a new-paradigm image of change from within. The primary responsibility of leadership in the era now upon us is to hold a space for the genius of others. In the presence of someone who believes in us, we move more quickly into who we might become. But the major work to be done is still up to each of us.

In the words of Francis Bacon, "Knowledge is power." There are universal laws of consciousness that apply to social change. I think of them as the Rules of Renaissance.

1. It is always our prerogative, as individuals and as nations, to choose again: to say no to a direction we've been moving in and yes to a new one. Our greatest power is our capacity to change our minds.
2. Alignment with higher principle is always supported by invisible forces.

3. If an energy is not in alignment with divine Truth, it is ultimately temporary. It will not last forever, and is more vulnerable than it appears.

4. The universe is impersonally invested in evolving toward goodness, and uses any available conduit for the purposes of doing so. Willingness to be so used, activates the conduit. You're as good for the job as anyone else, and your past is totally irrelevant.

In the words of Dr. King, "Even though the arc of the moral universe is long, it bends toward justice."

5. Don't expect the old order to like you.

6. A life of love and effort on behalf of the collective good promises the satisfaction of knowing that you are doing what you were born to do. You are not, however, promised specific results as you might define them.

7. Your happiness regarding the reality that's coming is a more potent method of social conversion than is your anger regarding the reality now.

As my father used to say, "You know. Now do."

# 7

# HOME

## OF THE

# BRAVE

*"And crown thy good with brotherhood..."*
——FROM
''AMERICA THE BEAUTIFUL''

I HEARD U.S. Congressman Walter Capps tell the following story. It is a traditional rabbinical tale.

A rabbi was giving instruction to some children, when he posed this question: how do you know the night is over and the day has come? Puzzled, the children took some time to answer. Then one of them ventured, "You know the night is over and the day has come when, at dawn, you look out at a tree, and you can tell whether it is an apple or a pear tree." The rabbi acknowledged this response, but repeated the question. A second student offered, "You know the night is over and the day has come when you see an animal in the distance, and you can tell whether it is a donkey or a horse." The rabbi acknowledged this response too, then repeated the question. At this the students, too puzzled to know how to answer, asked the rabbi to solve the dilemma he had posed. The rabbi said, "You know the night is over and the day has come when you look into the eyes of any human being, and you see there your brother or your sister; for, if you do not see your brother or your sister, it is still night—the day hasn't come."

Dr. King said this in the 1960s:

We are witnessing in our day the birth of a new age, with a new structure of freedom and justice.

———

Now, as we face the fact of this new, emerging world, we must face the responsibilities that come along with it. A new age brings with it new challenges....

First, we are challenged to rise above the narrow confines of our individualistic concerns to the broader concerns of all humanity. The new world is a world of geographical togetherness. This means that no individual or nation can live alone. We must all learn to live together, or we will be forced to die together.

... Through our scientific genius we have made of the world a neighborhood; now through our moral and spiritual genius we must make of it a brotherhood. We are all involved in the single process. Whatever affects one directly affects all indirectly. We are all links in the great chain of humanity.... We have before us the glorious opportunity to inject a new dimension of love into the veins of our civilization.

## The Whole World in His Hands

If we could, at this time, shrink the earth's population to a village of precisely 100 people, with all existing human ratios remaining the same, it would look like this:

- There would be 57 Asians, 21 Europeans, 14 from the Western Hemisphere (North and South), and 8 Africans.
- 70 would be nonwhite; 30 white.
- 70 would be non-Christian; 30 Christian.
- Fifty percent of the entire world wealth would be in the hands of only 6 people. All 6 would be citizens of the United States.
- 70 would be unable to read.
- 50 would suffer from malnutrition.
- 80 would live in substandard housing.
- Only 1 would have a college education.

# American Eyes

I've led several group tours abroad. It has been one of my most satisfying professional experiences, watching it dawn on a group of Americans that the world outside our borders isn't quite what they thought. We tend to have a very myopic worldview in America.

Even our most boastful President, Theodore Roosevelt, knew better. He used to bring guests at his home, Sagamore Hill, on Long Island, out onto the lawn on a fine, clear summer night and say, "Look, look at the stars." They'd just stand and look for minutes or even hours. Then Roosevelt would flash his famous grin and say, "All right, I think we feel insignificant enough now —let's go to bed."

America needs a truer sense of our relationship to a world much larger than we are. We are neither alone nor better than anyone else. Americans are so propagandized to think that certain things are the better way simply because they are our way. This places us in almost ridiculous situations vis-à-vis the rest of the world, and other nations tend to look at us with rolled eyes more than most Americans seem to have any idea. We are a two-hundred-year-old society in the habit of giving lectures about high civilization to people who have been around for hundreds, even thousands of years. Our own homelessness, poverty, violence, and crisis in health care make living in certain other nations look like a day at the beach compared to America, yet we hold forth on how the citizens of those nations could have what we have, if only they would do what we do.

The average American is less well-read and informed about world events and situations than are our European counterparts, our children are less well educated, and we are the only Western industrialized nation that does not have universal health care.

We lecture others about human rights (sometimes legitimately), while other nations regard health care as a human right. We go about singing the praises of democracy, but we don't ask ourselves why, if we love it so much, we don't make it easier for people to vote. We talk endlessly about family values in this country, while taking less good care of our children than any other nation with similar resources to do so.

"I am certain," said President Kennedy, "that after the dust of centuries has passed from our cities, we, too, will be remembered not for victories or defeats in battle or politics, but for our contribution to the human spirit."

## Soldiers of Peace

The guardians of the status quo intimidate us with their analytical, left-brain power. It is not there, but in our hearts and our imaginations that we will find a way to renew the world. When King Saul offered young David his armor to wear in doing battle with the giant, David put it on but then removed it. He wasn't comfortable with the old way of battle: he had to trust his own heart, and do things another way.

Soldiers of peace will create a new world.

I saw a photograph on the front page of a newspaper in the fall of 1996, showing an American soldier in Bosnia physically keeping apart two women who were having a violent argument. One woman was a Muslim seeking to return to her home, and the other was a Serb trying to keep her away. The soldier, one of America's "peacekeepers" in the region, was a valiant referee.

And yet I thought, as I looked at that picture, wouldn't it be wonderful if the soldier himself had the tools to actually help these women heal their relationship? The armies and police of our future will include conflict resolution as a part of their training. In some places, they already do. Then we will be most prepared to help those in the Middle East, Ireland, Bosnia, East Los Angeles, Washington, D.C., and elsewhere find the capacity to move beyond the barriers that divide us so dangerously to the peace that lies beyond.

The fact that the term "peacekeeper" was invented means our society has evolved to the point where we are ready to embrace its potential meaning. Conflict resolution is to peace what guns are to war. The full actualization of its potential, however, remains on the horizon.

IMAGINE if every member of the United Nations kept one delegate permanently stationed there to spend all day silently blessing every other nation of the world. Imagine that, instead of soldiers of war, we had soldiers of peace: lines of people committed to universal love, meditating on peace for the rest of the world, studied and practiced in the cultural, educational, artistic, philosophical, and diplomatic arts of waging peace. Imagine a world in which war no longer exists. That world is not just around the corner, obviously. But we begin a journey of a thousand miles by taking one step. "More than an end to war, we want an end to the beginnings of all wars," wrote President Franklin Roosevelt, who died before delivering this speech for a Jefferson Day broadcast in 1945. Only thoughts of peace can eradicate the beginnings of war. The dominant thinking in international politics is not yet based on a policy of peace creation. NATO, for instance, is not a creator or even a keeper of the peace. It merely manages the effects of a war mentality.

Only a new political sensibility arising throughout the world can counter the war machine always lurking in the background of international politics. We must be bold enough to state what kind of world we want, instead of always trying to accomplish small gains within a system we know is ultimately destructive.

Traveling in India with a group of fellow Americans, I spent quite a bit of time in meditation and prayer near the Taj Mahal. There is a mosque right next to the Taj, and all true houses of worship, of whatever religion, hold spiritual power for people of faith. We had already found that, while we were meditating, Indian people would frequently come and join us, sit down in the group and start meditating with us as though it was the most natural thing in the world. One particular day, as we came out of a deep period of silence, a line of about thirty or so Indians stood at the edge of the patio where we sat. We stood as if in a trance and faced our Indian counterparts. What followed, in a sublime silence, was an exchange of mutual honor and respect that was almost mind-altering. All of us were profoundly moved.

In a meeting with His Holiness the Dalai Lama, I learned some things about foreign policy. His Holiness told me that a German physicist had said to him that we should remove the concept of "foreign policy" from our minds, and think of all nations as our "domestic partners."

We shouldn't be overimpressed by terms like "foreign policy," huge secretive counterintelligence agencies, and government departments that play the world like a giant chessboard and view it as no more than a game we're trying to win. *Our* consciousness should drive *them;* their consciousness shouldn't drive *us.*

According to the esoteric wisdom of the ages, every nation carries with it a facet of divine light as it streams from the Mind of God to earth. The soulful function associated with the United States is to "light the way."

We must find again our own light. We are no longer known around the world as the great champion of democracy. We are known as the great underminer of communism, to be sure, but that is far from synonymous with being a champion of democracy. We have sabotaged democratic governments as well as communist governments when they did not move in the direction we wanted them to move, and even today we sell out oppressed democratic forces for a greater market share in their country's economies.

"The people of the world," the Dalai Lama told me, "no longer look at America as a champion of democracy. Too many times we have seen you take the side of undemocratic forces."

In our international relations, we have become in most ways just like any other world player, seeking political and economic advantage, manipulating events according to what some would call our "vital national interests," though those interests seem clearly defined more by economics than values.

## Egyptian Eyes

Another interesting thing happened to me at the Taj Mahal. The Mufti—Egypt's highest Muslim cleric—was visiting Agra at the time, and happened to pass our group as he walked through the area with his entourage. Seeing a group of Westerners meditating at the Taj Mahal made him curious, and he asked who we were. Upon being told we were a group of Christians and Jews from the United States, many of us clergy, he asked if he could meet with a small group of us later at his hotel.

The meeting was very formal and the Mufti spoke through an interpreter. His basic message to us was this: "I am aware that for most Americans, when you hear the word *Islamic*, you usually hear the word *terrorist* in the same sentence. I wanted to speak with you to make sure you understand that Islam is a religion of peace.

"Every people has a dark element—a group which does not

represent the larger group well. Obviously, we have ours. But please do not think that Islamic terrorists represent true Islam, any more than Christians who commit violence in the name of God represent true Christianity, or Jews who commit violence in the name of God represent true Judaism."

He offered to send someone to speak to our whole group about Islam any time we were visiting Egypt, that we might learn more about Islam and its message to the world. I did go to Egypt again several months after my trip to India. Our group heard a lecture on Islam while we were there, and we came to understand more deeply the larger religious story trying to reveal itself to the human heart.

After our meeting with the Mufti, as I made my way through the lobby of the hotel, one of the Egyptians who was attending His Eminence tapped me on the shoulder and asked if we could speak. In the most gentle, gracious tones, he said that he wanted to tell me something.

During the very week that we were in India, a group of Indian women threatened to burn themselves alive in protest of the Miss Universe pageant being held in New Delhi. What they were protesting was the imposition of Western standards of beauty on Indian women, expressing the resentment that many Indians—indeed, many people throughout the Third World—feel toward America.

The Egyptian diplomat whom I met in the lobby of the hotel in Agra said to me, "I do not mean this as a criticism of the United States. I know the Americans are good men and women. But please try to make them understand: many people in my part of the world feel that they have been forced to try to keep up with you, in a race that we do not really care to run. Your technology is amazing, but America seems spiritually polluted to many of us. Your ways are not our ways, and while we were tempted for a while to think that your ways *should* be our ways, we do not think that way anymore.

"This is the problem, Ms. Williamson, and there will be terrible consequences in the world if Americans do not come to understand this. Islamic terrorists have had such success—if you would call their campaigns a success—because they have been able to persuade millions of peasants that America is bad. It was not too difficult to do, Ms. Williamson. All they have to do is describe the television programs you export to this part of the world, and millions of our people are very horrified.

"Your government does not understand. They do not see how the people feel. We need the American people to understand. Perhaps you will bring more Americans to our part of the world. If they come to understand us, then they will respect us. We would feel that respect, and then I don't think that the terrorists would have such success. This is not a job the CIA can do. It is only a job which people can do."

I thanked him for telling me those things, and I promised him I would pass the information on.


AMERICA is not now the home of the brave, but I think we are the home of those who wish to be brave.

Coming back from Cairo to JFK Airport at the beginning of 1997, I handed my landing card to the agent at the Customs counter. He read what I had written.

"What do you do?" he asked me.

"I'm a writer," I replied.

"What do you write?"

"I'm writing a book called *The Healing of America*."

He looked at me. "Well, America is *shot*," he said.

I didn't say anything.

"You ought to come here for a day, to do research for your book. Come see what I see. These people are terrible."

I was rather shocked. "Do you mean immigrants?"

"Well," he hesitated, "Americans are the worst. But they're all bad. I came here wanting to like everybody, you know, thinking everybody's fairly decent. But immigrants now aren't like the immigrants fifty years ago. They might be good when they first come here, but after being around Americans for a couple of months, they're just as bad as we are."

I thought for a few moments, then ventured a comment. "Well, I have an idea that might help."

"Really?" he asked.

"When people come up to you here, look them in the eye and silently say, 'The goodness in me salutes the goodness in you.' "

He thought for a moment.

"Would that maybe really work, you think?"

"Oh, yes," I said. "Really."

He smiled and stamped my card, showing me which way to exit.

As I reached the door leading out, I looked back at the agent. He was looking at me. We both stood still for a moment, and both of us were silent.

The ancient Egyptians believed the stars in our eyes are reflections of the stars in the sky, and that the stars in the sky are our home. I had heard that in Egypt, but I learned it's true in America. I saw the stars in my brother's eyes, and I knew that I was home.

# APPENDIX A

## RESOURCES FOR ACTIVISM

*"Those who wish to reap the blessings of liberty must undergo the fatigues of supporting it."*

— THOMAS PAINE

# Organizations

**Earthsave International**
706 Frederick Street
Santa Cruz, CA 95062-2205
Phone (408) 423-4069
Web page: www.earthsave.org

**Sojourner magazine**
2401 Fifteenth Street NW
Washington, D.C. 20009
Phone: (202) 328-8842

**Center for Mind-Body Medicine**
5225 Connecticut Avenue,
No. 414
Washington, D.C. 20015
Phone: (202) 966-7338
Fax: (202) 966-2589

**Center For Visionary
Leadership**
3408 Wisconsin Avenue NW,
Suite 200
Washington, D.C. 20016
Phone: (202) 237-2800
Fax: (202) 237-1339

**Friends Committee on
National Legislation**
245 Second Street NE
Washington, D.C. 20002
Phone: (202) 547-6000
Legislative Action Message:
(202) 547-4343
Web page: www.fcnl.org

**People for the American Way**
People for the American Way is a grass-roots organization dedicated
to fighting for "pluralism, individuality, freedom of thought,
expression, and religion, a sense of community, and tolerance and
compassion for others."
2000 M Street NW, Suite 400
Washington, D.C. 20036
Phone: (202) 467-4999
Web page: www.pfaw.org

**American Civil Liberties Union**
An organization dedicated to protecting individual liberties as stipulated in the Bill of Rights.
132 West Forty-third Street
New York, NY 10036-6599
Phone: (212) 549-2500
Web page: www.aclu.org

**Public Citizen**
The original watchdog organization, founded by Ralph Nader, this organization is the "consumer's eyes and ears in Washington."
1600 Twentieth Street NW
Washington, D.C. 20009
Phone: (202) 558-1000
Web page: www.citizen.org

**Southern Poverty Law Center**
400 Washington Ave.
Montgomery, AL 36104
Phone: (334) 264-0286
Fax: (334) 264-0629
Web Page: www.splcenter.org

**Rainforest Action Network**
221 Pine Street, Suite 500
San Francisco, CA 94104
Phone: 1-800-989-7246
Fax: (415) 398-2732
Web page: www.ran.org

**Tikkun** *magazine*
26 Fell Street
San Francisco, CA 94102
Phone: (415) 575-1200
Fax: (415) 575-1434

**Natural Step**
4000 Bridgeway, Suite 102
Sausalito, CA 94965
Phone: (415) 332-9394
Fax: (415) 332-9395
Web page: www.emis.com/tns

**We the People**
200 Harrison Street
Oakland, CA 94607
Phone: (510) 836-3273
1-800-426-1112
Fax: (510) 836-8797
Web page: www.wtp.org

**Common Cause**
1250 Connecticut Avenue NW
Washington, DC 20036
Phone: (202) 833-1200
Web page:
www.commoncause.org

**Co-op America**
1612 K Street NW, No. 600
Washington, DC 20006
Phone: (202) 872-5307
Web page: www.coopamerica.org

# Appendix B

~~~~~~~

# FOUNDING
# DOCUMENTS

# Declaration of Independence

When in the course of human events it becomes necessary for one people to dissolve the political bands which have connected them with another, and to assume among the powers of the earth, the separate and equal station to which the Laws of Nature and of Nature's God entitle them, a decent respect to the opinions of mankind requires that they should declare the causes which impel them to the separation.

We hold these truths to be self-evident, that all men are created equal, that they are endowed by their Creator with certain unalienable rights, that among these are life, liberty and the pursuit of happiness. That to secure these rights, governments are instituted among men, deriving their just powers from the consent of the governed. That whenever any form of government becomes destructive of these ends, it is the right of the people to alter or to abolish it, and to institute new government, laying its foundation on such principles and organizing its powers in such form, as to them shall seem most likely to effect their safety and happiness. Prudence, indeed, will dictate that governments long established should not be changed for light and transient causes; and accordingly all experience hath shown, that mankind are more disposed to suffer, while evils are sufferable, than to right themselves by abolishing the forms to which they are accustomed. But when a long train of abuses and usurpations, pursuing invariably the same object, evinces a design to reduce them under absolute despotism, it is their right, it is their duty, to throw off such government, and to provide new guards for their future security. Such has been the patient sufferance of these Colonies; and such is now the necessity which constrains them to alter their former systems of government. The history of the present King of Great Britain is a history of repeated injuries and usurpations, all having, in direct object, the establishment of an absolute tyranny over these States. To prove this, let facts be submitted to a candid world.

He has refused his assent to laws, the most wholesome and necessary for the public good.

He has forbidden his Governors to pass laws of immediate and pressing importance, unless suspended in their operation till his assent should be obtained; and when so suspended, he has utterly neglected to attend to them.

He has refused to pass other laws for the accommodation of large districts of people, unless those people would relinquish the right of representation in the legislature, a right inestimable to them and formidable to tyrants only.

He has called together legislative bodies at places unusual, uncomfortable, and distant from the depository of their public records, for the sole purpose of fatiguing them into compliance with his measures.

He has dissolved representative houses repeatedly, for opposing with manly firmness his invasions on the rights of the people.

He has refused for a long time, after such dissolutions, to cause others to be elected; whereby the legislative powers, incapable of annihilation, have returned to the people at large for their exercise; the State remaining in the meantime exposed to all the dangers of invasion from without and convulsions within.

He has endeavoured to prevent the population of these States; for that purpose obstructing the laws of naturalization of foreigners; refusing to pass others to encourage their migration hither, and raising the conditions of new appropriations of lands.

He has obstructed the administration of justice, by refusing his assent to laws for establishing judiciary powers.

He has made judges dependent on his will alone, for the tenure of their offices, and the amount and payment of their salaries.

He has erected a multitude of new offices, and sent hither swarms of officers to harass our people, and eat out their substance.

He has kept among us, in times of peace, standing armies without the consent of our legislatures.

He has affected to render the military independent of, and superior to, the civil power.

He has combined with others to subject us to a jurisdiction foreign to our constitution, and unacknowledged by our laws; giving his assent to their acts of pretended legislation:

For quartering large bodies of armed troops among us:

For protecting them, by a mock trial, from punishment for any murders which they should commit on the inhabitants of these States:

For cutting off our trade with all parts of the world:

For imposing taxes on us without our consent:

For depriving us, in many cases, of the benefits of trial by jury:

For transporting us beyond seas to be tried for pretended offences:

For abolishing the free system of English laws in a neighbouring Province, establishing therein an arbitrary government, and enlarging its boundaries so as to render it at once an example and fit instrument for introducing the same absolute rule into these Colonies:

For taking away our Charters, abolishing our most valuable laws, and altering fundamentally the forms of our governments:

For suspending our own legislatures, and declaring themselves invested with power to legislate for us in all cases whatsoever.

He had abdicated government here, by declaring us out of his protection and waging war against us.

He has plundered our seas, ravaged our coasts, burnt our towns, and destroyed the lives of our people.

He is, at this time, transporting large armies of foreign mercenaries to complete the works of death, desolation and tyranny, already begun, with circumstances of cruelty and perfidy scarcely paralleled in the most barbarous ages, and totally unworthy the head of a civilized nation.

He has constrained our fellow citizens taken captive on the high seas to bear arms against their country, to become the executioners of their friends and brethren, or to fall themselves by their hands.

He has excited domestic insurrections amongst us, and has endeavoured to bring on the inhabitants of our frontiers, the merciless Indian savages, whose known rule of warfare is an undistinguished destruction of all ages, sexes, and conditions.

In every stage of these oppressions we have petitioned for redress in the most humble terms: our repeated petitions have been answered only by repeated injury. A prince whose character is thus marked by every act which may define a tyrant is unfit to be the ruler of a free people.

Nor have we been wanting in attention to our British brethren. We have warned them from time to time of attempts by their legislature to extend an unwarrantable jurisdiction over us. We have reminded them of the circumstances of our emigration and settlement here. We have appealed to their native justice and magnanimity, and we have conjured them by the ties of our common kindred to disavow these usurpations, which would inevitably interrupt our connections and correspondence. They too have been deaf to the voice of justice and of consanguinity. We must, therefore, acquiesce in the necessity, which denounces our separation, and hold them, as we hold the rest of mankind, enemies in war, in peace, friends.

We, therefore, the Representatives of the United States of America, in General Congress assembled, appealing to the Supreme Judge of the world for the rectitude of our intentions, do, in the name, and by authority of the good people of these Colonies, solemnly publish and declare, That these United Colonies are, and of right ought to be, Free and Independent States; that they are absolved from all allegiance to the British Crown, and that all political connection between them and the State of Great Britain, is and ought to be totally dissolved; and that as Free and Independent States, they have full power to levy war, conclude peace, contract alliances, establish commerce, and to do all other acts and things which Independent States may of right do. And for the support of this declaration, with a firm reliance on the protection of Divine Providence, we mutually pledge to each other our lives, our fortunes, and our sacred honor.

*John Hancock*

NEW HAMPSHIRE
*Josiah Bartlett*
*Wm. Whipple*
*Matthew Thornton*

RHODE ISLAND
*Step. Hopkins*
*William Ellery*

CONNECTICUT
*Roger Sherman*
*Sam'el Huntington*
*Wm. Williams*
*Oliver Wolcott*

NEW YORK
*Wm. Floyd*
*Phil. Livingston*
*Frans. Lewis*
*Lewis Morris*

NEW JERSEY
*Richd. Stockton*
*Jno. Witherspoon*
*Fras. Hopkinson*
*John Hart*
*Abra. Clark*

PENNSYLVANIA
*Robt. Morris*
*Benjamin Rush*
*Benja. Franklin*
*John Morton*
*Geo. Clymer*
*Jas. Smith*
*Geo. Taylor*
*James Wilson*
*Geo. Ross*

MASSACHUSETTS BAY
*Saml. Adams*
*John Adams*
*Robt. Treat Paine*
*Elbridge Gerry*

DELAWARE
*Caesar Rodney*
*Geo. Read*
*Tho. M'Kean*

MARYLAND
*Samuel Chase*
*Wm. Paca*
*Thos. Stone*
*Charles Carroll of Carrollton*

VIRGINIA
*George Wythe*
*Richard Henry Lee*
*Th. Jefferson*
*Benja. Harrison*
*Ths. Nelson, Jr.*
*Francis Lightfoot Lee*
*Carter Braxton*

NORTH CAROLINA
*Wm. Hooper*
*Joseph Hewes*
*John Penn*

SOUTH CAROLINA
*Edward Rutledge*
*Thos. Heyward, Junr.*
*Thomas Lynch, Junr.*
*Arthur Middleton*

GEORGIA
*Button Gwinnett*
*Lyman Hall*
*Geo. Walton*

# The Constitution of the
# United States of America

We, the people of the United States, in order to form a more perfect union, establish justice, insure domestic tranquility, provide for the common defense, promote the general welfare, and secure the blessings of liberty to ourselves and our posterity, do ordain and establish this Constitution for the United States of America.

## ARTICLE I

*Section 1.* All legislative powers herein granted shall be vested in a Congress of the United States, which shall consist of a Senate and House of Representatives.

*Section 2.* 1. The House of Representatives shall be composed of members chosen every second year by the people of the several States, and the electors in each State shall have the qualifications requisite for electors of the most numerous branch of the State legislature.

2. No person shall be a representative who shall not have attained to the age of twenty-five years, and been seven years a citizen of the United States, and who shall not, when elected, be an inhabitant of that State in which he shall be chosen.

3. Representatives and direct taxes shall be apportioned among the several States which may be included within this Union, according to their respective numbers, which shall be determined by adding to the whole number of free persons, including those bound to service for a term of years, and excluding Indians not taxed, *three fifths of all other persons.* The actual enumeration shall be made within three years after the first meeting of the Congress of the United States, and within every subsequent term of ten years, in such manner as they shall by law direct. The number of representatives shall not exceed one for

every thirty thousand, but each State shall have at least one representative; and until such enumeration shall be made, the State of New Hampshire shall be entitled to choose three, Massachusetts eight, Rhode Island and Providence Plantations one, Connecticut five, New York six, New Jersey four, Pennsylvania eight, Delaware one, Maryland six, Virginia ten, North Carolina five, South Carolina five, and Georgia three.

4. When vacancies happen in the representation from any State, the executive authority thereof shall issue writs of election to fill such vacancies.

5. The House of Representatives shall choose their speaker and other officers; and shall have the sole power of impeachment.

*Section 3.* 1. The Senate of the United States shall be composed of two senators from each State, *chosen by the legislature thereof,* for six years; and each senator shall have one vote.

2. Immediately after they shall be assembled in consequence of the first election, they shall be divided as equally as may be into three classes. The seats of the senators of the first class shall be vacated at the expiration of the second year, of the second class at the expiration of the fourth year, and of the third class at the expiration of the sixth year, so that one third may be chosen every second year; and if vacancies happen by resignation, or otherwise, during the recess of the legislature of any State, the executive thereof may make temporary appointments until the next meeting of the legislature, which shall then fill such vacancies.

3. No person shall be a senator who shall not have attained to the age of thirty years, and been nine years a citizen of the United States, and who shall not, when elected, be an inhabitant of that State for which he shall be chosen.

4. The Vice-President of the United States shall be President of the Senate, but shall have no vote, unless they be equally divided.

5. The Senate shall choose their other officers, and also a president *pro tempore,* in the absence of the Vice-President, or when he shall exercise the office of the President of the United States.

6. The Senate shall have the sole power to try all impeachments. When sitting for that purpose, they shall be on oath or affirmation. When the President of the United States is tried, the chief justice shall preside: and no person shall be convicted without the concurrence of two thirds of the members present.

7. Judgment in cases of impeachment shall not extend further than to removal from office, and disqualifications to hold and enjoy any office of honor, trust or profit under the United States: but the party convicted shall nevertheless be liable and subject to indictment, trial, judgment and punishment, according to law.

*Section 4.* 1. The times, places, and manner of holding elections for senators and representatives, shall be prescribed in each state by the legislature thereof; but the Congress may at any time by law make or alter such regulations, except as to the places of choosing senators.

2. The Congress shall assemble at least once in every year, and such meeting shall be on the first Monday in December, unless they shall by law appoint a different day.

*Section 5.* 1. Each House shall be the judge of the elections, returns and qualifications of its own members, and a majority of each shall constitute a quorum to do business; but a smaller number may adjourn from day to day, and may be authorized to compel the attendance of absent members, in such manner, and under such penalties as each House may provide.

2. Each House may determine the rules of its proceedings, punish its members for disorderly behavior, and, with the concurrence of two thirds, expel a member.

3. Each House shall keep a journal of its proceedings, and from time to time publish the same, excepting such parts as may in their judgment require secrecy; and the yeas and nays of the members of either House on any question shall, at the desire of one fifth of those present, be entered on the journal.

4. Neither House, during the session of Congress, shall, without the consent of the other, adjourn for more than three days, nor to any other place than that in which the two Houses shall be sitting.

*Section 6.* 1. The senators and representatives shall receive a compensation for their services, to be ascertained by law, and paid out of the Treasury of the United States. They shall in all cases, except treason, felony, and breach of the peace, be privileged from arrest during their attendance at the session of their respective Houses, and in going to and returning from the same; and for any speech or debate in either House, they shall not be questioned in any other place.

2. No senator or representative shall, during the time for which he was elected, be appointed to any civil office under the authority of the United States, which shall have been created, or the emoluments

whereof shall have been increased during such time; and no person holding any office under the United States shall be a member of either House during his continuance in office.

*Section 7.* 1. All bills for raising revenue shall originate in the House of Representatives; but the Senate may propose or concur with amendments as on other bills.

2. Every bill which shall have passed the House of Representatives and the Senate, shall, before it becomes a law, be presented to the President of the United States; if he approve he shall sign it, but if not he shall return it, with his objections, to that House in which it shall have originated, who shall enter the objections at large on their journal, and proceed to reconsider it. If after such reconsideration two thirds of that House shall agree to pass the bill, it shall be sent, together with the objections, to the other House, by which it shall likewise be reconsidered, and if approved by two thirds of that House, it shall become a law. But in all such cases the votes of both Houses shall be determined by yeas and nays, and the names of the persons voting for and against the bill shall be entered on the journal of each House respectively. If any bill shall not be returned by the President within ten days (Sundays excepted) after it shall have been presented to him, the same shall be a law, in like manner as if he had signed it, unless the Congress by their adjournment prevent its return, in which case it shall not be a law.

3. Every order, resolution, or vote to which the concurrence of the Senate and the House of Representatives may be necessary (except on a question of adjournment) shall be presented to the President of the United States; and before the same shall take effect, shall be approved by him, or being disapproved by him, shall be repassed by two thirds of the Senate and House of Representatives, according to the rules and limitations prescribed in the case of a bill.

*Section 8.* The Congress shall have the power

1. To lay and collect taxes, duties, imposts, and excises, to pay the debts and provide for the common defense and general welfare of the United States; but all duties, imposts, and excises shall be uniform throughout the United States;

2. To borrow money on the credit of the United States;

3. To regulate commerce with foreign nations, and among the several States, and with the Indian tribes;

4. To establish a uniform rule of naturalization, and uniform laws on the subject of bankruptcies throughout the United States;

5. To coin money, regulate the value thereof, and of foreign coin, and fix the standard of weights and measures;

6. To provide for the punishment of counterfeiting the securities and current coin of the United States;

7. To establish post offices and post roads;

8. To promote the progress of science and useful arts, by securing for limited times to authors and inventors the exclusive right to their respective writings and discoveries;

9. To constitute tribunals inferior to the Supreme Court;

10. To define and punish piracies and felonies committed on the high seas, and offenses against the law of nations;

11. To declare war, grant letters of marque and reprisal, and make rules concerning captures on land and water;

12. To raise and support armies, but no appropriation of money to that use shall be for a longer term than two years;

13. To provide and maintain a navy;

14. To make rules for the government and regulation of the land and naval forces;

15. To provide for calling forth the militia to execute the laws of the Union, suppress insurrections and repel invasions;

16. To provide for organizing, arming, and disciplining the militia, and for governing such part of them as may be employed in the service of the United States, reserving to the States respectively, the appointment of the officers, and the authority of training the militia according to the discipline prescribed by Congress;

17. To exercise exclusive legislation in all cases whatsoever, over such district (not exceeding ten miles square) as may, by cession of particular States, and the acceptance of Congress, become the seat of the government of the United States, and to exercise like authority over all places purchased by the consent of the legislature of the State in which the same shall be, for the erection of forts, magazines, arsenals, dockyards, and other needful buildings; and

18. To make all laws which shall be necessary and proper for carrying into execution the foregoing powers, and all other powers vested by this Constitution in the government of the United States, or in any department or officer thereof.

*Section 9.* 1. The migration or importation of such persons as any of the States now existing shall think proper to admit, shall not be prohibited by the Congress prior to the year one thousand eight hundred and eight, but a tax or duty may be imposed on such importation, not exceeding ten dollars for each person.

2. The privilege of the writ of *habeas corpus* shall not be suspended, unless when in cases of rebellion or invasion the public safety may require it.

3. No bill of attainder or *ex post facto* law shall be passed.

4. No capitation, or other direct, tax shall be laid, unless in proportion to the census or enumeration hereinbefore directed to be taken.

5. No tax or duty shall be laid on articles exported from any State.

6. No preference shall be given by any regulation of commerce or revenue to the ports of one State over those of another: nor shall vessels bound to, or from, one State be obliged to enter, clear, or pay duties in another.

7. No money shall be drawn from the treasury, but in consequence of appropriations made by law; and a regular statement and account of the receipts and expenditures of all public money shall be published from time to time.

8. No title of nobility shall be granted by the United States: and no person holding any office of profit or trust under them, shall, without the consent of the Congress, accept of any present, emolument, office, or title, of any kind whatever, from any king, prince, or foreign State.

*Section 10.* 1. No State shall enter into any treaty, alliance, or confederation; grant letters of marque and reprisal; coin money; emit bills of credit; a make anything but gold and silver coin a tender in payment of debts; pass any bill of attainder, *ex post facto* law, or law impairing the obligation of contracts, or grant any title of nobility.

2. No State shall, without the consent of the Congress, lay any imposts or duties on imports or exports, except what may be absolutely necessary for executing its inspection laws; and the net produce of all duties and imposts laid by any State on imports or exports, shall be for the use of the Treasury of the United States; and all such laws shall be subject to the revision and control of the Congress.

3. No State shall, without the consent of the Congress, lay any duty of tonnage, keep troops, or ships of war in time of peace, enter into any agreement or compact with another State, or with a foreign power, or engage in war, unless actually invaded, or in such imminent danger as will not admit of delay.

## ARTICLE II

*Section 1.* 1. The executive power shall be vested in a President of the United States of America. He shall hold his office during the term of four years, and, together with the Vice President, chosen for the same term, be elected as follows:

2. Each State shall appoint, in such manner as the legislature thereof may direct, a number of electors, equal to the whole number of senators and representatives to which the State may be entitled in the Congress: but no senator or representative, or person holding an office of trust or profit under the United States, shall be appointed an elector.

The electors shall meet in their respective States, and vote by ballot for two persons, of whom one at least shall not be an inhabitant of the same State with themselves. And they shall make a list of all the persons voted for, and of the number of votes for each; which list they shall sign and certify, and transmit sealed to the seat of the government of the United States, directed to the President of the Senate. The President of the Senate shall, in the presence of the Senate and House of Representatives, open all the certificates, and the votes shall then be counted. The person having the greatest number of votes shall be the President, if such number be a majority of the whole number of electors appointed; and if there be more than one who have such majority, and have an equal number of votes, then the House of Representatives shall immediately choose by ballot one of them for President; and if no person have a majority, then from the five highest on the list the said House shall in like manner choose the President. But in choosing the President, the votes shall be taken by States, the representation from each State having one vote; a quorum for this purpose shall consist of a member or members from two thirds of the States, and a majority of all the States shall be necessary to a choice. In every case, after the choice of the President, the person having the greatest number of votes of the electors shall be the Vice President. But if there should remain two or more who have equal votes, the Senate shall choose from them by ballot the Vice President.

3. The Congress may determine the time of choosing the electors, and the day on which they shall give their votes; which day shall be the same throughout the United States.

4. No person except a natural born citizen, or a citizen of the United States at the time of the adoption of this Constitution, shall be eligible to the office of President; neither shall any person be eligible

—

to that office who shall not have attained to the age of thirty-five years, and been fourteen years a resident within the United States.

5. In case of the removal of the President from office, or of his death, resignation, or inability to discharge the powers and duties of the said office, the same shall devolve on the Vice President, and the Congress may by law provide for the case of removal, death, resignation, or inability, both of the President and Vice President, declaring what officer shall then act as President, and such officer shall act accordingly, until the disability be removed, or a President shall be elected.

6. The President shall, at stated times, receive for his services a compensation, which shall neither be increased nor diminished during the period for which he shall have been elected, and he shall not receive within that period any other emolument from the United States, or any of them.

7. Before he enter on the execution of his office, he shall take the following oath or affirmation:—"I do solemnly swear (or affirm) that I will faithfully execute the office of President of the United States, and will to the best of my ability, preserve, protect and defend the Constitution of the United States."

*Section* 2. 1. The President shall be Commander-in-chief of the Army and Navy of the United States, and of the militia of the several States, when called into the actual service of the United States; he may require the opinion, in writing, of the principal officer in each of the executive departments, upon any subject relating to the duties of their respective offices, and he shall have power to grant reprieves and pardons for offenses against the United States, except in cases of impeachment.

2. He shall have power, by and with the advice and consent of the Senate, to make treaties, provided two-thirds of the senators present concur; and he shall nominate, and by and with the advice and consent of the Senate, shall appoint ambassadors, other public ministers and consuls, judges of the Supreme Court, and all other officers of the United States, whose appointments are not herein otherwise provided for, and which shall be established by law: but the Congress may by law vest the appointment of such inferior officers, as they think proper, in the President alone, in the courts of law, or in the heads of departments.

3. The President shall have power to fill up all vacancies that may happen during the recess of the Senate, by granting commissions which shall expire at the end of their next session.

*Section 3.* He shall from time to time give to the Congress information of the state of the Union, and recommend to their consideration such measures as he shall judge necessary and expedient; he may, on extraordinary occasions, convene both Houses, or either of them, and in case of disagreement between them with respect to the time of adjournment, he may adjourn them to such time as he shall think proper; he shall receive ambassadors and other public ministers; he shall take care that the laws be faithfully executed, and shall commission all the officers of the United States.

*Section 4.* The President, Vice President, and all civil officers of the United States, shall be removed from office on impeachment for, and conviction of, treason, bribery, or other high crimes and misdemeanors.

## ARTICLE III

*Section 1.* The judicial power of the United States shall be vested in one Supreme Court, and in such inferior courts as the Congress may from time to time ordain and establish. The judges, both of the Supreme and inferior courts, shall hold their offices during good behavior, and shall, at stated times, receive for their services, a compensation which shall not be diminished during their continuance in office.

*Section 2.* 1. The judicial power shall extend to all cases, in law and equity, arising under this Constitution, the laws of the United States, and treaties made, or which shall be made, under their authority;—to all cases affecting ambassadors, other public ministers and consuls;—to all cases of admiralty and maritime jurisdiction;—to controversies to which the United States shall be a party;—to controversies between two or more States;—between a State and citizens of another State;—between citizens of different States;—between citizens of the same State claiming lands under grants of different States, and between a State, or the citizens thereof, and foreign States, citizens or subjects.

2. In all cases affecting ambassadors, other public ministers and consuls, and those in which a State shall be party, the Supreme Court shall have original jurisdiction. In all the other cases before mentioned, the Supreme Court shall have appellate jurisdiction, both as to law and to fact, with such exceptions, and under such regulations as the Congress shall make.

3. The trial of all crimes, except in cases of impeachment, shall be by jury; and such trial shall be held in the State where the said crimes shall have been committed; but when not committed within any State,

the trial shall be at such place or places as the Congress may by law have directed.

*Section 3.* 1. Treason against the United States shall consist only in levying war against them, or in adhering to their enemies, giving them aid and comfort. No person shall be convicted of treason unless on the testimony of two witnesses to the same overt act, or on confession in open court.

2. The Congress shall have power to declare the punishment of treason, but no attainder of treason shall work corruption of blood, or forfeiture except during the life of the person attained.

## ARTICLE IV

*Section 1.* Full faith and credit shall be given in each State to the public acts, records, and judicial proceedings of every other State. And the Congress may by general laws prescribe the manner in which such acts, records and proceedings shall be proved, and the effect thereof.

*Section 2.* 1. The citizens of each State shall be entitled to all privileges and immunities of citizens in the several States.

2. A person charged in any State with treason, felony, or other crime, who shall flee from justice, and be found in another State, shall, on demand of the executive authority of the State from which he fled, be delivered up to be removed to the State having jurisdiction of the crime.

3. No person held to service or labor in one State under the laws thereof, escaping into another, shall, in consequence of any law or regulation therein, be discharged from such service or labor, but shall be delivered up on claim of the party to whom such service or labor may be due.

*Section 3.* 1. New States may be admitted by the Congress into this Union; but no new State shall be formed or erected within the jurisdiction of any other State; nor any State be formed by the junction of two or more States, or parts of States, without the consent of the legislatures of the States concerned as well as of the Congress.

2. The Congress shall have power to dispose of and make all needful rules and regulations respecting the territory or other property belonging to the United States; and nothing in this Constitution shall be so construed as to prejudice any claims of the United States, or of any particular State.

*Section 4.* The United States shall guarantee to every State in this Union a republican form of government, and shall protect each of them against invasion; and on application of the legislature, or of the executive (when the legislature cannot be convened), against domestic violence.

## ARTICLE V

The Congress, whenever two thirds of both Houses shall deem it necessary, shall propose amendments to this Constitution, or, on the application of the legislatures of two-thirds of the several States, shall call a convention for proposing amendments, which, in either case, shall be valid to all intents and purposes, as part of this Constitution, when ratified by the legislatures of three-fourths of the several States, or by conventions in three fourths thereof, as the one or the other mode of ratification may be proposed by the Congress; Provided that no amendment which may be made prior to the year one thousand eight hundred and eight shall in any manner affect the first and fourth clauses in the ninth section of the first article; and that no State, without its consent, shall be deprived of its equal suffrage in the Senate.

## ARTICLE VI

1. All debts contracted and engagements entered into, before the adoption of this Constitution, shall be as valid against the United States under this Constitution, as under the Confederation.

2. This Constitution, and the laws of the United States which shall be made in pursuance thereof, and all treaties made, or which shall be made, under the authority of the United States, shall be the supreme law of the land; and the Judges in every State shall be bound thereby, anything in the Constitution or laws of any State to the contrary notwithstanding.

3. The senators and representatives before mentioned, and the members of the several State legislatures, and all executive and judicial officers, both of the United States and of the several States, shall be bound by oath or affirmation to support this Constitution; but no religious test shall ever be required as a qualification to any office or public trust under the United States.

## ARTICLE VII

The ratification of the conventions of nine States shall be sufficient for the establishment of this Constitution between the States so ratifying the same.

Done in Convention by the unanimous consent of the States present the seventeenth day of September in the year of our Lord one thousand seven hundred and eighty-seven, and of the independence of the United States of America the twelfth. In witness whereof we have hereunto subscribed our names.

*George Washington*, President,
and Deputy from Virginia

NEW HAMPSHIRE
*John Langdon*
*Nicholas Gilman*

MASSACHUSETTS
*Nathaniel Gorham*
*Rufus King*

CONNECTICUT
*William Samuel Johnson*
*Roger Sherman*

NEW YORK
*Alexander Hamilton*

NEW JERSEY
*William Livingston*
*David Brearley*
*William Paterson*
*Jonathan Dayton*

PENNSYLVANIA
*Benjamin Franklin*
*Thomas Mifflin*
*Robert Morris*
*George Clymer*
*Thomas FitzSimons*
*Jared Ingersoll*
*James Wilson*
*Gouverneur Morris*

DELAWARE
*George Read*
*Gunning Bedford, Junior*
*John Dickinson*
*Richard Bassett*
*Jacob Broom*

MARYLAND
*James McHenry*
*Daniel of St. Thos. Jenifer*
*Daniel Carroll*

VIRGINIA
*John Blair*
*James Madison, Junior*

NORTH CAROLINA
*William Blount*
*Richard Dobbs Spaight*
*Hugh Williamson*

SOUTH CAROLINA
*John Rutledge*
*Charles Cotesworth Pinckney*
*Charles Pinckney*
*Pierce Butler*

GEORGIA
*William Few*
*Abraham Baldwin*

# The Bill of Rights

## ARTICLE I

Congress shall make no law respecting an establishment of religion, or prohibiting the free exercise thereof; or abridging the freedom of speech, or of the press; or the right of the people peaceably to assemble, and to petition the government for a redress of grievances.

## ARTICLE II

A well regulated militia being necessary to the security of a free State, the right of the people to keep and bear arms shall not be infringed.

## ARTICLE III

No soldier shall, in time of peace, be quartered in any house, without the consent of the owner, nor in time of war, but in a manner to be prescribed by law.

## ARTICLE IV

The right of the people to be secure in their persons, houses, papers, and effects, against unreasonable searches and seizures, shall not be violated, and no warrants shall issue, but upon probable cause, supported by oath or affirmation, and particularly describing the place to be searched, and the persons or things to be seized.

## ARTICLE V

No person shall be held to answer for a capital, or otherwise infamous crime, unless on a presentment or indictment of a grand jury, except in cases arising in the land or naval forces, or in the militia, when in actual service in time of war or public danger; nor shall any person be subject for the same offense to be twice put in jeopardy of life or limb; nor shall be compelled in any criminal case to be a witness against himself, nor be deprived of life, liberty, or property, without due process of law; nor shall private property be taken for public use without just compensation.

## ARTICLE VI

In all criminal prosecutions, the accused shall enjoy the right to a speedy and public trial, by an impartial jury of the State and district wherein the crime shall have been committed, which district shall have been previously ascertained by law, and to be informed of the nature and cause of the accusation; to be confronted with the witnesses against him; to have compulsory process for obtaining witnesses in his favor, and to have the assistance of counsel for his defense.

## ARTICLE VII

In suits at common law, where the value in controversy shall exceed twenty dollars, the right of trial by jury shall be preserved, and no fact tried by a jury shall be otherwise reexamined in any court of the United States, than according to the rules of the common law.

## ARTICLE VIII

Excessive bail shall not be required, nor excessive fines imposed, nor cruel and unusual punishments inflicted.

## ARTICLE IX

The enumeration in the Constitution of certain rights shall not be construed to deny or disparage others retained by the people.

## ARTICLE X

The powers not delegated to the United States by the Constitution, nor prohibited by it to the States, are reserved to the States respectively, or to the people.

# Selected Bibliography

Bernstein, Richard B., with Kym S. Rice. *Are We to Be a Nation? The Making of the Constitution.* Cambridge, Mass.: Harvard University Press, 1987.

Boorstin, Daniel J. *The Americans,* 3 vol. New York: Random House, 1958–1973.

Carey, Ken. *Third Millennium.* San Francisco: Harper San Francisco, 1996.

Donald, David Herbert. *Lincoln.* New York: Simon & Schuster, 1995.

Elgin, Duane. *Awakening Earth.* New York: Morrow, 1993.

Gandhi, M. K. *An Autobiography or The Story of My Experiments with Truth.* London: Penguin Books, 1927.

Gordon, James S. *Manifesto for a New Medicine.* New York: Addison-Wesley Publishing Company, Inc., 1996.

Guthman, Edwin O., and C. Richard Allen, eds. *RFK: Collected Speeches.* New York: Viking, 1993.

Hawken, Paul. *The Ecology of Commerce: A Declaration of Sustainability.* New York: Harper Business, 1993.

Henderson, Hazel. *Building a Win-Win World: Life Beyond Global Economic Warfare.* San Francisco: Berrett-Koehler Publishers, 1996.

Houston, Jean. *Public Like a Frog: Entering the Lives of Three Great Americans.* Wheaton, Ill.: Quest Books, 1993.

Iyer, Raghavan. *The Essential Writings of Mahatma Gandhi.* Delhi: Oxford University Press, 1991.

Jefferson, Thomas. *Writings.* Merrill D. Peterson, ed. New York: Library of America, 1984.

Lerner, Michael. *The Politics of Meaning.* Indianapolis: Addison Wesley, 1996.

Lincoln, Abraham. *Speeches and Writings,* 2 vol., Don E. Fehrenbacher, ed. New York: The Library of America, 1989.

Oates, Stephen B. *Let the Trumpet Sound: The Life of Martin Luther King, Jr.* New York: Harper & Row, 1982.

Paine, Thomas. *Writings,* Eric Foner, ed. New York: Library of America, 1995.

Rifkin, Jeremy. *The End of Work: The Decline of the Global Labor Force and the Dawn of the Post-Market Era.* New York: G. P. Putnam's Sons, 1995.

Schechter, Stephen L., Richard B. Bernstein, and Donald S. Lutz, eds. *Roots of the Republic.* Madison, Wisc.: Madison House, 1990.

Secretan, Lance H. K. *Reclaiming Higher Ground.* New York: McGraw-Hill, 1997.

Slater, Phillip. *A Dream Deferred: America's Discontent and the Search for a New Democratic Ideal.* Boston: Beacon Press, 1991.

Smith, Hedrick. *Rethinking America.* New York: Random House, 1995.

Smith, Huston. *The World's Religions.* San Francisco: Harper San Francisco, 1991.

Tarnas, Richard. *The Passion of the Western Mind: Understanding the Ideas That Have Shaped Our World View.* New York: Ballantine Books, 1991.

Walsch, Neale Donald. *Conversations with God: An Uncommon Dialogue, Book 2.* Charlottesville: Hampton Roads Publishing Company, Inc., 1997.

Washington, George. *Writings.* John Rhodehamel, ed. New York: The Library of America, 1997.

Washington, James M., ed. *A Testament of Hope. Selected Writings of Martin Luther King, Jr.* San Francisco: HarperCollins, 1986.

# Acknowledgments

Many people provided invaluable kindnesses to me as I wrote this book. My most sincere thanks to Richard B. Bernstein, David Bender, and Naomi Wolf for their wise and generous tutelage, counsel, and editorial comments. Each one of them has been a profound teacher and friend, for which I am deeply grateful.

Thanks to Oprah Winfrey, whose generous support of my career has given me a far wider exposure to people and places in America than I otherwise would have had.

Thanks to both Jack Romanos and Harry Evans for believing in this book.

Thanks to my wonderful editor, Mary Ann Naples, and to Carolyn Reidy, Michele Martin, Jackie Seow, and all those at Simon & Schuster who helped to bring the finished book into the world. I have felt very welcomed and supported. Thanks also to Rosemary Morris and Mitchell Ivers for help with my efforts along the way.

Thanks to Al Lowman for literary midwifery of the highest order and precious friendship throughout the years.

Thanks to Lane Bowes for very kind and sagacious help with the manuscript.

Thanks to Robert Barnett, Jacqueline Maitland Davies, and Alan Weil for most excellent counsel.

Thanks to Tammy Vogsland for both friendship and support.

Thanks to Jean Houston, David Perozzi, and Jeanne Milstein for information, inspiration, and encouragement.

Thanks to B. G. Dilworth, Carlene Bauer, Robin Webb, Charlotte Patton, Dean Williamson, Kate Plaugher, Courtney Carlson, Cheryl

LaBrucherie, Hal Sparks, Jim Breen, Don Thompson, T. J. Plaugher, Bob Labanara, and Todd Shroeder all for very valuable help.

Thanks to Richard Cooper, David Kessler, Norma Ferrara, Victoria Pearman, Rod Ostrom, Walter Capps, Daphne Rose Kingma, Jean Houston, and Diane Simon for being my companions along the way.

To my mom and to Emma, deeper thanks than I have words for. And thanks to Jennifer, who makes it all more fun.

''WITH a good conscience our only sure reward, with history the final judge of our deeds, let us go forth to lead the land we love, asking His blessing and His help, but knowing that here on earth God's work must truly be our own.''

— PRESIDENT JOHN F. KENNEDY

## *The American Renaissance Alliance*

If you are interested in more information concerning holistic politics and its principles in action, please contact:

The American Renaissance Alliance
1187 Coast Village Road, Suite 1-492
Santa Barbara, CA 93108
(805) 565-8757
Visit www.marianne.com

# INDEX